Great Newspaper Graphics

Great Newspaper Graphics

by the Editors of PBC International
& The Society of Newspaper Design

PBC International, Inc. • Glen Cove, New York

Distributor to the book trade in the United States and Canada:

Publishers Group West
4065 Hollis Street
Emeryville, CA 94608

Distributor to the art trade in the United States:

Letraset USA
40 Eisenhower Drive
Paramus, NJ 07652

Distributor to the art trade in Canada:

Letraset Canada Limited
555 Alden Road
Markham, Ontario L3R 3L5, Canada

Distributed throughout the rest of the world by:

Hearst Books International
105 Madison Avenue
New York, NY 10016

Library of Congress Cataloging-in-Publication Data

Great newspaper graphics / [compiled by] The Society of
  Newspaper Design.

      p.   cm.
Includes indexes.
ISBN 0-86636-120-0
1. Newspaper layout and typography.
2. Pictures—Printing.   3. Graphic Arts.   I. Society of
Newspaper Design.
Z246.G73   1990
686.2'252—dc20   90-38143
                          CIP

Printing and binding by Toppan Printing Co. (H.K.) Ltd.

PRINTED IN HONG KONG
10 9 8 7 6 5 4 3 2 1

Contents

The Judges

ROBERT LOCKWOOD
Founder, First President, Society of Newspaper
Design
Principal, News Graphics, New Tripoli

CLAUDIO RODRIGUEZ
Director of Art, NOVEDADES, Mexico City
President, National Foundation of Design
Associations of Mexico

CHRISTINA BRADFORD
Managing Editor/News
Detroit News

C. THOMAS HARDIN
Director of Photography, Louisville
Courier-Journal and Times
President, National Press Photographers
Association (1984–85)

SARA GIOVANITTI
Founding member, Society of Newspaper
Design
Principal, Sara Giovanitti Design, New York City

GERARD SEALY
Design Director, Sunday Magazine
Cleveland Plain Dealer

JOHN BODETTE
Executive News Editor
St. Cloud Times

MAGGIE BALOUGH
Assistant Managing Editor
Austin American Statesman
Society of Newspaper Design President

EDWIN TAYLOR
Managing Editor
U.S. News and World Report
Washington D.C.

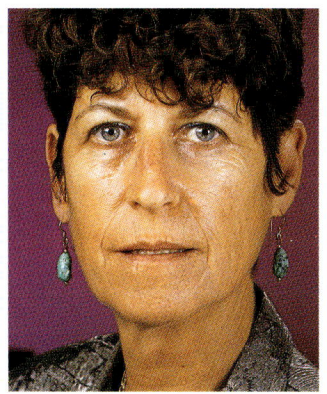

JUDY CROOK
Color Consultant/Instructor
Art Center College of Design
Pasadena, CA

N. CHRISTIAN ANDERSON
Editor, The Orange County Register
Pulitzer Prize for News Photography, 1985

NIGEL HOLMES
Executive Art Director
Time magazine, New York City

CHAPTER 1

News
Categories

"The people putting the award-winning pages together are thinking of the reader first, trying to take the reader through the news, whether it's a photograph or a drawing. If they do it on a day-in and day-out basis, the reader is the winner."

C. THOMAS HARDIN

"Readers visually expect more from newspapers today. The challenge for designers is to enhance a story graphically, but not overwhelm the message of that story."

GERALD SEALY

"All share energy, decisions have been made and there's a hand in control. The reader will see the order and understand what is being conveyed."

SARA GIOVANITTI

Main

Award of Excellence
THE SUNDAY TIMES
London, England
Gordon Beckett

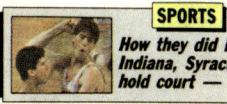

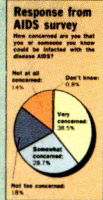
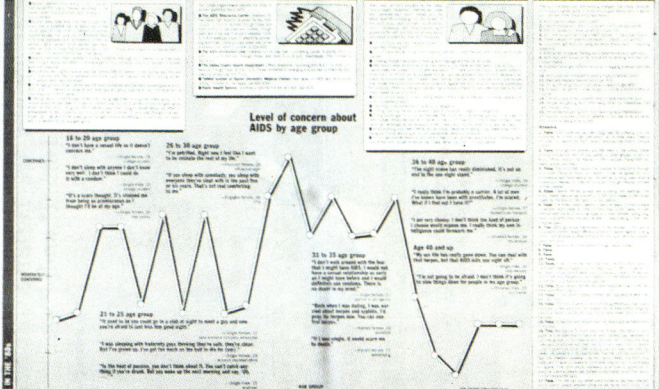

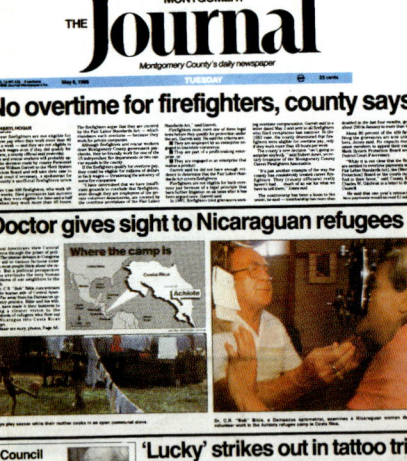

A man of vision
County optometrist gives sight to refugees fleeing Nicaragua

Photos and story by Danielle Pallotta

THE MONTGOMERY Journal
Montgomery County's daily newspaper

No overtime for firefighters, county says

Doctor gives sight to Nicaraguan refugees

Where the camp is

'Lucky' strikes out in tattoo trial

Council vote hit as cop-out on school integration

Scull opens books, blasts Kramer

OUTSIDE · INSIDE · SPORTS STATS · INDEX

TACKLING TERROR

HOW SHE RUNS

A NEW FACE

TOMORROW! Making Mom's special breakfast a success, in Tempo

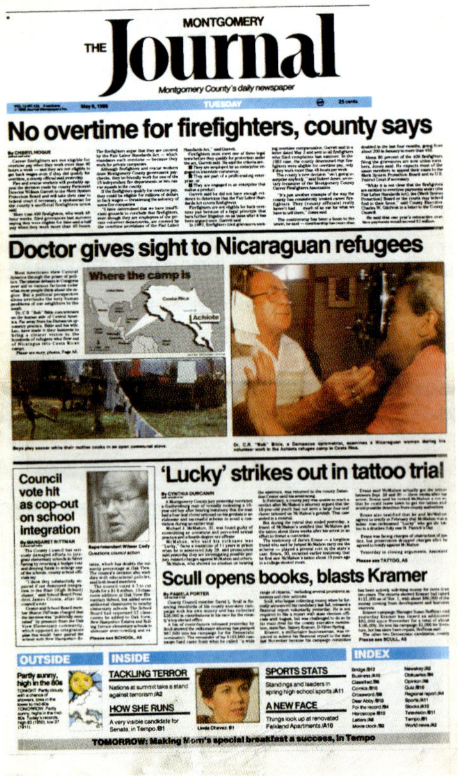

Award of Excellence

THE REGISTER-GUARD
Eugene, Oregon
Larry May,
George Millener,
Carl Davaz

The Register-Guard

EUGENE, OREGON   THURSDAY, MAY 15, 1986   25 CENTS

Hope fading for lost climbers

Heroic efforts fail to revive 3 taken from Mount Hood

Search goes on; prayers offered

Surgeon survived 1970 ordeal

Gorbachev tells of 'sinister force'

MOSTLY CLOUDY
High 35, low 25
Cloudy Saturday
Details on Page 2A

Ohio State's Woody Hayes dies at 74
Story below

Lance Parrish signs with the Phillies
Page 1D

NCAA Round 1: U-M scuttles Navy, UCLA routs CMU
Page 1D

IN SPORTS

20¢
For home delivery call 222-6500.

Detroit Free Press

* 1987, Detroit Free Press, Inc.
ON GUARD FOR 155 YEARS **
Volume 156, Number 312

Friday
March 13, 1987
Metro final

FIRE TRAGEDY

Blaze kills 3 fire fighters

Fire fighters battle a five-alarm blaze Thursday at a vacant warehouse in Detroit. At least three fire fighters were killed and six others injured in the blaze.

RICHARD LEE/Detroit Free Press

5-alarm fire injures 6, destroys 2 buildings

Full report

■ A history of other major fires in Detroit. **Page 13A.**
■ Lt. Paul Schimeck was "a very good person." **Page 13A.**
■ The hurt shoots through family, friends at hospital. **Page 14A.**
■ Fire fighters at the scene are shocked at the deaths. **Page 13A.**

At least three Detroit fire fighters were killed and six others were injured Thursday while fighting a five-alarm blaze that engulfed two buildings on the city's near west side.

One arson investigator said fire fighters who responded to the first alarm found several separate small blazes on the third floor of a vacant warehouse making arson a possibility. Fire officials also said a rubbish fire started by several vagrants who camped in the building, which overlooks the Jeffries Freeway and is south of the Edsel Ford Freeway, may have ignited the blaze, which spread to a second building, Continental Paper & Supply Co.

Lt. Paul Schimeck, 46, a 26-year veteran, was dead on arrival at Southwest Detroit Hospital at 3:35 p.m., a hospital spokesman said. Schimeck suffered massive head injuries and a broken neck, the spokesman said.

About 2½ hours later, at least two other fire fighters died when the Continental roof collapsed and dropped into the basement, burying them under five feet of rubble, officials said.

"They're dead. Yes, they're dead already. They're dead," one fire fighter yelled to another as he ran to the front of the building shortly after the roof collapsed.

Killed when the roof collapsed were 31-year-veteran Lt. David Lau and Trial Fire Fighter Larry McDonald Jr., 24, whose father is a fire engine operator, said Deputy Fire Commissioner Phillip Gorak.

McDonald was to receive his badge as a fire fighter in ceremonies March 23. Gorak said. McDonald was fulfilling a four-month on-the-job training program, Gorak said.

FIRE DEPARTMENT Senior Chief Jack Stelzer ordered all fire fighters out of the burning Continental building at 9 p.m. and said then that the fire was out of control. Stationary hoses outside the building continued to pour water onto the blaze.

Stelzer said Lau and McDonald were killed when they were fighting the blaze on one of the floors of the three-story building and the roof and part of a wall collapsed, crashing to the ground floor and carrying the fire fighters with

See FIRE, Page 12A

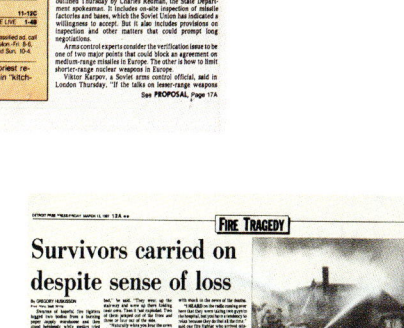

Two fire fighters walk away from the blaze that killed three fellow workers.

Gone to glory: Ohio State's Woody Hayes dies at 74

"I don't want to be known as a character. Some people think I'm just a good-natured fat boy. I don't like that. I'm not a glamor boy ... I don't last long in the coaching profession and I'm planning to be around for a long time."
Woody Hayes, 1955

By JOE LAPOINTE
Free Press Sports Writer

Woody Hayes, who was born on St. Valentine's Day in 1913 and died of an apparent heart attack Thursday, was more than just a successful football coach at Ohio State University.

He was an American archetype, a man of his times, a passionate person who inspired love and hate and many emotions in between. And he was a winner.

Hayes could be a loyal friend, a concerned educator and an inspirational, charming speaker. He also

See WOODY, Page 17A

■ Full report, 8-9D.

Woody Hayes' life spanned two world wars and the Depression.

PAGE ONE

Inside today

ANN LANDERS	2D
BRIDGE	14D
BUSINESS NEWS	8-13B
CLASSIFIED ADS	13-17C
COMICS	16-17D
CROSSWORD PUZZLE	16D
DATELINE MICHIGAN	5A
DEATH NOTICES	15C
EDITORIALS	6A
ENTERTAINMENT	1-10C
FEATURE PAGE	15B
HEALTH & FITNESS	15B
HOROSCOPE	14D
JUMBLE	16C
METRO DATELINE	4A
MOVIE GUIDE	15D
NAMES & FACES	14D
OBITUARIES	15C
SPORTS	1-12D
STOCK MARKETS	8-13B

MSL
THURSDAY: 339 and 9045
SAT JACKPOT $2 million

Lotto info
Computer analysis of lottery numbers, out-of-state numbers. 11C.

TELEVISION 11-12C
THE WAY WE LIVE 1-4B

To close a classified ad, call 222-6500, Mon.-Fri. 8-6, Sat. 9-5 and Sun. 10-4.

■ Freed priest re-calls day in "kitchen." 10A.

U.S. proposes 6 steps to arms verification

By JOHN H. CUSHMAN Jr.
New York Times

WASHINGTON — The United States proposed in Geneva Thursday elaborate verification measures that the Reagan administration will insist the Soviet Union agree to before signing any treaty removing American and Soviet intermediate-range nuclear missiles from Europe.

The six-point package of verification measures was outlined Thursday by Charles Redman, the State Department spokesman. It includes on-site inspection of missile factories and bases, which the Soviet Union has indicated a willingness to accept. But it also includes provisions on inspection and other matters that could prompt long negotiations.

Arms control experts consider the verification issue to be one of two major points that could block an agreement on medium-range missiles in Europe. The other is how to limit shorter-range nuclear weapons in Europe.

Viktor Karpov, a Soviet arms control official, said in London Thursday, "If the talks on lower-range weapons

See PROPOSAL, Page 17A

FIRE TRAGEDY

Survivors carried on despite sense of loss

3 fire fighters die in warehouse blaze

FIRE TRAGEDY

Neighbors lament loss of fallen fire fighter

The hurt shoots through family, friends at hospital

City motto reflects history of tragic fires

Detroit warehouse fire

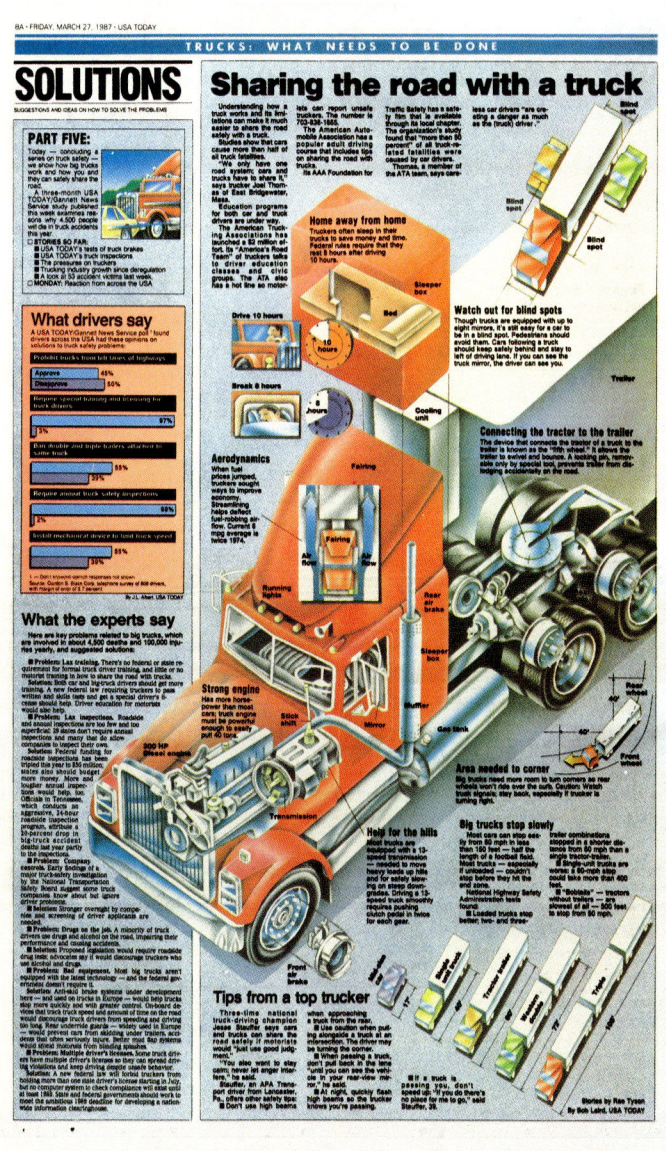

Local

Award of Excellence
THE WASHINGTON TIMES
Washington, D.C.
The Washington Times staff

Silver Award
NEWS/SUN-SENTINEL
Fort Lauderdale, Florida
News/Sun-Sentinel staff

News Categories 19

Sports

Gold Award
HELSINGIN SANOMAT
Helsinki, Finland
Helsingin Sanomat staff

Helsingin Sanomat, maanantaina 11. toukokuuta 1987 — 29

URHEILU

Murtunut solisluu hurjan ilmalennon seuraus

Heikki Kotilainen

Ismo Vehkosen sairaalareissu alkaa: Mies tömähtää Ruskeasannan MM-osakilpailun avauserässä rajusti tantereeseen olkapää edellä murtaen solisluunsa ja saa hetken päästä vielä oman pyöränsä niskaansa.

Vehkoselle kolmen viikon pakkolepo

Ismo Vehkosen epäonni motocrossin isoimman luokan (500 ksm) MM-mittelöissä jatkuu. Vehkosen kotiradalla Vantaan Ruskeasannalla ajettu neljäs osakilpailu päättyi sairaalareissuun kuten päättyi myös edellinen osakilpailu Sittendorfissa Itävallassa.

Sittendorfissa saamastaan polvivammasta Vehkonen toipui viikossa, Ruskeasannalla kävi köpelömmin.

Ensimmäinen erä Ruskeasannalla ehti vanheta vain parikymmentä minuuttia, kun Vehkonen ajoi hurjasti nurin. Vehkonen tömähti tantereeseen olkapää edellä. Pahaksi onneksi pyörä rämähti vielä nuorukaisen niskaan. Alkoi matka Töölön sairaalaan, jossa todettiin solisluun murtuma. Nyt Vehkosella on edessään kolmen viikon pakkolepo.

Liian kovaa syvään monttuun

"Nurin mentiin niin pirusti. Ajoin monttuun liian kovaa ja sitten vietiin", 18-vuotias Vehkonen muisteli käsi kantositeessä.

Moottoripyörän iskemän jäljiltä myös Vehkosen selkää kolotti melkoisesti. Selässä oli kuitenkin "vain" lihasvamma, joka paranee nopeasti.

"Yksi osakilpailu jää nyt varmasti väliin eikä mitenkään varmaa ole sekään, että toivun kolmen viikon päästä ajettavaan L-Saksan kilpailuun. Pakkolepo on aina pahasta."

Seuraava osakilpailu ajetaan jo viikon päästä Kristianstadissa Ruotsissa.

Vehkonen johti ensimmäistä erää pari kierrosta, kaatui ja putosi kolmanneksi. Oliko yritys takaisin kärkeen liian raju ?

"Mitään ei saa, jos mitään ei yritä"

"Ei ollut. Mitään ei saa, jos ei mitään yritä. Minulla oli selvät suunnitelmat miten ohitan edelläni ajaneen Kees van der Venin. Uskon, että erävoittokin olisi ollut mahdollinen, jos onni olisi hymyillyt."

Eränhän voitti lopulta Kurt Ljungqvist.

Viime aikojen loukkaantumiset eivät kuitenkaan ole vantaalaisnuorukaista täysin tyrmänneet, vaikka ilme sairaalamatkan jälkeen pysyikin peruslukemilla. "Nyt on aikaa mennä ongelle. Koukin Mikasta taidan saada kaverin."

Mika Kouki on toinen Vantaan huippuajaja, joka kulkee käsi kantositeessä. Koukin käsi on kipsattu kuudeksi viikoksi. Niin pitkästä lomasta Vehkonen ei kuitenkaan ole kiinnostunut.

Ruskeasannan tulokset sivulla 34.

Murheinen Ismo Vehkonen pohtii, oliko yrittäminen liian rajua.

Ensimmäinen MM-erävoitto irrotti hymyn

Kurt Ljungqvist lähestyy huippua

Kurt Ljungqvist säteili tyytyväisyyttään sunnuntaina Ruskeasannan motocrossradalla, vaikka vettä vihmoi taivaan täydeltä ja lämpötila lähenteli nollaa. Ljungqvistin ilon syynä oli uran ensimmäinen MM-erävoitto, jonka 24-vuotias espoolainen nappasi 500-luokan neljänneen osakilpailun avauserässä.

Toisessa erässä Ljungqvist kaatuili ja kärsi lisäksi tehottomasta takajousesta. Sijoitus oli kymmenes. Hetken espoolainen harmitteli toisen erän epäonnea, mutta manailu vaihtui nopeasti iloksi.

"Olen tyytyväinen päivän saaliiseen. Pääsin historian kirjoihin kahdeksantena suomalaisena MM-erävoittajana. Lisäksi tiedän, että tallini (Yamaha) on odottanut kovasti ensimmäistä voittoa tällä pyörällä. Tulevaisuudessa voi olla hyötyä siitä, että onnistuin avausvoiton hankkimaan", Ljungqvist pohdiskeli.

Tehdaskalusto on, sopimusta ei

Ljungqvistilla on käytössään nyt Yamahan tehdaskalusto. Japanilaistalli päätyi suomalaiseen, kun ilmeni, että varsinaiseksi tehdaskuskiksi palkattu Ranskan Jacky Vimond ei pysty ajamaan pitkään aikaan. Tehdassopimusta Ljungqvistilla ei kuitenkaan ole. Jos tahti jatkuu nykyisellään, ensi kaudeksi sopimus kuitenkin syntyy vaivatta.

Ruskeasannan kilpailun jälkeen Ljungqvist on pisteissä edelleen neljäs. Kärki tiivistyi kuitenkin melkoisesti, kun mestaruutta puolustava ja pistetilastoa edelleen johtava Englannin David Thorpe jäi kytkinmurheitten ja nurinajojen takia kokonaan pisteittä.

Ensimmäisen erän ratkaisuhetket lähestyvät. Hollannin Kees van der Ven (5) on hetkeksi livahtanut Kurt Ljungqvistin edelle.

Käsivaivainen ruotsalainen Håkan Carlqvist putosi kolmanneksi. Carlqvist kaatui heti ensimmäisen erän lähtökiihdytyksessä ja keskeytti. Toisessa erässä Carlqvist sinnitteli kuudenneksi.

Georges Jobe kohensi asemiaan

Belgian Georges Jobe voitti toisen erän ja nousi samalla yhteispisteissä toiseksi. Ljungqvist johti toistakin erää pari kierrosta, mutta kaatui ja takana väijynyt Jobe pääsi keulaan. Sen jälkeen ei kokeneella belgialaisella ollut vaikeuksia varmistella kauden ensimmäistä erävoittoaan.

"Ljungqvist juuttui mutaan pyöränsä alle. Pääsin helposti keulaan ja sen jälkeen keskityin vain ajamaan virheettömästi", Jobe sanoi.

Ljungqvist sanoi nurinajon johtuneen reistailevista jarruista. "Vauhtia oli kaarteessa liikaa."

Koko toinen erä oli espoolaiselle tuskien taivalta. Takaiskuvaimentimeen säädettiin erätauolla vaimennusta lisää. Se oli virhe. Joustoa tuli liikaa. Ajaminen kävi vaikeaksi. "Jokainen hyppy sattui selkään, kun iskunvaimennin rämähti pohjaan. Saattoi näyttää siltä, että olin väsynyt, mutta näin ei ollut. Iskunvaimentimen takia ajo oli vain niin vaikeata", Ljungqvist sanoi.

Kaksinkamppailu van der Venin kanssa

Ensimmäisessä erässä Ljungqvist kävi kovan kamppailun Hollannin Kees van der Venin kanssa. Hollantilainen ajoi kärjen tuntumassa koko alkumatkan siirtyen uhkaavan tuntuisesti johtoon kolme kierrosta ennen maalia. 10 000-päisen yleisön riemuksi Ljungqvist pääsi kuitenkin uudestaan johtoon ennen viimeistä kierrosta.

"Van der Ven teki virheen samassa mutkassa, jossa hän ohitti minut. Jarrutus meni pitkäksi ja pääsin sisäkautta ohi", Ljungqvist muisteli.

Alkuviikolla testit Ruotsissa

Ljungqvist lupasi juhlia elämänsä ensimmäistä erävoittoa rauhallisesti. Vapaata ei liiemmälti ole luvassa, sillä jo tiistaina alkaa matka seuraavaan osakilpailuun, joka ajetaan Kristianstadissa Ruotsissa ensi sunnuntaina.

"Viikolla on ajettava Ruotsissa testejä. Iskunvaimennus on saatava kuntoon ennen sunnuntain kilpailua."

Ljungqvist onkin kielitaitoisena miehenä oiva testikuski. Kokemus on osoittanut, että hyvä kielitaito on iso etu ammattilaisten kovassa maailmassa. Ljungqvist on nyt työntänyt jalkansa ovenrakoon, josta avautuu pääsy ehdottomalle huipulle. Seuraavat kilpailut ratkaisevat paljon. Syntyperäinen espoolainen on toiveikas. Kunto on vahvassa nousussa ja kalusto varmasti kilpailukykyinen.

KAARLO SUNDELL

Niittymäki hallitsee rallicrossin EM-sarjaa

Tomelilla (HS) Seppo Niittymäki ajoi kolme lähtöä rallicrossin Ruotsin EM-osakilpailussa Tomelillan Svampabananilla. Hän voitti ne kaikki; kaksi alkuerää ja kivikovan II divisioonan finaalin. Edellisen viikonlopun voitto Itävallan avauskilpailussa sai seurakseen toisen ja näin Niittymäki johtaa EM-sarjaa puhtaalla pelillä.

Matti Alamäki uusi myös Itävallan sijoituksensa eli kolmannen sijan ja on siitä syystä toisena yhteispisteissä, sillä avauskilpailun kakkonen, Ruotsin Olle Arnesson oli Tomelillassa vasta kuudes.

Jälleen ylivoimainen

Ruotsin osakilpailu oli Niittymäelle Itävallan toisinto. Tuusulalainen johti lähdöstä maaliin. Jo alkuerät lupailivat hyvää. Kaksi voittoa ja nopeimmat ajat.

"Ensimmäisen erän ajo oli vähän hermostunutta. Ajo olikin sen mukaista. Radan takaosassa muutin toiseen erään hieman ajolinjoja. Toiseksi tullut Ruotsin Rolf Nilsson tuntee radan hyvin. Onhan Tomelilla hänen kotiratansa", Niittymäki raportoi.

"Kaiken kaikkiaan tykkään tästä radasta. Tämä on ajajan rata ja vaihteleva korkeuseroineen."

"Kuin korkki pullosta"

Finaalissa Niittymäen Peugeot lähti kuin tykinsuusta. Ensimmäiseen pahaan kaarteeseen hän tuli ykkösenä ja piti sijan ruutulipulle asti.

"Auto lähti kuin korkki pullosta. Viikon takainen voitto oli helpompi, sillä nyt kantaani tuli Rolf Nilsson. Kisa oli todella hermoja kutkuttavaa. Mutta tarkka ajo ja kisakaarteen kiinnipitäminen takasi voiton", Niittymäki selvitti taktiikkaansa.

"Ei tämä helpolla tullut eikä jarruttelemalla. Töitä sai tehdä olan takaa."

Lähettäjälle sapiskaa

Kilpailun lähettäjä sai melkoista sapiskaa usealta kilpailijalta. Myös Niittymäeltä.

"Säännöissä sanotaan selvästi, että punaisen valon on annettava palaa vähintään 2–5 sekuntia. Tämä lähettäjä vaihtoi valon vihreäksi jo puolen sekunnin kuluttua."

"Mutta kaiken kaikkiaan päivä oli tiimilleni aurinkoinen. Tästä on taas hyvä jatkaa", Niittymäki sanoi.

Kolmanneksi sijoittunut Matti Alamäki oli myös melko tyytyväinen, vaikka sijoitukseksi tulikin kolmas.

"Kerrankin sain hyvän lähdön. Taisi syy aikaisemmin olla ratin ja penkin välissä. Aluksi yritin ohittaa Nilssonin mutta huomasin sen melko mahdottomaksi. Ei hänen ohitse pääse ilman toisen virhettä. Ja sitähän ei Nilsson tällä radalla tee", Alamäki myönsi.

Alamäellä aikapula

"Auton tekemisessä on paljon suunnittelua vielä. Ei minun Lanciani vielä valmis ole. Kun olisi vain aikaa. Nyt olen kahden kuukauden aikana ollut kolme yötä kotona. Hotellikuolemahan tässä uhkaa", porilainen naureskeli.

Jotain Alamäkikin voitti. Viiden parhaan aika-ajossa sijoittuneen kesken oli kierroksen kilpailu, josta palkintona oli tuhat Ruotsin kruunua ja pokaali. Kilpailu ajettiin yksitellen ja Alamäki oli paras.

"Mekaanikot halusivat tänään juhlia ja jostainhan minun piti rahat hankkia", Alamäki vitsaili.

Yhdeksän suomalaisajajaa

Mukana oli kaikkiaan yhdeksän suomalaisajajaa. C-finaalissa heitä oli peräti kolme, Porsche-kuskit Mauno Jokinen ja Jarmo Lähteenmäki sekä Ford-kuljettaja Pekka Rantanen. Rantanen kolaroi Ruotsin Bengt Wiklundin kanssa ja sijoittui 14:nneksi. Lähteenmäeltä meni rengas ja hän oli 16:s.

Mauno Jokinen voitti C-finaalin ja oli B-finaalissa viides eli kokonaiskilpailussa kymmenes.

"Kun opin auton metkut, niin ruuvaan turboruuvia hieman lisää. Ahveniston radan pitäisi olla parempi tälle autolleni", Jokinen arveli.

Kallio seitsemäs

Jukka Pelttari ja Lasse Lehtinen eivät II divisioonassa päässeet finaaleihin.

I divisioonan suomalaiskunkku oli jälleen kerran Jouko Kallio, mutta nyt sijoitukseksi tuli seitsemäs. Se ei ollut Kallion mieleen, mutta osansa siihen oli teipatulla olkapäällä, joka tahtoo jatkuvasti mennä sijoiltaan. Ari Jykylä ei finaaleihin päässyt.

Jari Nurminen jaksoi maaliin Vallelungassa

Vallelunga Italia (HS) Jari Nurminen ajoi pitkästä aikaa maaliin kilpa-autoilun F3000-luokan kilpailussa. Tämän vuoden toisessa mannertenvälisen sarjan osakilpailussa Vallelungassa Nurminen pääsi ruutulipulle 16:ntena. Saavutus oli Nurmisen uran toiseksi paras luokassa; viime vuonna Itävallassa hän oli sijaa parempi.

Kilpailu alkoi suomalaisittain heikosti. Jo lähtökiihdytyksessä Nurmisen Dallaran vaihdelaatikosta katosivat sekä ykkös- että kakkosvaihde.

Paalupaikalta startannut Ranskan Yannick Dalmas ajoi pahasti ulos, jolloin kilpailu keskeytettiin raivaustöiden ajaksi. Uusi startti ei muuttanut Nurmisen sijoitusta.

Kilpailun voitti eturivistä startannut Italian Stefano Modena Marchilla. Toinen oli espanjalainen Luis-Perez Sala.

Sarjan kolmas osakilpailu ajetaan ensi lauantaina Span radalla Belgiassa F1:n MM-osakilpailun yhteydessä.

Floessellin kevätkunto rautaa SM-trialissa

Trialin SM-sarja alkoi sunnuntaina kun Toijalan–Valkeakosken seudulla ajettiin kauden ensimmäinen SM-osakilpailu. Staffan Floessell osoitti jälleen vahvaa kevätkuntoa jättämällä taakseen koko viime vuoden SM-kärkikolmikon.

19-vuotias Jakomäen trialkaartin vahva nimi Juha Porali hallitsi kilpailun alkuvaiheita johtaen selvästi viimeiselle kierrokselle lähdettäessä. Ero toisena taituroineeseen Floesselliin oli kuusi pistettä.

Poralin konseptit sekosivat ratkaisujaksoilla perusteellisesti, sillä kolmas kierros toi hänelle virhepisteitä yhtä paljon kuin kaksi ensimmäistä yhteensä. Tarkasti ajanut Floessell kiristi ensin tasoihin ja sitten viimeisillä jaksoilla kolmen pinnan erolla voittoon.

Kolmea edellistä Suomen mestaruutta puolustava Peter Jahn on sekoillut ajosopimustensa kanssa eikä yhteistyö uuden ajokin kanssa ainakaan vielä ole niin saumatonta, että mestaruusputken jatkuminen olisi näköpiirissä.

Luokka A1: 1) Staffan Floessell Tapiolan MMK 57 virhepistettä (15 SM-pistettä), 2) Juha Porali JakomMK 60 (12), 3) Peter Jahn MP-taito 65 (10), 4) Mika Oksanen MP-taito 74 (8), 5) Petri Hartman JakomMK 80 (6), 6) Harri Hoittinen TeMK 97 (3), 7) Raimo Eräkare EspMK 100 (2), 8) Marko Jaatinen VantMK 103 (1), 9) Sakari Sipponen JakomMK 107, 10) Panu Leppo EspMK 112.

Pekka Vehkonen MM-kärkeen

Hawkstone Park, Englanti (HS) Epäonnisen Ismo Vehkosen serkku Pekka Vehkonen onnistui lähes täydellisesti motocrossin 250-luokan kolmennessa MM-osakilpailussa Hawkstone Parkissa. Hän sijoittui erissä ensimmäiseksi ja toiseksi ja siirtyi MM-sarjan kärkeen.

Ennen kilpailua sarjaa johtanut Eric Geboers voitti toisen erän, mutta pistesaalis jäi laihaksi, koska avauserässä belgialainen ei mahtunut pisteille eli 15 parhaan joukkoon.

Seuraavan kerran Vehkonen ajaa jo ensi sunnuntaina Bestissä Hollannissa.

Award of Excellence
THE WASHINGTON TIMES
Washington, D.C.
The Washington Times
sports staff

Award of Excellence
LOS ANGELES TIMES
Los Angeles, California
Rick Jaffe

Award of Excellence

DEMOCRAT AND CHRONICLE
Rochester, New York
Ted Haider

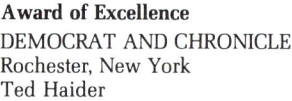

Business

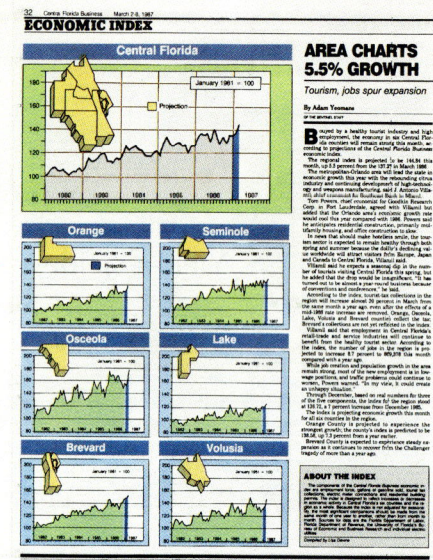

Award of Excellence
THE ORLANDO SENTINEL
Orlando, Florida
Bruce Carden

Award of Excellence
THE VIRGINIAN-PILOT/LEDGER-STAR
Norfolk, Virginia
Lynn Feigenbaum, Chris Kouba,
Sam Hundley

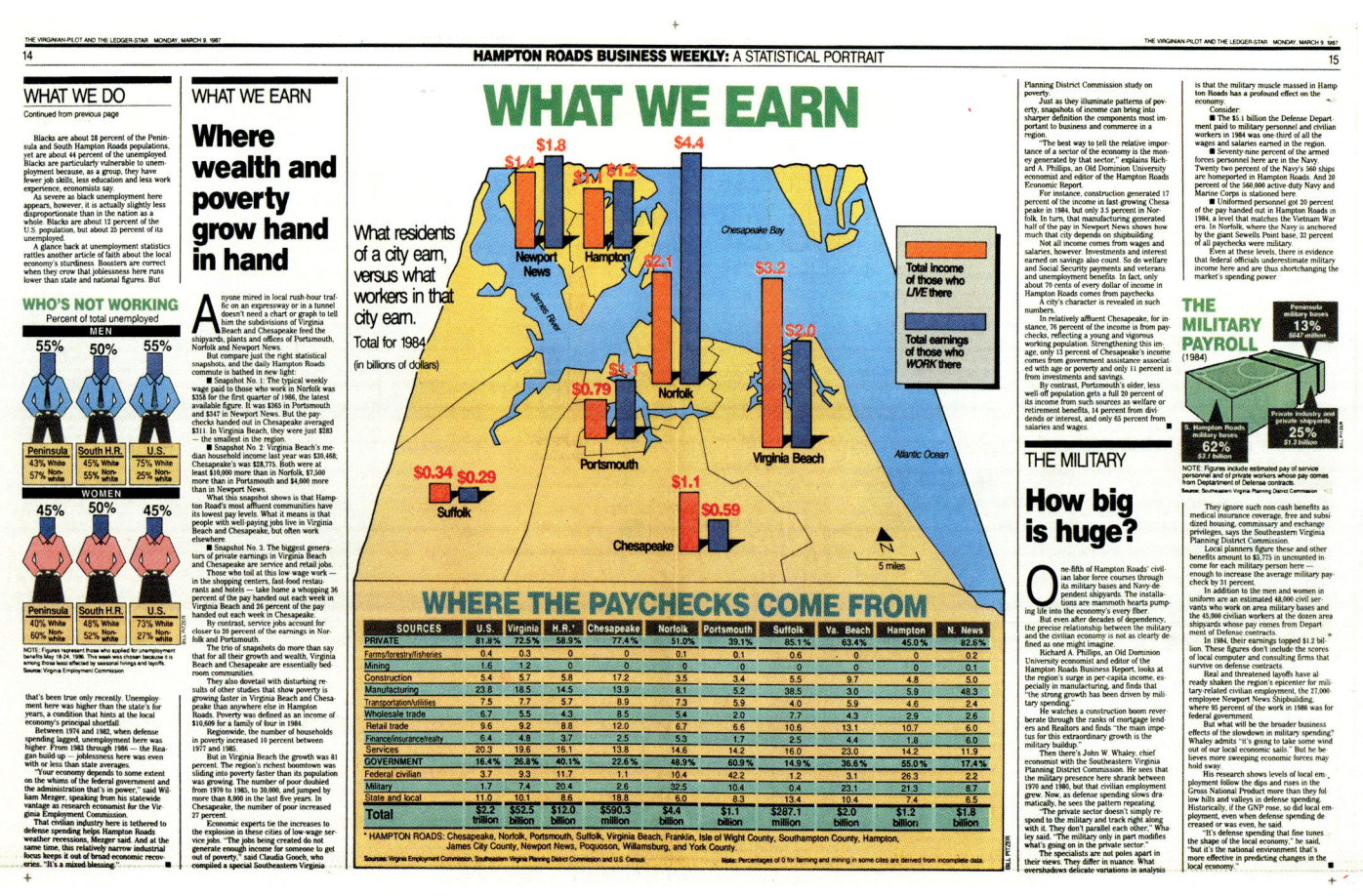

Page Design

Front Pages

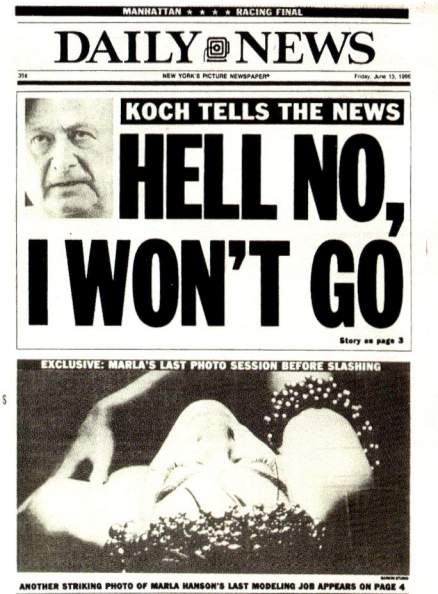

4 STAR ★ ★ ★ FINAL

WEDNESDAY'S CLOSE 1879.50

JAZZ LIVES ON
in FRIDAY EXTRA section

DAILY◉NEWS

35¢   NEW YORK'S PICTURE NEWSPAPER®   Friday, September 12, 1986

WALL STREET TAKES A BATH

Stocks plunge record **86** points

THURSDAY'S CLOSE 1792.89

Story on page 3

IS   **AREN'T YOU GLAD YOU'RE NOT IN THIS MAN'S SHOES?**

GUCCI JAILED

Aldo Gucci (right), patriarch of the Gucci fashion empire, walks into Manhattan Federal Court with attorney Milton Gould (rear). Gucci, 81, who was convicted of evading $7 million in income taxes, made a tearful plea for mercy before he was sentenced to a year and a day in jail.

Story on page 3

Award of Excellence
LEXINGTON HERALD-LEADER
Lexington, Kentucky
Jim Jennings, David Williams,
Malcolm Stallons

Wednesday

Grits get sophisticated
Around Derby time, the Southern staple is a menu favorite
— Lifestyle/Food

NFL drafts UK's Logan, Mayes — Sports

Pay raises outstrip inflation rate — Page B5

Winners, losers on prime time — Lifestyle/Food

Today's weather-A10
CHANCE OF PRECIPITATION
10%
Partly sunny — 75°

LEXINGTON HERALD-LEADER

Vol. 5, No. 117   Metro Final   Lexington, Kentucky, April 29, 1987   52 pages   35 cents

PTL board cuts off payments to Bakker, Hahn

Iran-contra probe targets top officials

Special prosecutor Walsh indicates he will seek conspiracy charges

Council decides not to name city street for King

Thoroughbred as machine

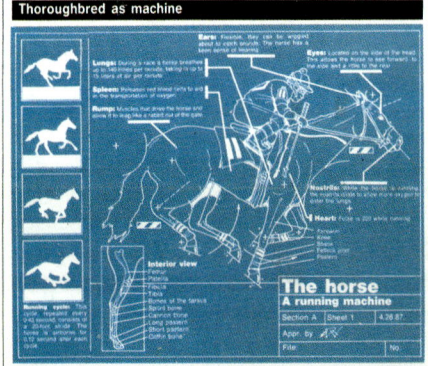

The horse
A running machine

Derby pushes horse's body to the limit

More inside

Police: Nudity common at accused man's camp

Inside

Truck crashes and explodes

Promises on education may be hard to pay for

ELECTION '87

Award of Excellence
THE HARTFORD COURANT
Hartford, Connecticut
Teddy Sherwood,
Ed LaFreniere

The Hartford Courant

Towering Offices Dwarf Apartments — 9 Yards Away

Senate Passes Defense Bill
Reagan's Request for 1987 Trimmed to $295 Billion

Stevie: A World Of Pride
Burn Victim, 9, Smiles Amid The Obstacles

A Relaxed Moffett Looks to the Future

Tests on President Reveal No Tumors

Local Fronts

Metro

■ Fort Lauderdale News
■ Section **B**
■ Wednesday, September 3, 1986

■ GARY STEIN
Staff Columnist

Once a candidate, now an observer

Even Poitier surprised by victory

By RICK PIERCE
Staff Writer

"I thought my opponent had it in the bag."
— Sylvia Poitier

Little lifesaver

Schwartz captures District 1

Newcomer victorious in School Board race

By ROBBIE MORGANFIELD
Staff Writer

Tense search for boy ends happily at YMCA

By RENEE KRAUSE
Staff Writer

Jewette Wynn of Hollywood gives son Brian a hug upon his return.

■ INSIDE

LOCAL

DADE

Sports Fronts

Business Fronts

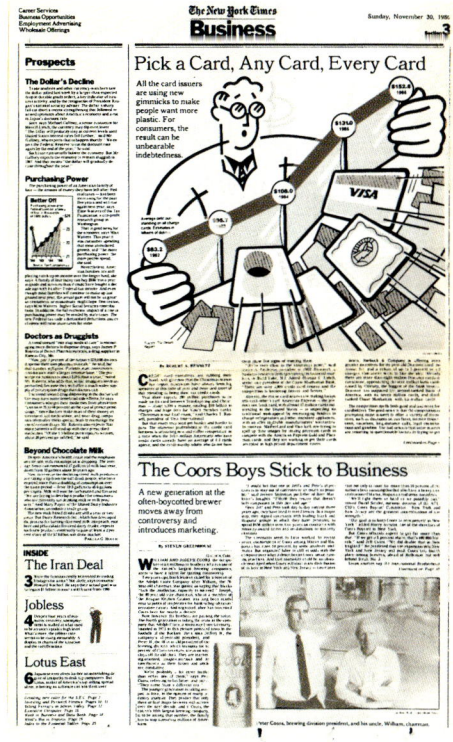

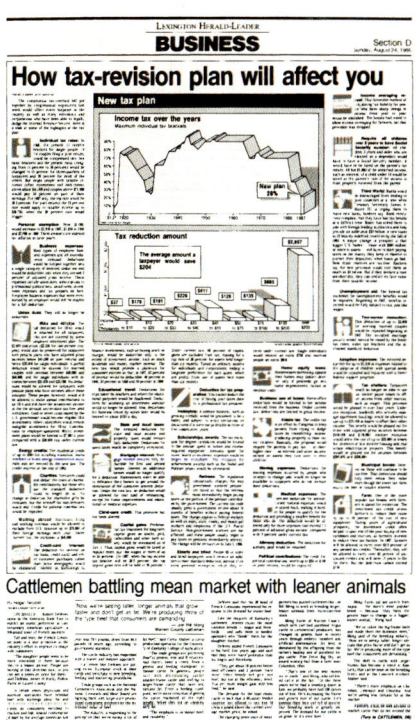

Inside Pages

Silver Award
THE ORANGE COUNTY REGISTER
Santa Ana, California
Neil Wertheimer

Silver Award
THE CHRISTIAN SCIENCE MONITOR
Boston, Massachusetts
Joan W. Forbes

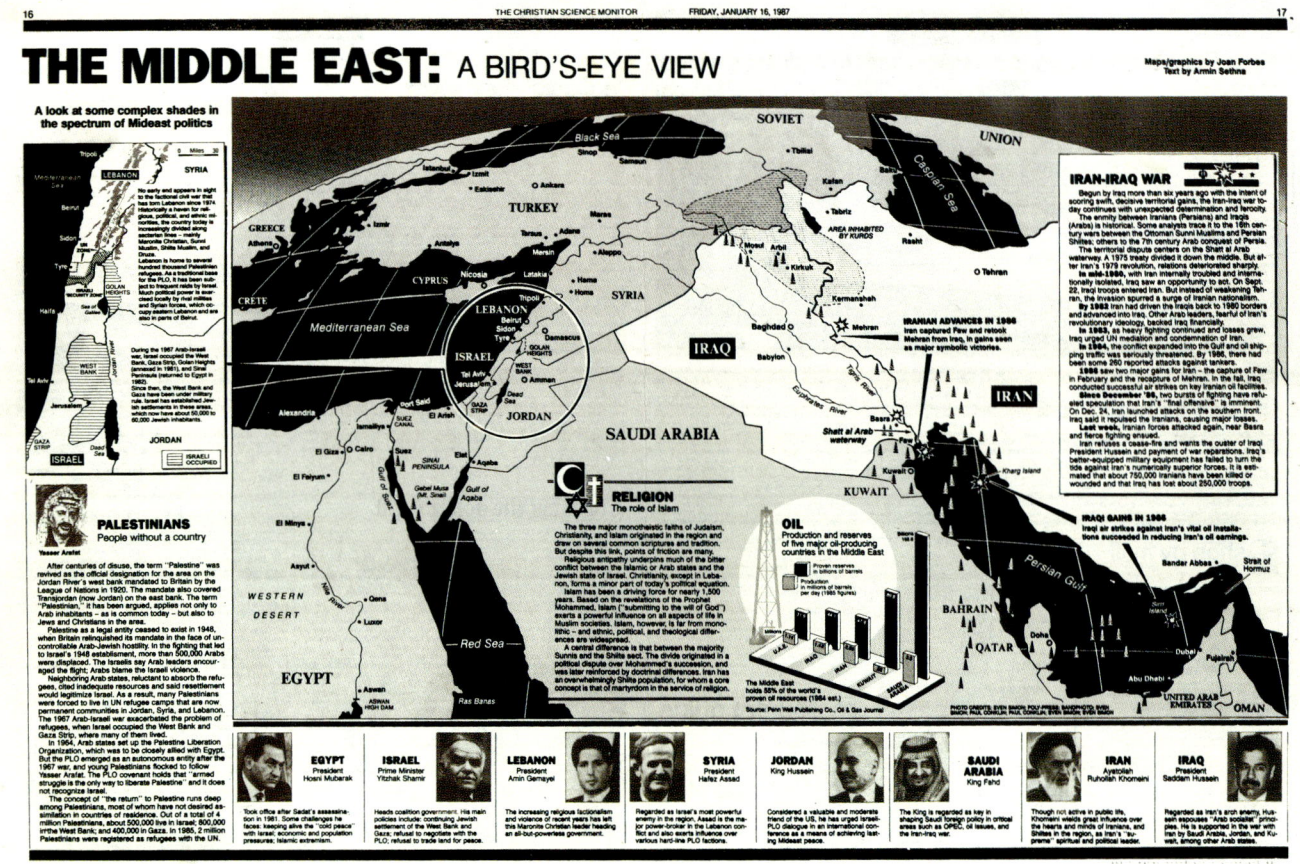

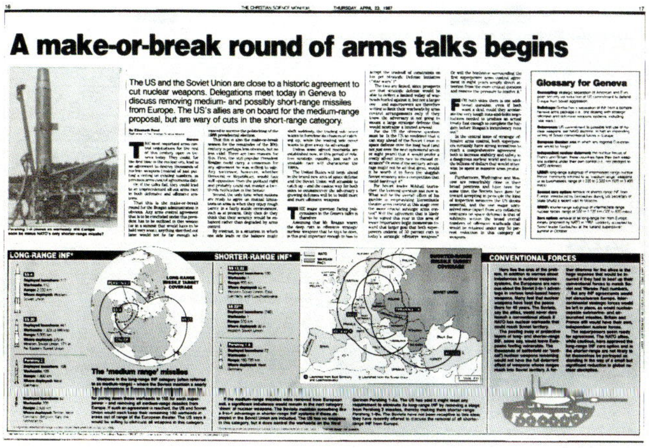

A make-or-break round of arms talks begins

Award of Excellence
THE CHRISTIAN SCIENCE MONITOR
Boston, Massachusetts
Lisa Remillard, Joan W. Forbes

LAWSON'S PARADISE LOST

A path to safety first

Award of Excellence
THE SUNDAY TIMES
London, England
David Gibbons

Award of Excellence
NEWSDAY
Melville,
New York
Jeff Massaro

THE CENTERPIECE

YAP! YAP! YAP!

Wimp Sanderson conducts a typical symphony of scream along the Alabama bench. Sanderson tops the officials' Most Unwanted list.

A Jekyll-and-Hyde type, Norm Sloan of Florida, left, is a different man when the game starts.

Billy Tubbs of Oklahoma, right, has a high opinion of himself, but the officials tend to disagree.

Some officials are said to be "scared to death" of the cream of scream, Indiana's Bobby Knight

COLLEGE BASKETBALL OFFICIALS FINGER THE BIG-MOUTH COACHES

By PAUL DAUGHERTY

All right for you, Billy Tubbs. Go ahead, give us that Jack Nicholson, half-weird, half-weird smile if you want. But we're on to you, Mr. Oklahoma basketball coach.

And you, Wimp Sanderson. Watch your back, bubba. All these years at Alabama, throwing side-line tantrums, conducting your little symphonies of scream. Don't think we haven't noticed.

The rest of you college basketball coaches — and you know who you are — listen up. You're not going to like this.

The referees are talking about you now. Blowing the whistle, so to speak.

It's about time, don't you think? For every technical foul they call, for every ejection, there's a coach trashing them in the press. Refs take more abuse than the Knicks. Refs rarely reply. Being a referee means never having the last word.

What to do? The ref goes home and socks the inflatable Bob Knight doll and sticks pins in the jaw of his plastic Jim Boeheim. He locks the Dale Brown watercolor in a closet with the NCAA manual and the autographed Polaroid of Tito Horford and he vows, the next time he works a game at Ohio State, to give Gary Williams a technical for breathing. Fine. Then what?

Only two kinds of people boo college basketball officials: col-

lege basketball coaches and everyone else.

But who do the refs boo?

In the spirit of fairness and objectivity (and for the purpose of encouraging a healthy animosity), Newsday asked 26 referees, from sea to whining sea, which coaches they considered the hardest to work for.

Among the participants were officials from the Big East, Atlantic Coast, Pac-10, Southeast, Metro, Southwest, Big 10, Big 8 and Western Athletic conferences. All were promised anonymity.

From their responses has come a definitive list of the top 10 bitchers, bellyachers and yappers in the college game. Nothing personal, Jim Boeheim, but one referee likened you to a toothache. He also said, "Jimmy would have made a great wife."

Bob Knight, said another ref, is "tough and insufferable." A "miniature Woody Hayes," said another. Bolt down the furniture.

Not that every major college coach is a certified wacko. Even a few on our Most Unwanted list earned high marks from some officials. Generally, coaches react more favorably to officials they know and who they believe to be fair.

"A big part of it is familiarity and acceptance," said one ref. "I've had coaches jump all over me the first time I worked for them. Then, after I'd had them for three or four games, they'd come up to me and

say, 'I know I'm going to get a fair shake tonight.'"

Also, most coaches "work" referees during a game, hoping to steal a call or two. But most outbursts are not premeditated. Few coaches hold grudges. "When it's over, it's over," Tubbs said. "I forget about it."

And really, if you're looking for theatrical mayhem, you'd do better at the roller derby. These guys like each other. Honest.

Well, most of them.

All right, some of them.

The list:

1. Wimp Sanderson, Alabama

Other than the dear, departed Dana Kirk of Memphis State (we'll get to him later), Sanderson was the only consensus pick. Everybody had nothing nice to say about him.

What the refs don't like about Wimp is his incessant and often irrational griping. Wimp whimpers. All the time.

"He screams about nonsensical things," said one official. "He has no credibility at all. I had him once last year and he was mad before the game started. He forgot about coaching and tried to officiate."

Sanderson also trashes the refs in the press, the cardinal no-no in coach-ref relations.

"By his own admission, he's paranoid. I don't think he means to be an angry person, but once the ball is tossed up, he can't control it," one ref said.

Another official said Sanderson once got so worked up over a call, Wimp actually forgot what the call was. "He asked me if I remembered when he was bitching about," said the ref. "Do you believe that?"

Sanderson was nonplussed.

"I don't guess that's something to be proud of," he said. "A majority of the officials that know me ... I won't say they like me, but they understand me. Every coach gets into it with officials. Maybe my facial expressions get me into trouble."

2. Gary Williams, Ohio St.

Listen now for a sigh of relief from every official east of West Lafayette, Indiana. In shifting from Boston College to Ohio State, Williams made a lot of Big Easterners happy. As for the Big 10 refs, what they don't know won't hurt them. At least not yet.

"The best set of lungs in the country," said a Big East official. "I thought I saw intensity until I saw Gary."

Another Big East official: "Since he's gone, I've forgotten about him. Gary who?"

Williams occasionally will try to embarrass an official with his outbursts and, like Sanderson, he can become irrational during a game.

And apparently Williams does not go out of his way to praise an official's job well done. "I've never heard a good comment from him regarding officials," said one.

To his credit, Williams' act is not premeditated. He just can't help himself. In his first game at Ohio State, Williams got a technical. His team was up by 31.

3. Billy Tubbs, Oklahoma

The nicest thing our panel would say about Tubbs was, "He was a

funny guy when he was [coaching] at Lamar."

Lots of other words were used to describe Tubbs. None was particularly funny.

"Wise ass ... Arrogant ... Obnoxious ... Jerk."

Other than that, they love the guy.

"I'm a great guy," said Tubbs, who was a good sport about this story. "I point out mistakes. Sometimes they don't like that. This [survey] just shows you referees are human.

"Really, though, I'm disappointed I'm not No. 1. I'll have to work on it. What did they say I was doing wrong?"

Many officials said they don't respect Tubbs' knowledge of the game, and that he tries to intimidate certain refs, especially when the Sooners are at home.

"He runs off at the mouth," said a ref, "and he usually has no idea what he's saying."

4. Bob Knight, Indiana

You didn't think we could get through this without him, did you?

Actually, several refs enjoyed working for Knight. "He demands perfection," said one. "That's certainly not bad."

Yet Knight detractors were so forceful in their critique that he ranks among the cream of the screamers.

Officials said Knight treats them in much the same fashion he treats sports writers. They are bugs on his life's windshield.

Some are truly afraid of him. "You don't know when he's going to go off the deep end," said one.

"There are officials who dread going to Indiana, mainly young guys who don't know how to take him," said another ref. "They're scared to death."

And another: "He's particularly

tough in runaway games because he loves to watch you."

5. Paul Evans, Pitt

Officials described Evans as paranoid and tightly wound from the opening tap. They said Evans was convinced that his largely unheralded teams at Navy (where he coached before moving to Pitt this year) would never get a break from them, particularly during the NCAA tournament.

They also said Evans could be nasty and profane. "The guy has a great vocabulary," said one.

"He borders on being dangerous when he's upset," said another. "You wonder, is this guy going to throw a punch?"

6. Norm Sloan, Florida

Apparently, Sloan has mellowed since he left North Carolina State in the mid '70s. Still, he can be a terror.

"I must have I'd him every game he was in the ACC," one ref said.

Said another: "Norman is one of the nicest guys in the world before the game starts, [but] he can get pretty incoherent during a game."

Yet another ref lumped Sloan with Sanderson: "They are explosive to the point that their opinion is biased and carries over to the next game, or even the next season."

Said Sloan: "Anybody that sits [on the bench] and works hard is going to be on that list. When I talk to an official, I mean it. A lot of guys are yappers, and officials don't pay any attention to them. I'm not a yapper."

7. Jud Heathcote, Mich. St.

And you thought Ozzy Osborne was loud. One referee did describe

—Continued on Page 25

—Continued on Page 25

GENTLEMEN AMONG COACHES

The referees also wanted it known that there were lots of coaches who were good to work with, coaches who appreciated what the officials were doing. Imagine that.

At the top of the list was ex-Maryland coach Lefty Driesell, who won the Big Bad Wolf Award.

"He huffs and puffs but never blows your house down," one official said.

Next was Louisville's Denny Crum: "He concerns himself with his players. He doesn't seem to care if the officiating is good, so long as it's fair. He knows he has enough good players to win if the officiating is fair."

Dean Smith of North Carolina fell into the same category, although one ref said that, in the past, Smith's political clout in the ACC was such that he didn't believe an official to be competent, he could assure that that ref would not work any

Lefty Driesell gone but not forgotten.

Denny Crum happy with a fair shake.

more UNC games.

"He could write a nasty letter" to the conference office, one ref said.

"He's fair on the floor and a gentleman off it. He knows what the officials are supposed to be doing, and his beefs are almost always legitimate."

The same could be said of Georgia Tech's Bobby Cremins, who received credit for being sympathetic to the demands of officiating. Auburn's Sonny Smith was "funny and fair," former South Florida coach Lee Rose was "the gentleman's gentleman."

Others with high marks were Bill Mulligan at Cal-Irvine, C. M. Newton at Vanderbilt, Jeff Mullins at UNC-Charlotte and Shelby Metcalfe at Texas A&M.

— Paul Daugherty

INDOOR GAMES

Keeping track of the meet

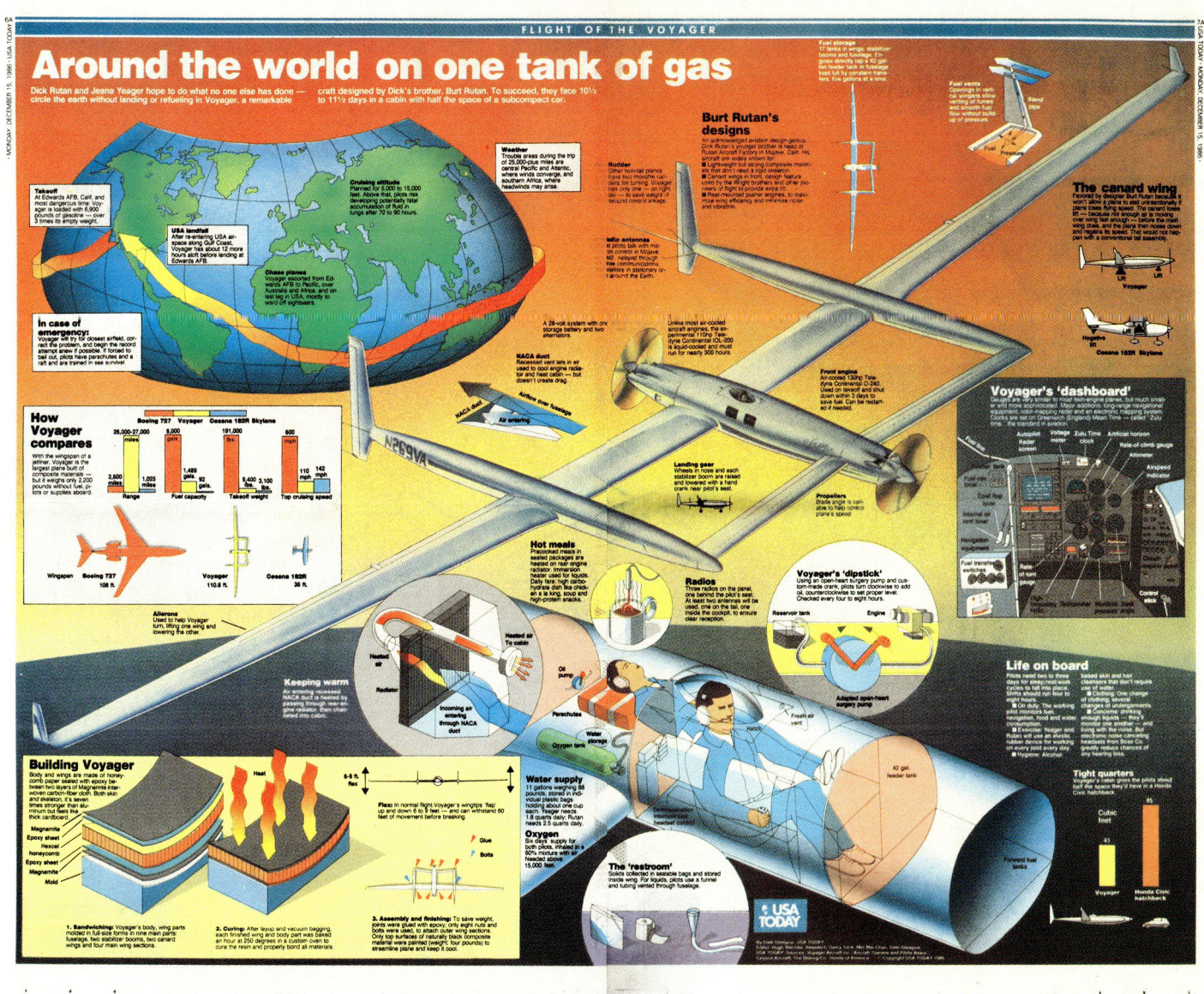

Award of Excellence
USA TODAY
Arlington,
Virginia
Dave Glasglow

Award of Excellence
THE NEW YORK TIMES
New York, New York
Ron Couture,
Anne Cronin

News Categories 33

Portfolios of Work

Award of Excellence
THE SEATTLE TIMES
Seattle, Washington
Marian Wachter

Silver Award
THE WASHINGTON POST
Washington, DC
Marty Barrick

Award of Excellence
LOS ANGELES TIMES
Los Angeles, California
James Owens

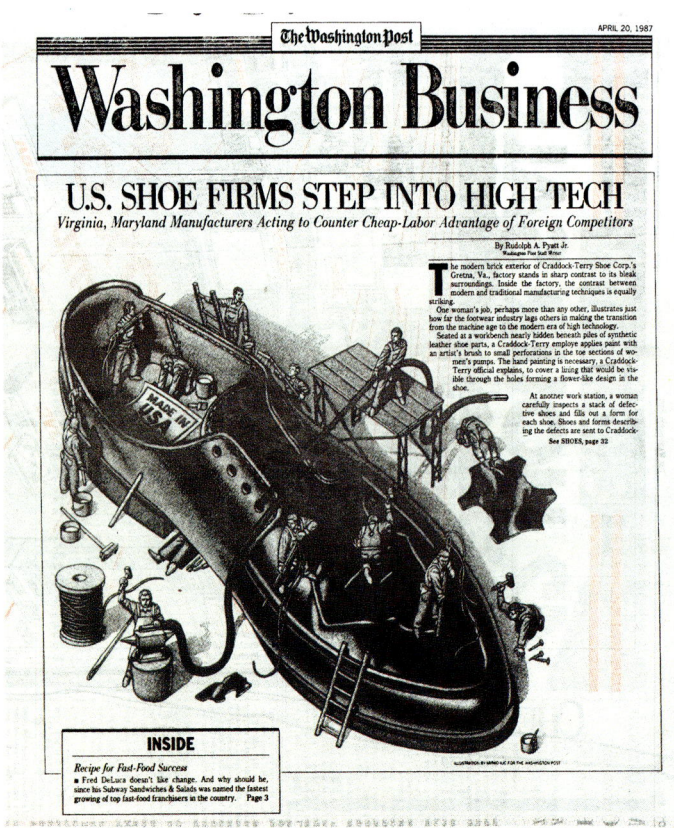

Award of Excellence
THE VIRGINIA-PILOT/LEDGER-STAR
Norfolk, Virginia
Alan Jacobson

GOOD MORNING
Recipe for a good July 4th: don't buy a fifth on the third.

The Virginian-Pilot AND THE LEDGER-STAR

WEATHER
Sunny with highs in the low 80s. Complete weather/A4

FRIDAY
JULY 4, 1986

NORFOLK, PORTSMOUTH, VIRGINIA BEACH, CHESAPEAKE AND SUFFOLK

Not like the brazen giant
of Greek fame
With conquering limbs
astride from land to land;
Here at our sea-washed,
sunset gates shall stand
A mighty woman with a torch,
whose flame
Is the imprisoned lightning,
and her name
Mother of Exiles.
From her beacon-hand
Glows world-wide welcome;
her mild eyes command
The air-bridged harbor that
twin cities frame.
"Keep ancient lands, your
storied pomp!" cries she
With silent lips.
"Give me your tired,
your poor,
Your huddled masses
yearning to breathe free,
The wretched refuse of your
teeming shore.
Send these, the homeless,
tempest-tost to me,
I lift my lamp beside
the golden door!"

"The New Colossus"
by Emma Lazarus, inscribed on a
tablet in the pedestal of
the Statue of Liberty in 1903.

© 1986 Dan Cornish/ESTO

'We are the keepers of the flame'

By ROBERT D. McFADDEN
New York Times News Service

NEW YORK — With the eyes of America on its most cherished symbol of freedom, the city and the nation rededicated the Statue of Liberty in a blaze of light Thursday night, marking its centennial as a beacon of hope in New York Harbor.

In a radiant crescendo to Liberty Weekend's opening ceremonies on Governors Island, President Reagan "unveiled" the monument by triggering a 1.4 million-watt series of laser beams that shot a mile across the harbor and bathed the statue in successive stages of light.

INSIDE
Take the Lady Liberty quiz/**A2**
A detailed look at the statue's restoration/**B1**
'What liberty means to me'/**D1**

Beams of bright red caught the base of the Lady first, then changed to red-amber as they caught the pedestal. Seconds later, a steel-blue wash revealed the full, 151-foot monument. Next 15 floodlights splashed the full statue in an intense white light.

Then, at 11:08 p.m., after a program of music and dance, speeches and swearing-in ceremonies for new citizens, came the dramatic finale: High above the harbor, stark against a black velvet sky, the statue's torch suddenly flamed into golden brilliance.

It was a tableau witnessed by millions lining the shores and aboard ships and boats riding at anchor in the light-flecked harbor, and by tens of millions of television viewers in the United States and abroad.

"We are the keepers of the flame of liberty," Reagan said, addressing a crowd of 4,000 celebrities and officials on the windswept island. "We hold it high tonight for the world to see — a beacon of hope, a light unto the nations."

Earlier in remarks to President Francois Mitterrand of France, Reagan declared: "Tonight, as we celebrate the friendship of our two nations, we also pray: May it ever be so. God bless America! Vive la France!"

Mitterrand struck a similar theme. "May the children of our children find themselves celebrating together in one hundred years' time, and longer still, the festival of free men in a peaceful world." Then, in English, he added: "Happy Birthday United States! Happy Birthday Miss Liberty!"

During the ceremonies, which featured performances by Shirley MacLaine, Elizabeth

Please see FLAME, Page A2

INDEX
Ann Landers B15, Bridge B14, Business C8, Classified D9, Portsmouth/Chesapeake classified D3, Comics B12, Crossword B12, Dr. Solomon B16, Editorials A14, Horoscope B15, Movies B8, National A3, Obituaries D4, People A2, TV B2, Virginia D6, World A17

HOLIDAY HOURS
The Classified Advertising Department of The Virginian-Pilot and The Ledger-Star will be open today from 8:30 a.m. until noon for telephone cancellations and corrections.

It's Broyhill: In the wake of John East's death, N.C. gets another GOP senator/**A3**

A24 THE HARTFORD COURANT Sunday, August 24, 1986

■ Tom Downing, 74, of Blues Old Stand, Ala., used to make a living plowing other people's fields with a mule. Now he uses a rototiller. He put in an acre of corn for himself this year, and although most of the farmers around him lost their crops, his survived. "I planted it and it come up and I got just a little rain on it," he said. "It didn't get too high, but I got 2-3 ears on each stalk." When asked why he got corn, he just smiled and said: "Prayed."

■ Bill, Lester Kennedy's dog, stands on the dried-out lake bed of his master's farm in Commerce, Ga. The lake, once fed by two natural springs, used to stand about 12 feet deep. Kennedy could fish for channel catfish and bass. The cracks, 10 to 12 inches deep, make it hard for Bill to walk across the lake bed.

From the rolling hills of southeast Alabama to the sloping piedmont of the Carolinas, the great drought of 1986 touched the lives of nearly every farmer and city dweller. Some, such as those whose wells went dry, merely were inconvenienced. For others the drought was a disaster that has changed their lives forever. Here are but a few of the faces and words that serve to document the hardships much of the South endured.

Faces Of the Drought

■ Lucy Arnold lugged drinking water home in gallon milk jugs after her well went dry; but she had gone two weeks without a bath. The Arnolds were among 800 families in Piedmont, S.C. whose wells either had gone completely dry or had been reduced to a trickle. "I'm 35 and feel like 56," she said. "You can't rest too good with all that sweat and dirt on you." Asked how she was doing her wash, she said, "Ain't."

■ Charles Jaemes, a student at Tuskegee Institute in Tuskegee, Ala., was riding his bicycle through town when he got caught in a sudden downpour. It rained so hard that he sought shelter on the porch of an abandoned house. After five minutes, the rain stopped. "That," Jaemes said, "was the best rain I've seen all summer."

■ Charlie Bouldin, 52, of Pittsboro, N.C., strummed his guitar in his empty barn after lenders had foreclosed on his dairy cows. The drought, which killed Bouldin's feed corn and sorghum, has cost him so much money that he is losing the farm that had been in his family for 47 years. His 90-year-old mother is taking it hard, he said. "I didn't tell her the cows were going till the day before they went. It's probably all she thinks about."

Photos by
BRAD CLIFT
Of The
Hartford Courant

Award of Excellence
THE HARTFORD COURANT
Hartford, Connecticut
Randy Cox

Breaking News

Election Night

Silver Award
THE SEATTLE TIMES
Seattle, Washington
Rob Covey, Staff

Award of Excellence
THE ORANGE COUNTY REGISTER
Santa Ana, California
Nanette Bisher, staff

Editor's Choice: Local

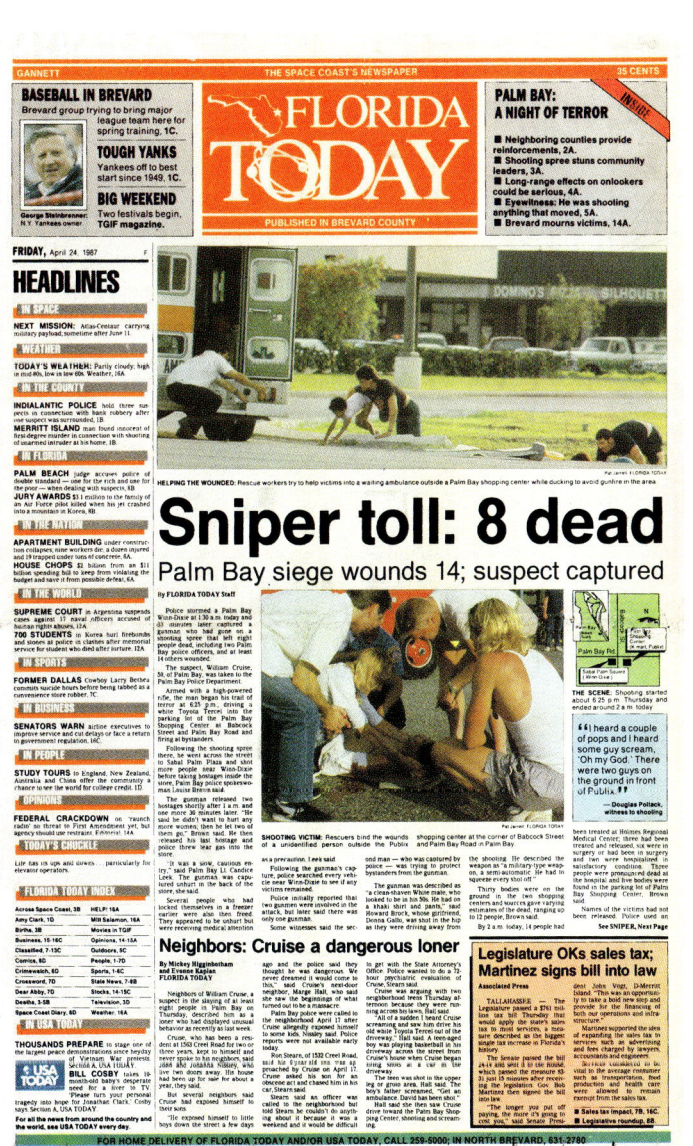

Award of Excellence
FLORIDA TODAY
Melbourne,
Florida
Florida Today
staff

Editor's Choice: Regional

Air disaster in Cerritos

At least 70 left dead after Aeromexico jet, small plane collide over residential area

Aeromexico Flight 498 smashed into a Cerritos neighborhood and triggered a fireball that damaged or destroyed 20 homes.

Those who survived: They watched helplessly

Gold Award

THE ORANGE COUNTY REGISTER
Santa Ana, California
David Petro

Quiet neighborhood becomes war zone

Editor's Choice: Local

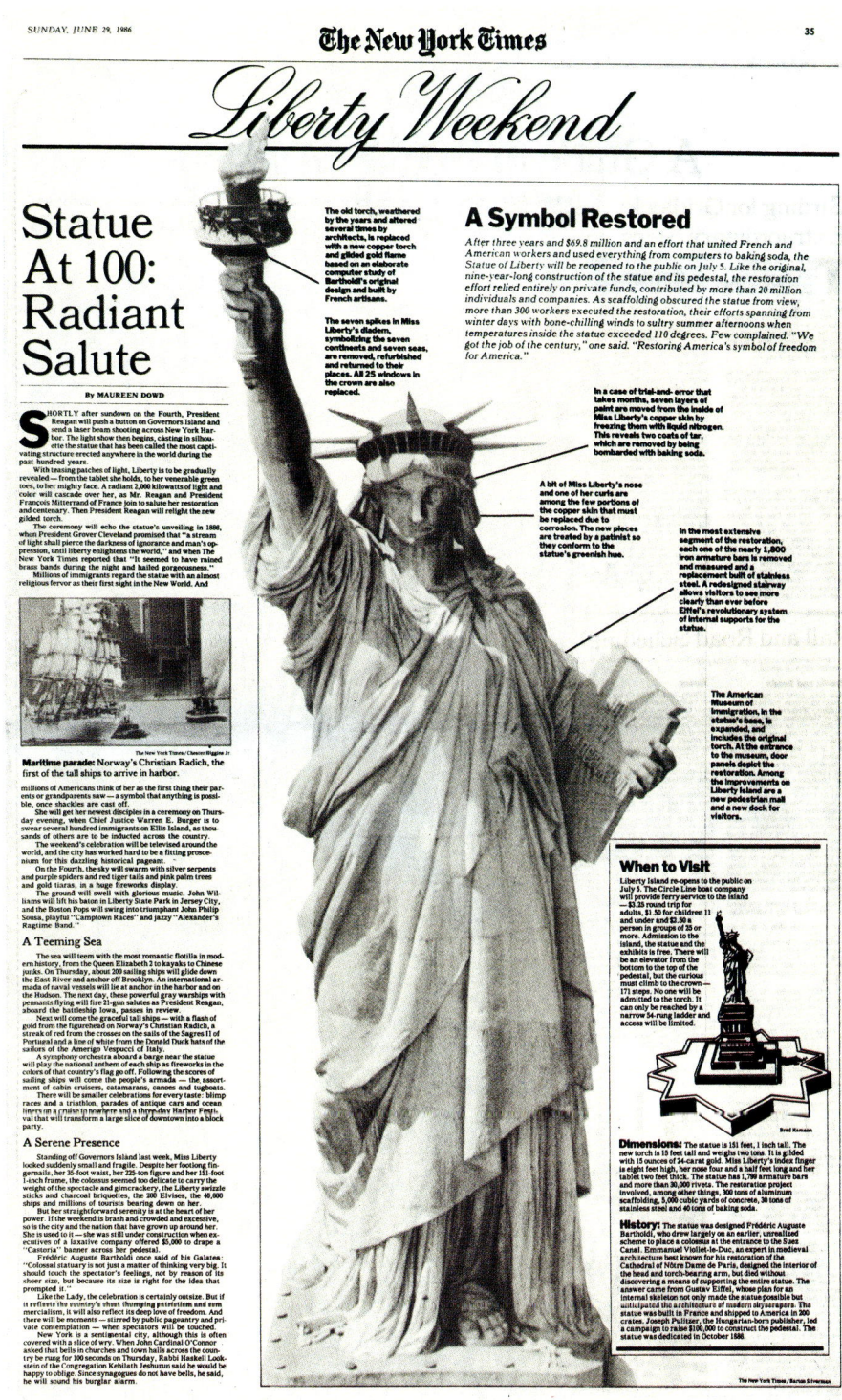

Editor's Choice: Regional

Editor's Choice: National

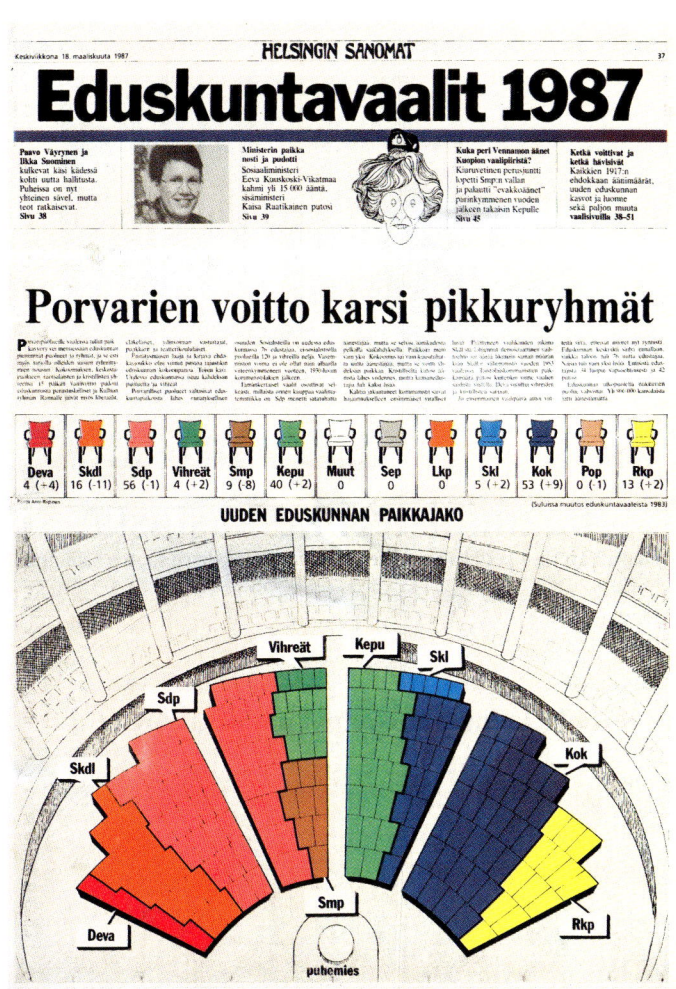

Silver Award
HELSINGIN SANOMAT
Helsinki, Finland
Carl Henning

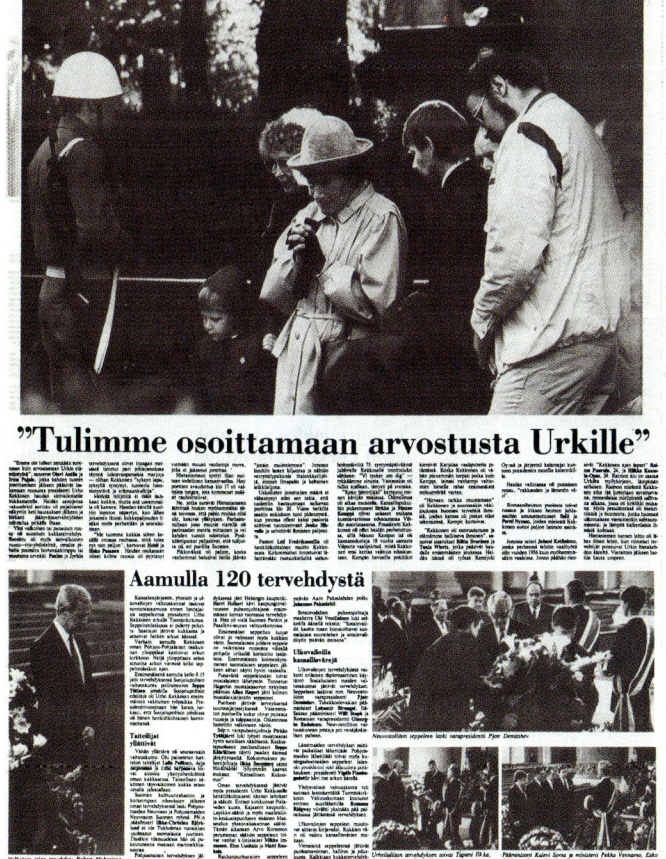

Silver Award
HELSINGIN SANOMAT
Helsinki, Finland
Helsingin Sanomat staff

Editor's Choice: International

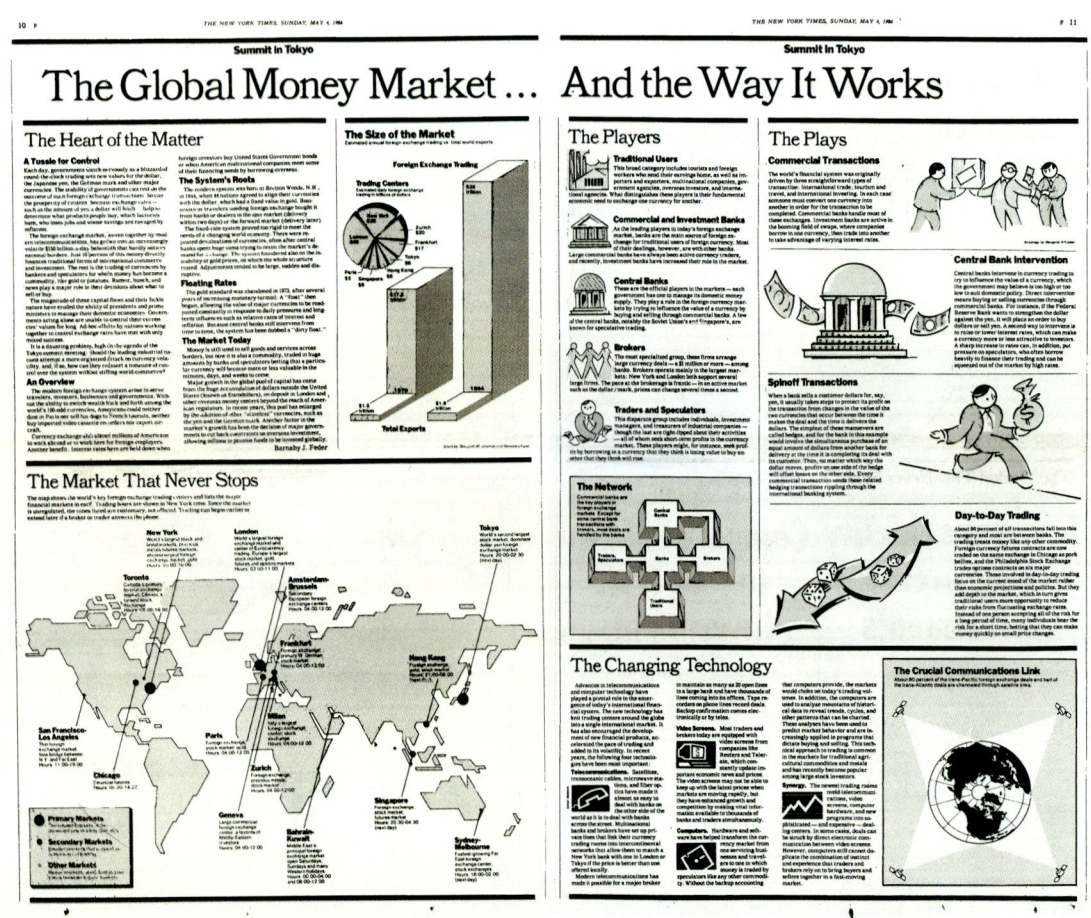

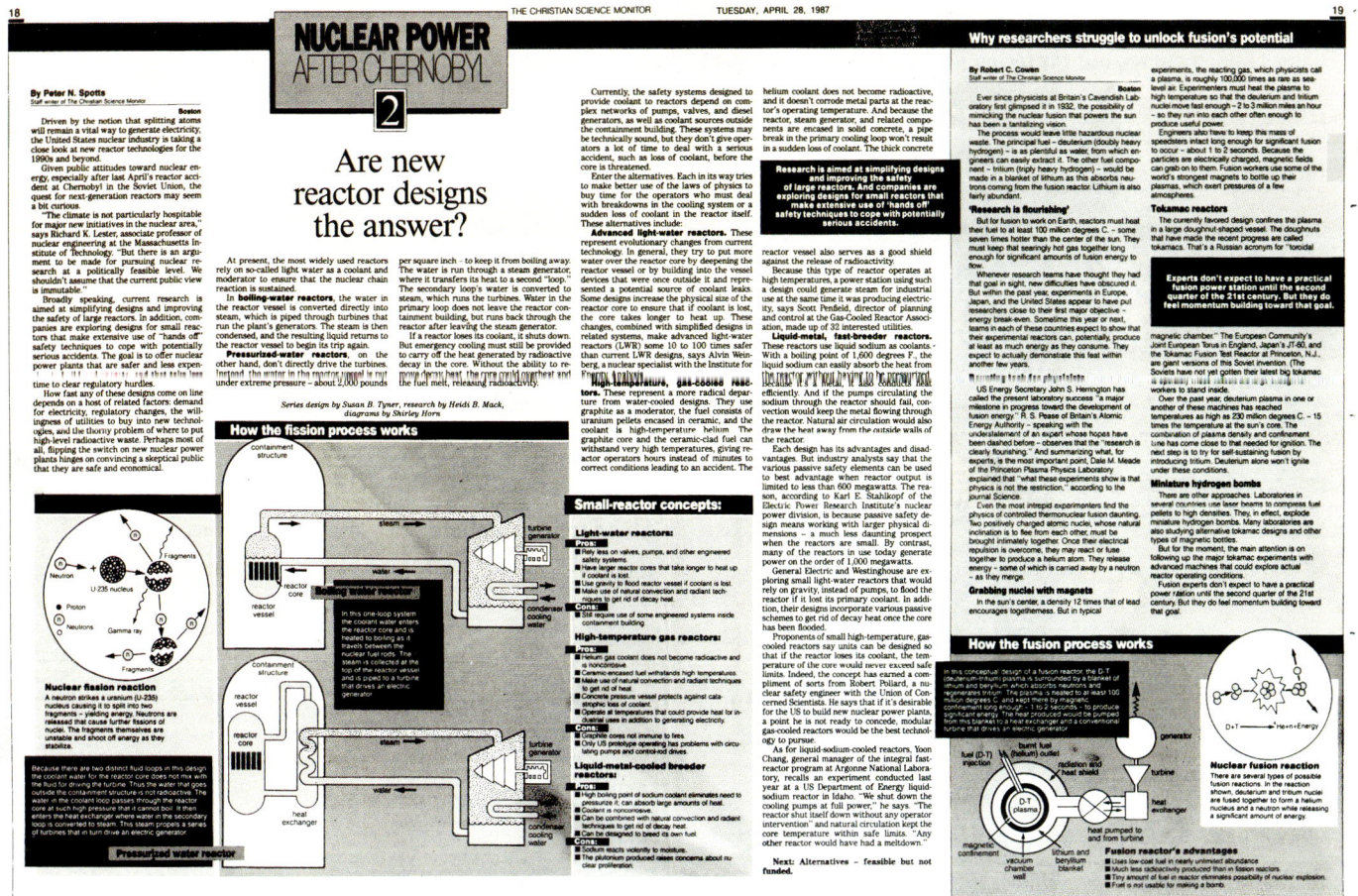

Award of Excellence

THE CHRISTIAN SCIENCE MONITOR
Boston, Massachusetts
Susan B. Tyner, Heidi B. Mack

Award of Excellence

EL NORTE
Monterrey,
Mexico
Eduardo Danilo,
Jaime Belden

CHAPTER 2

Feature
Sections

Regularly Appearing Sections
Page Design

"There's a sense of excitement to the work. Whoever was putting together the pages was excited—the editor, photographer, designer—they were all having a great day."

CHRISTIE BRADFORD

Some judgments reflected basic disagreements about the relationship between presentation and information. For example, this exchange took place between two judges in the Feature Sections category over a page of type that was heavily color-screened:
N. Christian Anderson: "This is not a well-designed page."
Robert Lockwood: "I think it's very ambitious, and its failure is one of reaching a little farther, which should be balanced by too many entries which don't reach far enough."
N. Christian Anderson: "I agree with you that it's ambitious, but if the reader picks it up and it's illegible, if the reader can't get the information, then the page is not successful."

Opinion, Commentary

Award of Excellence
THE DENVER POST
Denver, Colorado
Paul M. Keebler,
Eddie Thomas,
Andy Rogers

Award of Excellence
CHICAGO TRIBUNE
Chicago, Illinois
Tom Heinz

Award of Excellence
THE GLOBE AND MAIL
Toronto, Ontario,
Canada
F. Teskey, E. Nelson,
P. Martin,
J. Shuttleworth

Award of Excellence
SAN DIEGO UNION
San Diego,
California
Ken Marshall,
Bill Evans

Lifestyle

Silver Award
THE WASHINGTON TIMES
Washington, D.C.
Greg Groesch

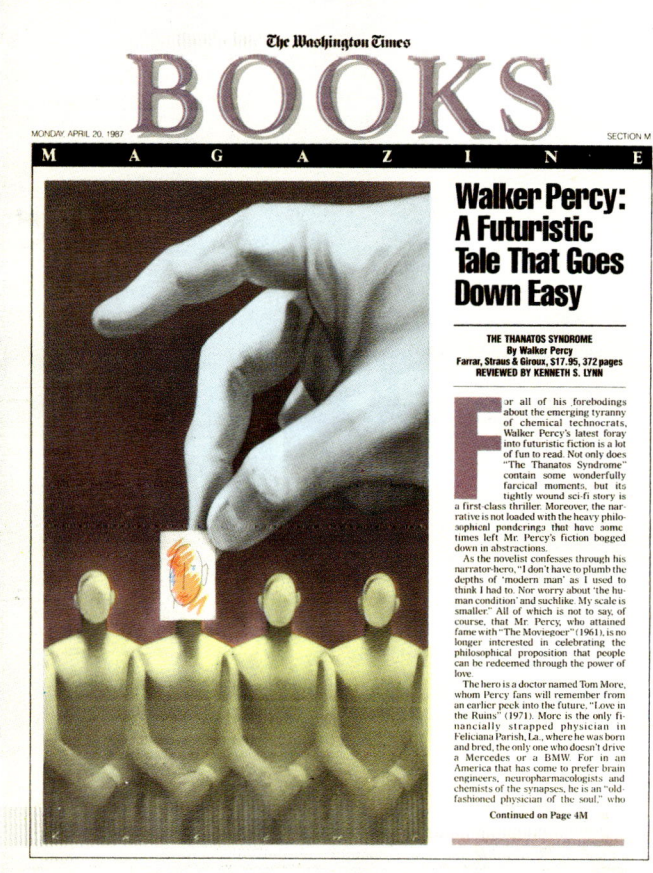

Entertainment

Silver Award
THE NEW YORK TIMES
New York, New York
Tom Bodkin,
Linda Brewer

Silver Award
THE HARTFORD COURANT
Hartford, Connecticut
Patti Nelson

Silver Award
THE HARTFORD COURANT
Hartford, Connecticut
Linda Shankweiler

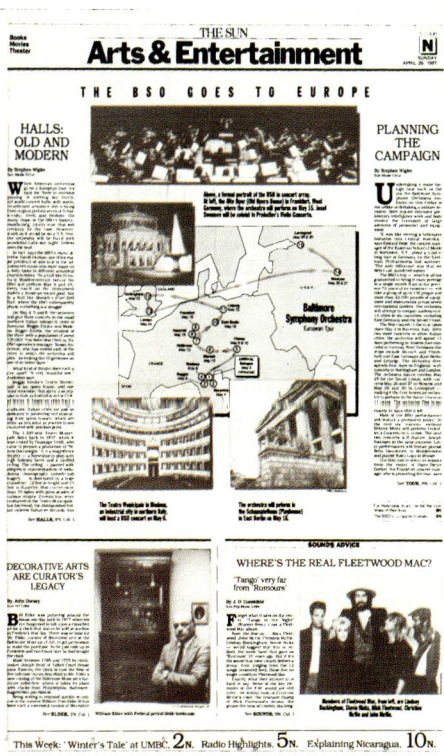

Fashion

Home, Real Estate

Travel

Model of a wedding scene at the museum in Kibbutz Lahav.

The Ways Of the Bedouins

A kibbutz museum of nomadic life. By Thomas L. Friedman. Page 33.

Peak Tram passengers get a view from the top.

Colonial Classics

Hong Kong's favorite rides are the oldest, too. By Sally Hassan. Page 9.

The New York Times

Travel

Sunday, November 16, 1986
Section 10

WINTER SUN ISSUE

Following the Breeze In the Caribbean

The crew takes down the spinnaker on board a 40-foot sailboat off Antigua.

A small-boat sailor on a big-boat adventure, with sandstorms and engine trouble. By Joan Gould/ Coddled on a crewed charter in the Grenadines. By Roxana Robinson/ Island action: Where to snorkel, hike and saddle up. By Stanley Carr. Pages 14 to 30.

| **Indian Jewelry** Shopper's World: A guide to the silver and stone pieces crafted by the tribes of the Southwest. By Deborah Blumenthal. | **6** | **A Taste of Sydney** At an Australian restaurant, purists relish lillypilly berries and witchetty grubs. By Noela Whitton. | **12** | **Always in Focus** A journey's important images are captured in the mind, not the lens of a camera. By Thomas Simmons. | **51** |

Silver Award
THE NEW YORK TIMES
New York, New York
Linda Brewer

TRAVEL

News/Sun-Sentinel, Sunday, September 21, 1986   Section J

CRUISING'S NEW WAVE

Only four in 100 Americans have ever been on a cruise. Passenger lines are hoping to draw on that untapped pool of travelers and are building new ships at a frenetic pace.

By JEAN ALLEN

Cruise passengers stretch value of their trip

By GEORGINA CRUZ

Passengers on the *Fairwind* fight cruise bulge by doing calisthenics.

"All people used to do on a ship was eat, play bridge, drink and gamble. Now you can get healthier and exercise instead of putting on weight."
— Jackie Park, cruise passenger

INSIDE

The Caribbean is one of the most popular areas for the world's cruise ships.

CRUISING
South Florida's ports are offering many maritime choices. **3J**

Several smaller ships are joining the cruising fleet this year. **3J**

A ship becomes a floating campus for college students. **3J**

Recalling the beauty and adventure of cruising. **11J**

PRINTED ON FLEXO

Award of Excellence
NEWS/SUN-SENTINEL
Fort Lauderdale, Florida
News/Sun-Sentinel staff

Science, Technology

Silver Award
THE WASHINGTON POST
Washington, D.C.
Peggy Robertson

Award of Excellence
THE ORANGE COUNTY REGISTER
Santa Ana, California
G. W. Babb, Thomas Ward,
Gwendolyn Wong, Elizabeth Rahe,
Sherry Stern, staff

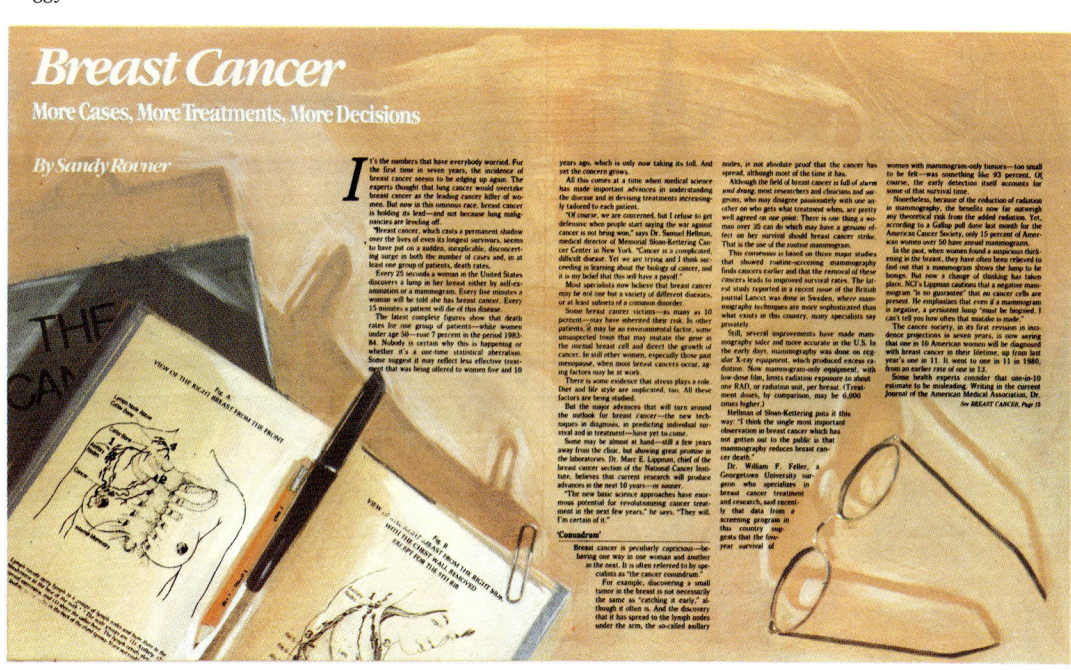

Opinion, Commentary

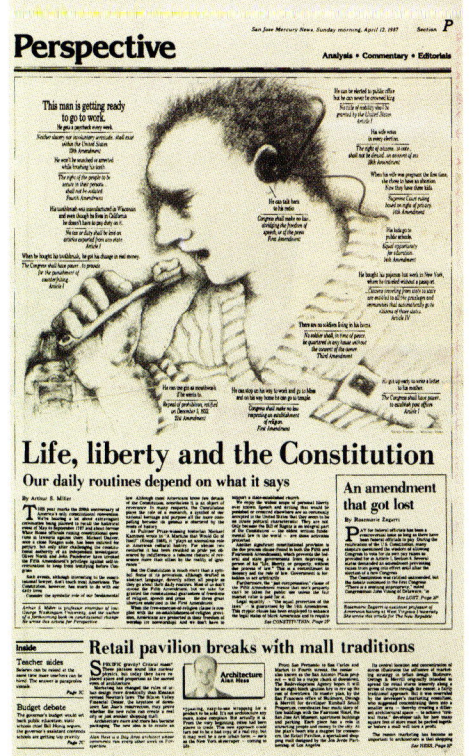

Award of Excellence
SAN DIEGO UNION
San Diego,
California
Ken Marshall

Silver Award
THE GLOBE AND MAIL
Toronto, Ontario,
Canada
Frank Teskey

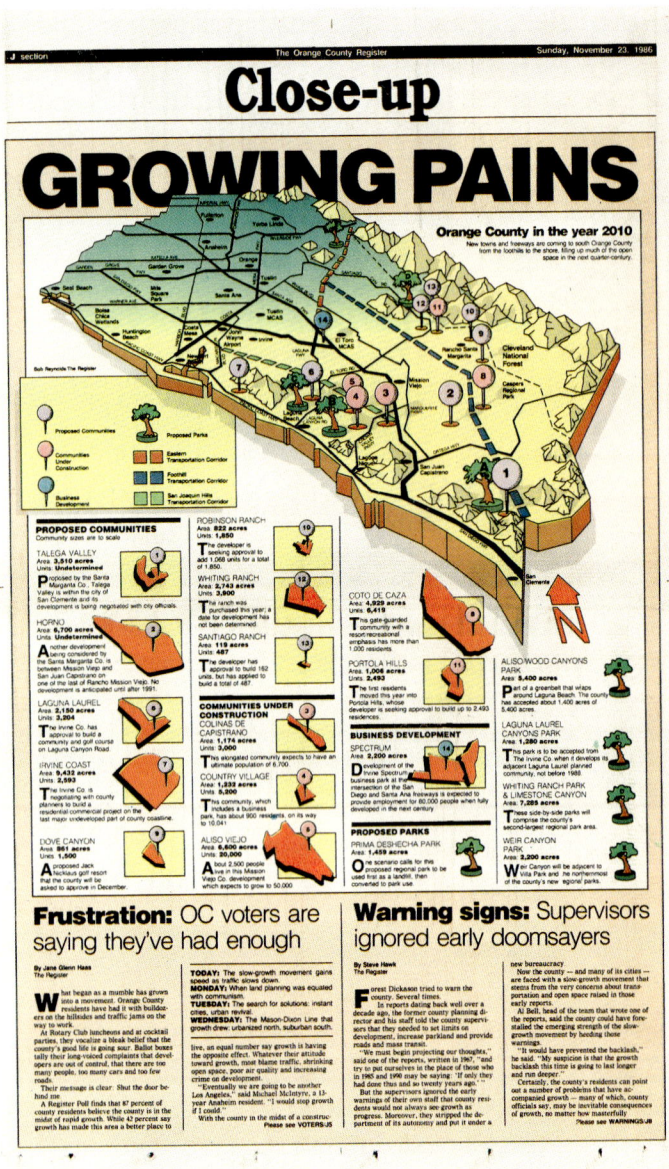

Close-up

GROWING PAINS

Orange County in the year 2010

New towns and freeways are coming to south Orange County from the foothills to the shore, filling up much of the open space in the next quarter-century.

Frustration: OC voters are saying they've had enough

Warning signs: Supervisors ignored early doomsayers

Award of Excellence
THE ORANGE COUNTY REGISTER
Santa Ana, California
Bob Reynolds, Nanette Bisher

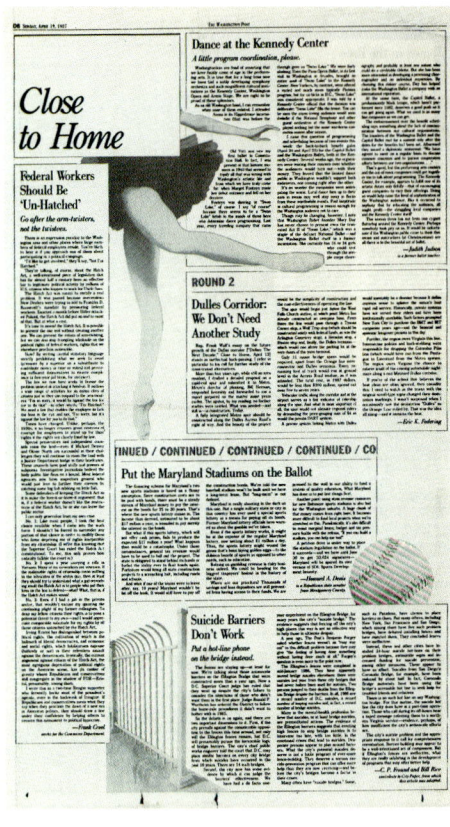

Close to Home

Federal Workers Should Be 'Un-Hatched'
Go after the arm-twisters, not the twistees.

ROUND 2

Dulles Corridor: We Don't Need Another Study

Put the Maryland Stadiums on the Ballot

Suicide Barriers Don't Work
Put a bed-line phone on the bridge instead.

Dance at the Kennedy Center
A little program coordination, please.

Award of Excellence
THE WASHINGTON POST
Washington, D.C.
David Gunderson

CLASSIFIED STARTS ON PAGE 5E

COMMENTARY

CORD MEYER

Tugging at the rug under Savimbi

A combination of brilliant strategy and effective American weaponry has now removed entirely the danger that a Soviet-directed offensive might overwhelm UNITA's main southern bases.

Cord Meyer is a nationally syndicated columnist.

JACK KEMP

State vs. the president

JOHN LOFTON

When Keith was brought home

John Lofton is a staff columnist for The Washington Times.

Award of Excellence
THE WASHINGTON TIMES
Washington, D.C.
Alexander Hunter

Lifestyle

Silver Award
THE WALL STREET JOURNAL
New York, New York
Jerry Litofsky

Award of Excellence
THE WASHINGTON TIMES
Washington, D.C.
David Bartlett

Award of Excellence
BERGENS TIDENDE
Bergen, Norway
Bergens Tidende
staff

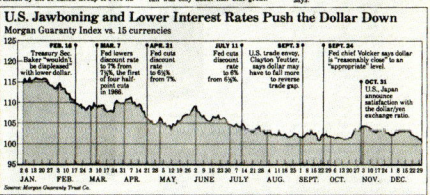

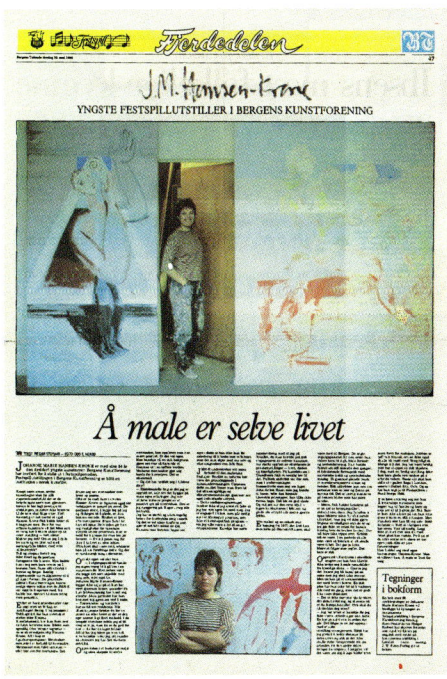

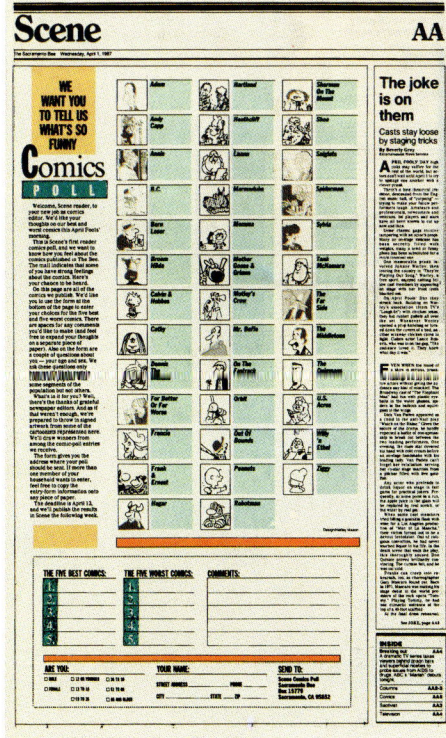

Entertainment

Silver Award
THE TORONTO STAR
Toronto, Ontario,
Canada
Therese Shechter

Award of Excellence
THE BOSTON GLOBE
Boston, Massachusetts
Jim Pavlovich

Award of Excellence
LOS ANGELES TIMES
Los Angeles, California
Terry Redknapp

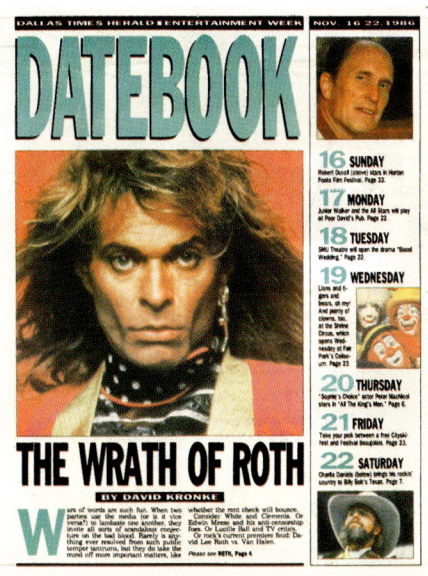

Award of Excellence
POLITIKEN
Copenhagen,
Denmark
Finn Nielsen

Award of Excellence
THE HARTFORD COURANT
Hartford, Connecticut
Patti Nelson

Award of Excellence
POLITIKEN
Copenhagen,
Denmark
Finn Nielsen

Award of Excellence
THE BOSTON PHOENIX
Boston, Massachusetts
Cleo Leontis

Award of Excellence
SANTA BARBARA NEWS-PRESS
Santa Barbara, California
Louis Silverstein

Award of Excellence
THE TORONTO STAR
Toronto, Ontario,
Canada
Therese Shechter

Award of Excellence
THE TORONTO STAR
Toronto, Ontario,
Canada
Therese Shechter

Food

Award of Excellence
NEWSDAY
Melville,
New York
Ned Levine

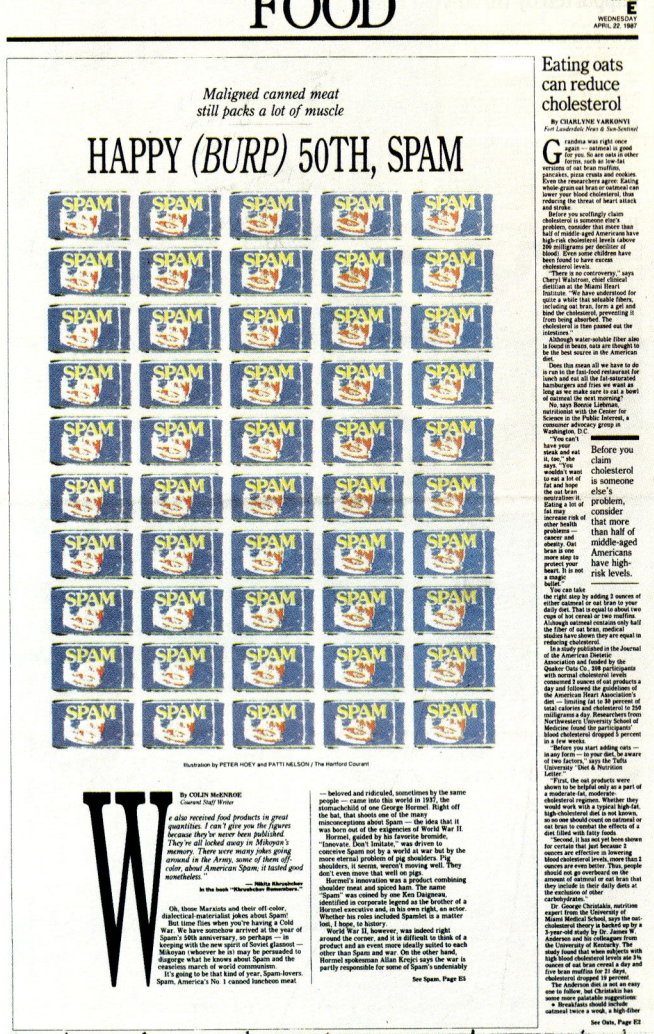

Award of Excellence
THE HARTFORD COURANT
Hartford, Connecticut
Patti Nelson, Peter Hoey

Fashion

Award of Excellence
THE PROVIDENCE JOURNAL
Providence, Rhode Island
Susan Huntemann

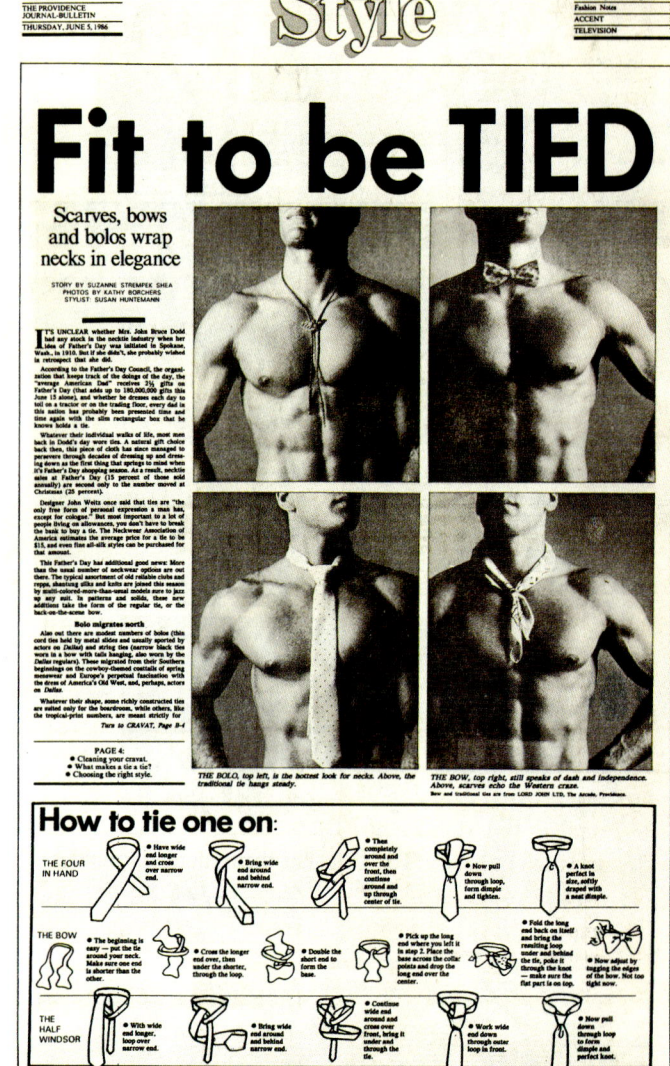

B Section
THE PROVIDENCE
JOURNAL-BULLETIN
THURSDAY, JUNE 5, 1986

Style

What They're Wearing	2
Fashion News	2
ACCENT	5
TELEVISION	7

Fit to be TIED

Scarves, bows and bolos wrap necks in elegance

STORY BY SUZANNE STREMPEK SHEA
PHOTOS BY KATHY BORCHERS
STYLIST: SUSAN HUNTEMANN

IT'S UNCLEAR whether Mrs. John Bruce Dodd had any stock in the necktie industry when her idea of Father's Day was initiated in Spokane, Wash., in 1910. But if she didn't, she probably wished in retrospect that she did.

According to the Father's Day Council, the organization that keeps track of the doings of the day, the "average American Dad" receives 2½ gifts on Father's Day (that adds up to 180,000,000 gifts this June 15 alone), and whether he dreams each day to tell on a tractor or on the trading floor, every dad is this nation has probably been presented time and time again with the slim rectangular box that he knows holds a tie.

Whatever their individual walks of life, most men back in Dodd's day wore ties. A natural gift choice back then, this piece of cloth has since managed to perservere through decades of dressing up and dressing down as the first thing that springs to mind when it's Father's Day shopping season. As a result, necktie sales at Father's Day (15 percent of those sold annually) are second only to the number moved at Christmas (25 percent).

Designer John Weitz once said that ties are "the only free form of personal expression a man has, except for cologne." But most important to a lot of people living on allowances, you don't have to break the bank to buy a tie. The Neckwear Association of America estimates the average price for a tie to be $15, and even fine all-silk styles can be purchased for that amount.

This Father's Day has additional good news: More than the usual number of neckwear options are out there. The typical assortment of old reliable clubs and repps, chambray silks and knits are joined this season by multi-colored-more-than-usual models sure to jazz up any suit. In patterns and solids, these new additions take the form of the regular tie, or the back-on-the-scene bow.

Bolo migrates north

Also out there are modest numbers of bolos (thin cord ties held by metal slides and usually sported by actors on *Dallas*) and string ties (narrow black ties worn in a bow with tails hanging, also worn by the *Dallas* regulars). These migrated from their Southern beginnings on the cowboy-themed cocktails of spring menswear and Europe's perpetual fascination with the dress of America's Old West, and, perhaps, actors on *Dallas*.

Whatever their shape, some richly constructed ties are suited only for the boardroom, while others, like the tropical-print numbers, are meant strictly for

Turn to CRAVAT, Page B-4

PAGE 4:
● Cleaning your cravat.
● What makes a tie?
● Choosing the right style.

THE BOLO, top left, is the hottest look for necks. Above, the traditional tie hangs steady.

THE BOW, top right, still speaks of dash and independence. Above, scarves echo the Western craze.
Bow and traditional ties are from LORD JOHN LTD. The Arcade, Providence.

How to tie one on:

THE FOUR IN HAND
● Have wide end longer and cross over narrow end.
● Bring wide end around and behind narrow end.
● Then completely around and over the front, then continue around and up through center of tie.
● Now pull down through loop, form dimple and tighten.
● A knot perfect to size, softly draped with a neat dimple.

THE BOW
● The beginning is easy — put the tie around your neck. Make sure one end is shorter than the other.
● Cross the longer end over, then under the shorter, through the loop.
● Double the short end to form the base.
● Pick up the long end where you left it in step 2. Place the base across the collar points and drop the long end over the center.
● Fold the long end back on itself and bring the resulting loop under and behind the tie, poke it through the loop — make sure the flat part is on top.
● Now adjust by tugging the edges of the bow. Not too tight now.

THE HALF WINDSOR
● With wide end longer, loop over narrow end.
● Bring wide end around and behind narrow end.
● Continue wide end around and cross over front, bring it under and through the tie.
● Work wide end down through outer loop in front.
● Now pull down through loop to form dimple and perfect knot.

THE TORONTO STAR
Thursday, February 19, 1987

FASHION

SECTION **B**
Pages B1-B8

canadian designers
WISTFULLY AVANT-GARDE

BY NANCY HASTINGS   PHOTOGRAPHY BY GEORGE WHITESIDE

Schoolgirl tunic in black linen, $105; cotton blouse, $95; linen knickers, $115.

Haysack linen duster coat, $360; collarless shirt, $120; linen pants, $102; Mennonite straw hat, $25.

Double pleated black linen shorts, $120; black suspenders, $18.

A-line, placket front Pilgrim dress in pre-wrinkled cotton, $210.

BABEL, Toronto's daring young design line, romanticizes Canada's "urban farmer" in its spring collection: a modern pastoral fashion fantasy. Sober, strong and spare chic. These sepia-toned family album images of Babel's schoolgirl heroines and strapping farm boys are inspired by the grace, innocence and simplicity inherent in the traditional garb of the Mennonite.

Babel's solid design foundation is built on the towering talent of three young designers — Karim Rashid, 26, an industrial designer by trade; Pauline Landriault, 27, and Scott Cressman, 27, both architects.

The creative trio became a team while studying at Carleton University in Ottawa, where a shared interest in innovative dressing led them to surface on the Toronto fashion scene.

Moonlighting nights away from the corporate drafting table, they formed World Enterprise Fashion Inc., industriously turning out the Babel label in a west-end warehouse.

A year later, in the fall of '86, Women's Wear Daily singled them out for a feature story in its Canadian supplement, praising their ambitious creative efforts. In New York,

See INNOVATIVE/page B4

Award of Excellence
THE TORONTO STAR
Toronto, Ontario,
Canada
Catherine Pike

Award of Excellence
THE BOSTON GLOBE
Boston, Massachusetts
Aldona Charlton

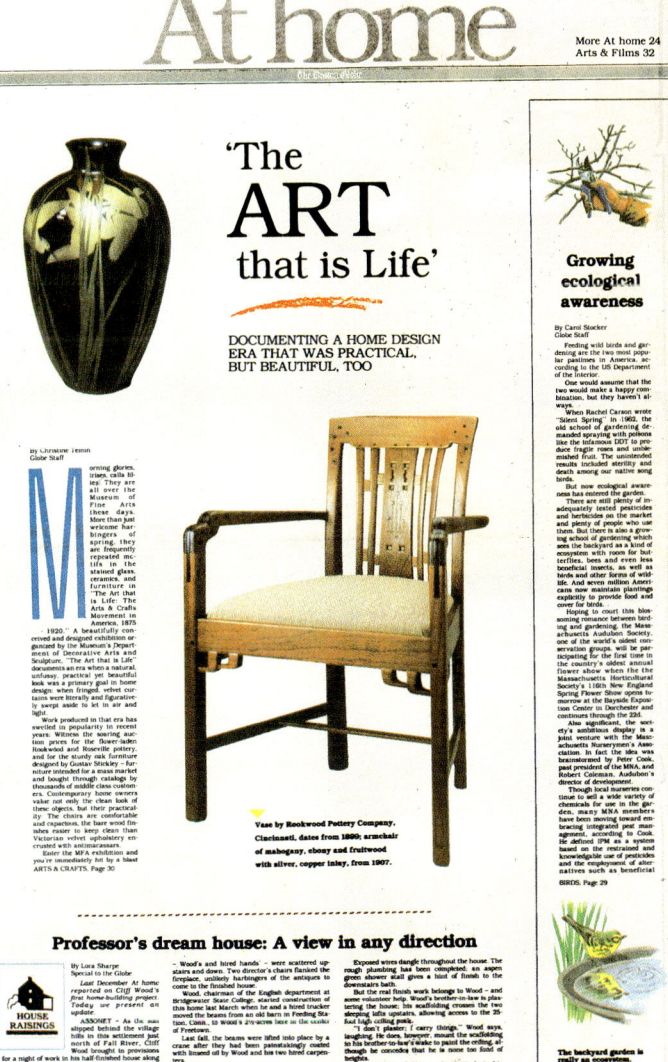

Award of Excellence
CHICAGO TRIBUNE
Chicago, Illinois
Nancy Donohue,
Art Director

Travel

SPECIAL ISSUE

Around the World In Springtime

NSD

Nancy Denizer

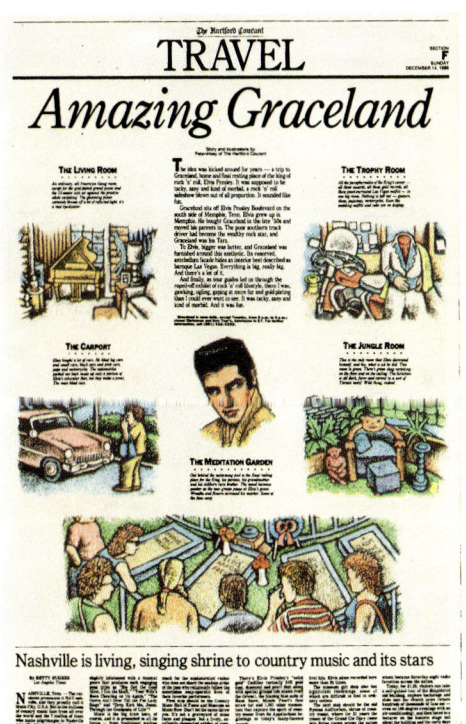

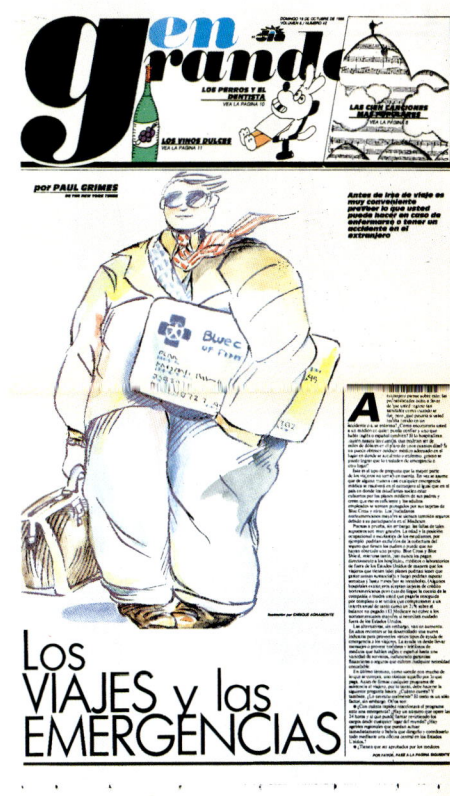

Science, Technology

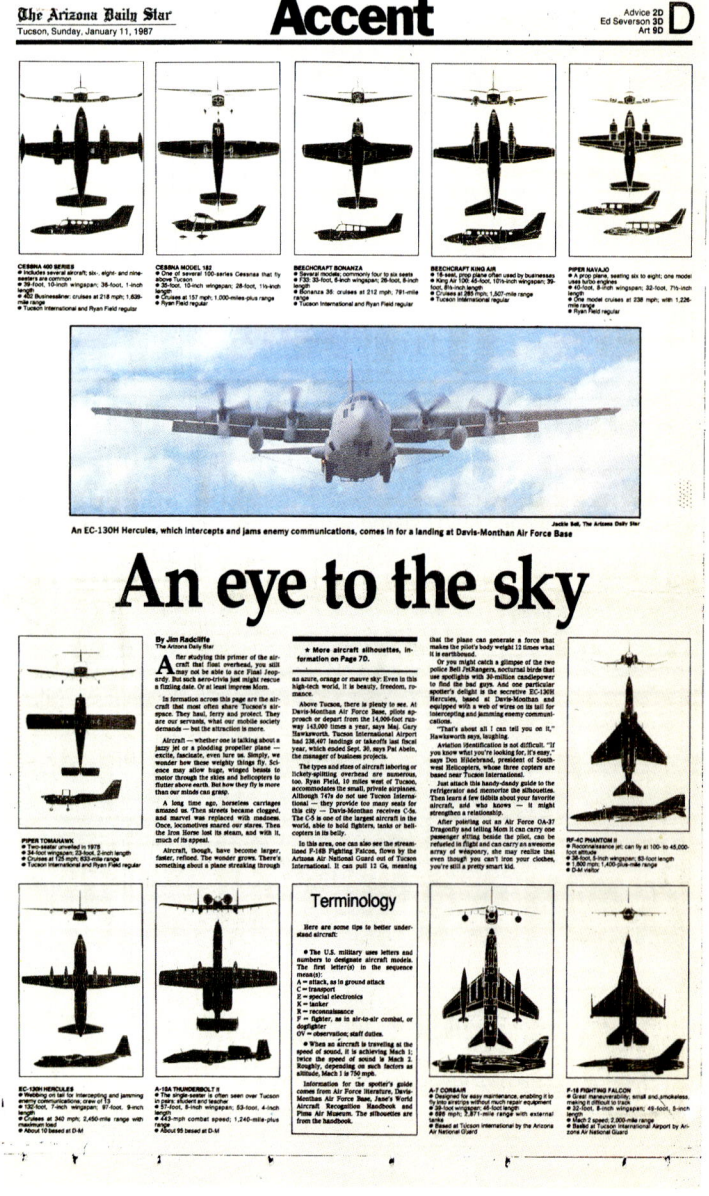

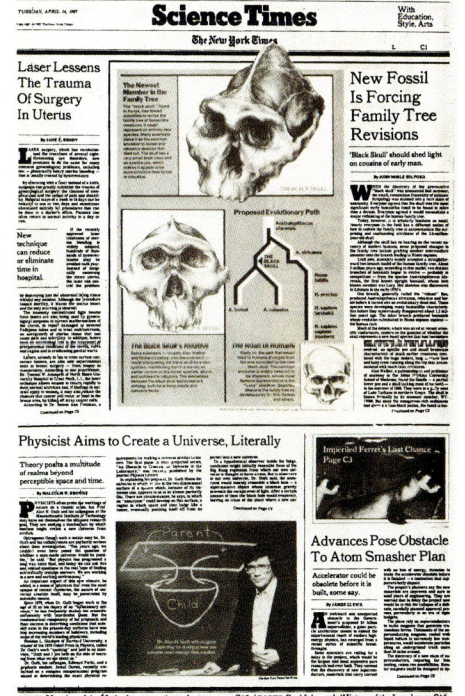

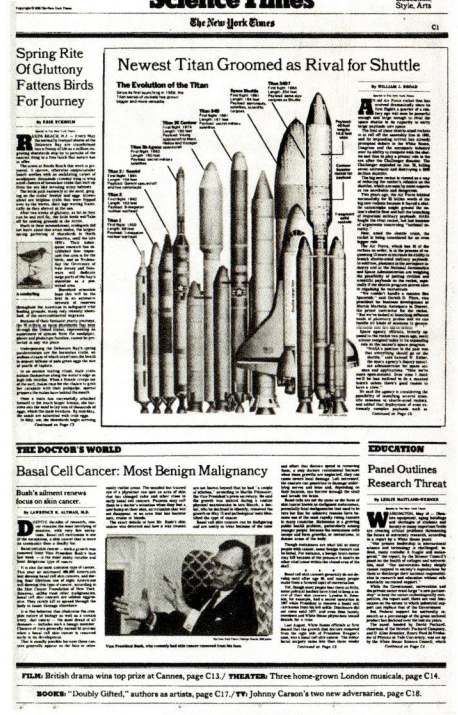

WHAT'S ON

THE STAR'S GUIDE TO ENTERTAINMENT IN TORONTO THIS WEEKEND AND NEXT WEEK

THE TORONTO STAR
FRIDAY, JULY 11, 1986

SECTION D
PAGES D1-D24 ★

EDDIE MURPHY

LOVE HIM

Ron Base applauds spunky, savvy, star

Eddie Murphy's rise to stardom happened so quickly, and so indisputably, that if I had not been there to see it for myself, I wouldn't have believed it. Nobody gets to be a star *that* fast. But one night early in December of 1982, Eddie Murphy, then about 21 years old and known only as one of the featured players on the new and not-very-good *Saturday Night Live*, walked into a theatre in midtown Manhattan for the premiere of his first movie, *48 Hrs.* When he walked out ... well, he couldn't walk out. He was mobbed by a crowd that loved the movie — and, more particularly, loved

CONTINUED: D16

HATE HIM

Peter Goddard can't stand the egomaniac

I don't like Eddie Murphy. Then again, I don't think I'm supposed to. That's not what he wants, from me or anybody else. What he is after, as far as I can tell — aside from megabucks-a-movie and a supernova stardom, is serious respect.

This is big-time respect we're talking about. Awe, the kind Liz Taylor gets by shaking her diamonds. He wants to be *that* big a star. Yachts. *National Enquirer* headlines. A sandwich named after him.

No, I've got that wrong. He already *is* that big a star, in his own head. Always has been. He's been that big a star since he was a kid chauffeured by his mother around Long Island to various tal-

CONTINUED: D16

PHOTOGRAPH FROM SYGMA. DESIGN BY THERESE SHECHTER/TORONTO STAR

Gold Award
THE TORONTO STAR
Toronto, Ontario, Canada
Therese Schechter

Silver Award

THE ORANGE COUNTY REGISTER
Santa Ana, California
Katharine Garraty

Silver Award

THE HARTFORD COURANT
Hartford, Connecticut
Linda Shankweiler

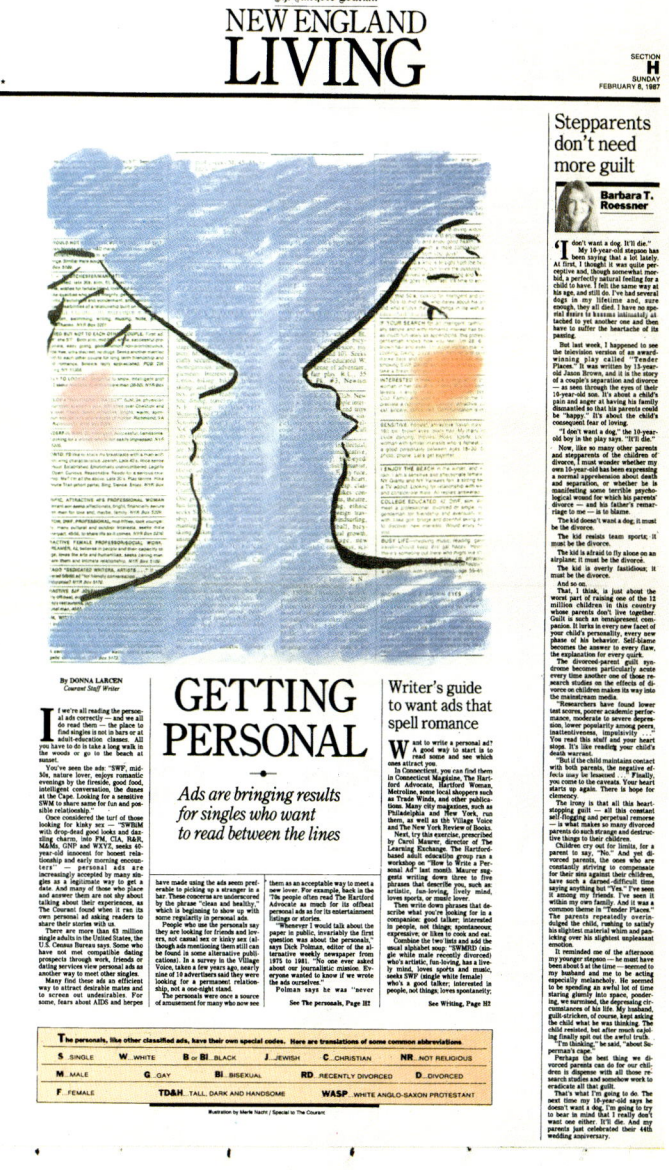

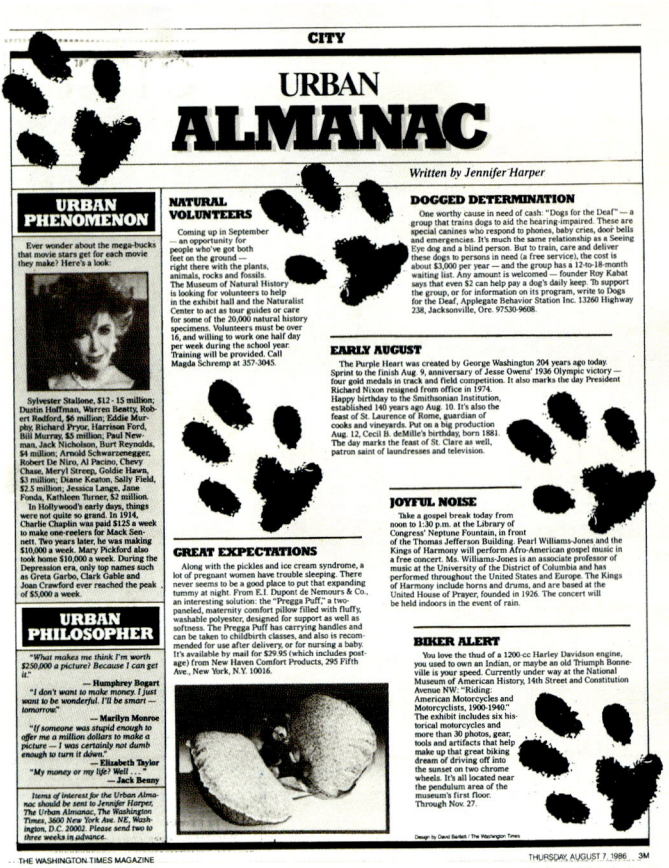

Award of Excellence
HOUSTON CHRONICLE
Houston, Texas
Kristina Poli

Award of Excellence
THE MIAMI HERALD
Miami, Florida
Sean Kelly, Rick Brownlee, Brian Smith,
Rich Barb, Steve Rice, Randy Stano

CHAPTER 3
Projects

"They all share a muscularity. The anatomy of the pages is clear. It's an edition I trust. They understand blackness and shades of blackness."

EDWIN TAYLOR

"There's so much energy on some of the fronts, but nothing inside. The fronts were so overdone that you wanted to peel away 60–70 percent and put it inside, to give you some information."

MAGGIE BALOUGH

Single Subject Series

Gold Award
THE SEATTLE TIMES
Seattle, Washington
Marian Wachter,
Rob Covey, staff

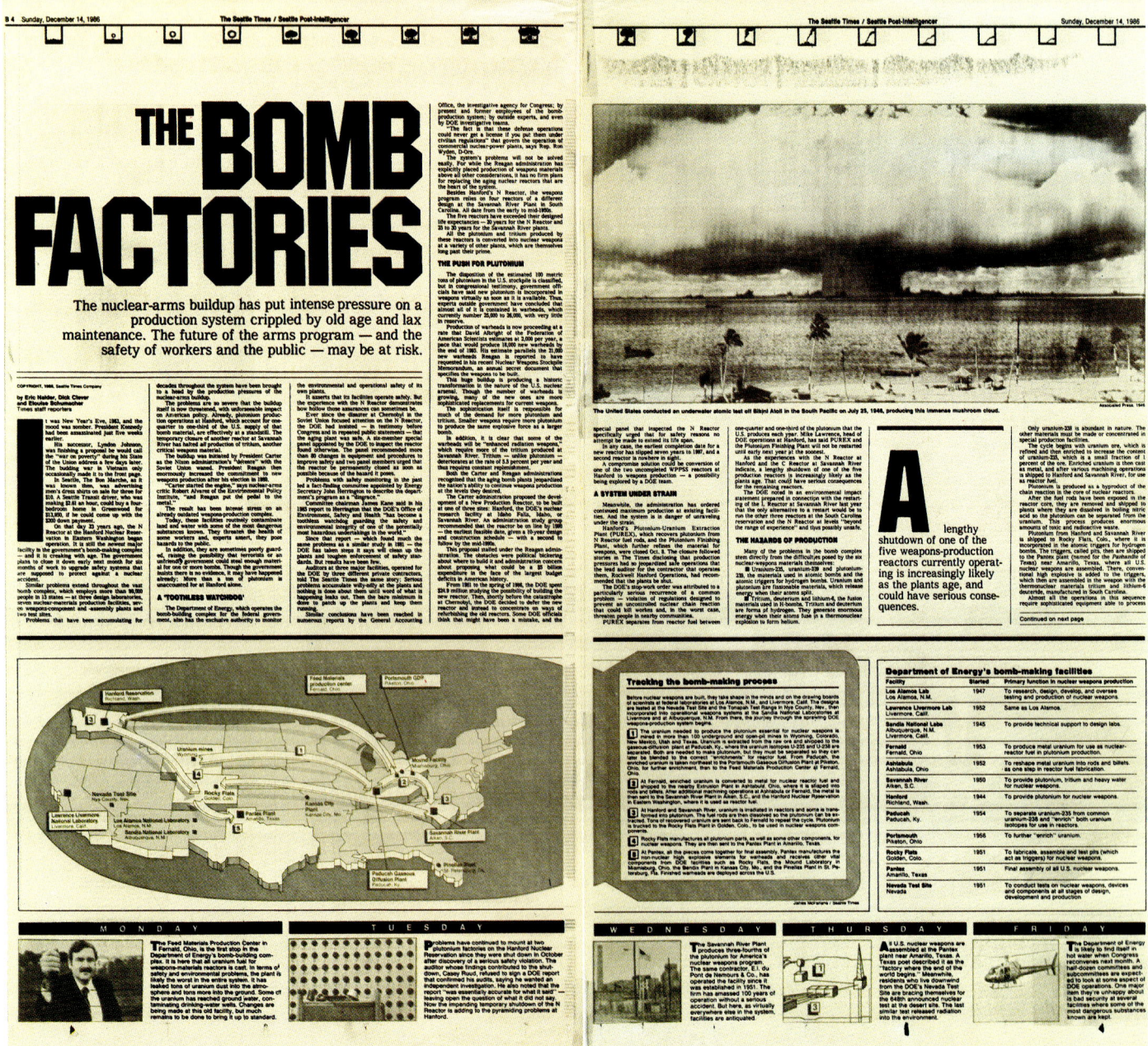

Friday, March 13, 1987 The Seattle Times E 5

A TIMES SPECIAL REPORT

ON THE STREET

STREET LIFE: PERSONAL NOTES

INSIDE THE STORY

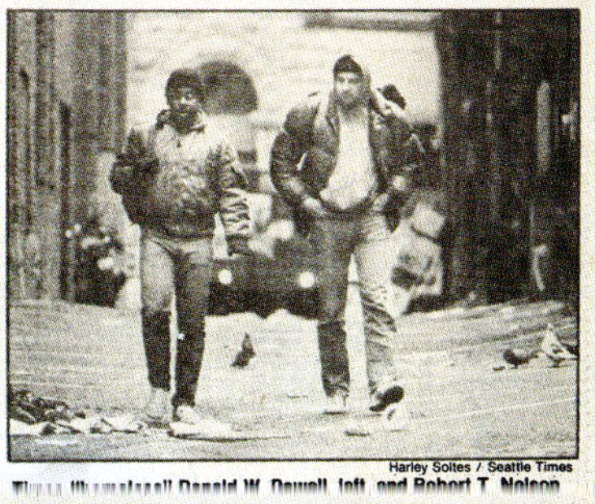

Harley Soltes / Seattle Times

[illegible] Ronald W. Powell, left, and Robert T. Nelson

Grim masquerade: Going 'undercover' to live on the streets

by Robert T. Nelson
Times staff reporter

At 10:30 p.m. the lights in the large room dim for the night. Several hundred men who have spent most of the day with nothing better to do but wander the streets and sit in this room shift positions and lie down on mats arranged for them on the dingy tile floor.

The smokers begin coughing, though none quite as loudly as a heavy-set man near the center of what once was the main ballroom of the Morrison Hotel. His hacking emanates from deep in his lungs, rumbling up through his body and escaping in a raspy, wet, tuberculin-sounding cough.

The coughing lasts until the boozy old man drifts off to sleep. As his body relaxes he passes gas, and when that ends, the snoring starts. The word doesn't really do justice to this noise. It sounds as though it is reverberating through a coffee can, and the pitch changes so often it is not a sound a person can get used to, as you would the ticking of an old clock.

The snoring eventually is interrupted by a groan, and then a shriek, which wakes him just enough so that he begins coughing again.

Outside the dirty, third-story windows it is snowing, and beneath the yellow street lamps Seattle seems an uninviting place. Among the homeless, the old ballroom is considered the least desirable place to sleep. But on this cold night it is a welcomed home to the 256 people sleeping there.

I had dreaded this. Ever since the idea of spending time as a vagrant on Seattle's streets came up as part of a Times series on the homeless, I would wake up at 2 o'clock each morning and lie there with the covers pulled up under my chin, imagining what it would feel like to awaken on the floor of the Morrison, or, worse, in an alley or beneath a viaduct.

There were ample opportunities to get out of this assignment, but not without sacrificing a certain amount of dignity. So on a chilly morning in mid-January the adventure began. With a week's growth of beard, dirty clothes and a tattered knapsack, I met a fellow reporter near the Seattle Center and together we walked to the Millionair Club. A group of men had gathered outside, and as we approached them we realized we weren't yet ready to come face to face with the people we were pretending to be. We walked past them, past a billboard featuring four pretty women promising it would be a "Cutters Kind of Night," and down to Alaskan Way, where we sat in a small park collecting our thoughts and courage.

The trick to surviving on the streets is to look fearless. Forget the fact you are 40 and haven't been in a fight since high school. Find that narrow space between looking tough and not looking for a fight and hold it. Don't stare at people, and don't sleep alone in the parks. The advice had come from an undercover cop, whose tone made it clear he thought we were in pursuit of a bad idea.

In the beginning, my overriding concern had been that I would be embarrassed by walking the streets as a bum, but people don't really look at you. They stare straight ahead, lest their eyes meet those of a vagrant, and the bum takes it as an opportunity to panhandle.

What I had become, down there, was invisible, and strangely enough, there was something enticing about it. I haven't quite figured out why, but my best guess is that for four days I didn't have to impress anybody, and nobody expected anything of me. On the street people pretty much accept you as you are, at your worst. The rules are simple. Pair up with a friend, don't crowd the Salvation Army soup line, and sit quietly through a mission's church service. You surrender virtually all your privacy, but in exchange for those simple tasks, and without a cent, you can stay warm, and clean, and fed on the streets.

But not loved.

By Thursday I knew what it was like to sleep in the Morrison; to shower naked in front of 25 men who were angry because they thought I was hogging the hot water; to sit through nightly sermons in exchange for a meal and a bed, and to stand on the fringe of a street fight as it erupted on a corner near Occidental Square.

What I hadn't felt, couldn't feel, was the loneliness these men and women live with each day. That point was dramatized on that first night in the Morrison's ballroom. A news crew from KING-TV dropped in to film conditions at the emergency shelter, and to ask residents how they felt about U.S. Rep.John Miller's having spent a night there.

The reporter would ask the innocuous question, and the men would stare back blankly, not really knowing what to say. As the reporter approached the corner of the room where I sat, the man next to me began to worry that the crew would film him, and put him on television.

"I know my wife and kids will see it, and they'll say, 'Daddy's a bum,' " the man said. "My brother will see it and tell my wife, 'See, I told ya he was no good.' "

Yet the chance to be on television proved too enticing. When the camera crew and reporter got to where we were sitting, he let them take his picture, and he answered her questions.

"I think it's a good thing that the congressman came down here to see what it's like," the man said. "Maybe he'll bring President Reagan with him next time."

The television crew moved on and the man turned to me. He looked about 35 years old, and he had the saddest eyes. He was broke, and had spent the better part of the evening trying to decide whether to hock his guitar. And now — on this, his most humiliating day ever — his family was going to see him on television.

"You know," he said, "a person can spend a night down here to get a feel for what it's like to be homeless, but they can't know what it's like to know that in the whole world nobody cares about you."

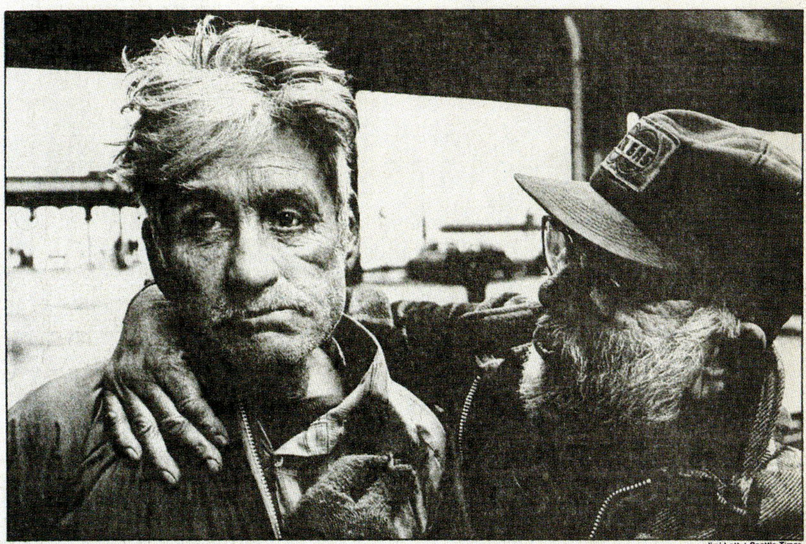

Jimi Lott / Seattle Times

Thuryl Green, left, cries as he talks of his survival in a World War II POW camp and today as a homeless man. Comforting him is buddy Felix Martinez.

Photographers find one word — homeless — is worth 3,500 pictures

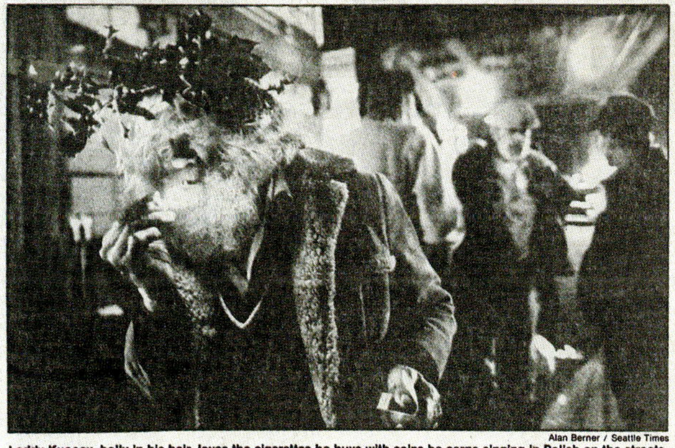

Alan Berner / Seattle Times

Laddy Kuecay, holly in his hair, loves the cigarettes he buys with coins he earns singing in Polish on the streets.

Robert T. Nelson
Times staff reporter

The call came early in the morning to The Times photo desk.

It was the wife of Times photographer Jimi Lott, asking if the newspaper knew his whereabouts.

The night before, Lott, all alone, had hit Seattle's streets to photograph the homeless for this series.

Lott hadn't shown up in the newsroom either.

He did turn up, however, a few hours later, inside an abandoned apartment building on Boren Avenue, where he had spent the night with two teen-age runaways.

For Times photographer Alan Berner, working the streets for the homeless series also had its moments.

More than 3,500 photographs had been taken for the series when Berner went out to get just one more — of a woman huddled beneath a blanket. As Berner prepared to shoot her picture, the young woman charged at him, breaking two of his cameras.

Berner and Lott each have had a longstanding interest in the homeless, shooting hundreds of photographs of street people long before the series was conceived.

Lott began as far back as 1968, when he was in San Diego. He found he had things in common with the street people, and he appreciated their lack of pretense.

"I could empathize with them," said Lott. "These were people who had nothing, and at one time of my life I didn't have anything either."

Like many photographers, Berner is rarely without his cameras. In the course of photographing Seattle, he found that a favorite photo subject was the city's homeless.

"It's not that I would go out and just shoot (photograph) transients," said Berner. Photography is "one of the ways I experience the world."

For this series, the photographers got closer to their subjects than they might have in other assignments.

Lott, for example, put one elderly woman up in an inexpensive downtown hotel room for two nights to help her get over a lingering cold. He estimates that in the five weeks he worked on the project he gave away $40 for food, cigarettes and booze.

Berner carried a pack of cigarettes with him, giving them freely to those he met. He also bought food for many of the people he met on the streets.

"Guys would say they needed 25 cents for lunch," says Berner. "No way they'd use it for that. I'd bring them back lunch."

Berner says the weeks on the street changed some of his perceptions.

"I used to see it (downtown) as destination points. Now I see it as more the turf of these people. These places where I used to go to are now a backdrop for the homeless."

And although photographing the homeless got so intense for Lott that at times that he couldn't wait for the project to end, he still goes back to take photographs of the people living on the streets.

"Without question I will continue an ongoing relationship," he said, "just to check on their welfare, share some words of encouragement and lose some change."

Being with the homeless means sharing the scorn they can't escape

by Ronald W. Powell
Times staff reporter

It was a blustery January day and chilling winds were whipping around the maze of steel and glass buildings that dominate downtown Seattle.

I had been panhandling in Pioneer Square with four others to get enough money for a "jug," a bottle of cheap wine. While passers-by weren't biting, the winds certainly were, easily cutting through our tattered clothes.

Pursuit of money soon gave way to pursuit of shelter.

My four companions were *straight-up concrete people*, those homeless who reject the network of downtown shelters for fear of rules, lice, scabies or all three. They choose instead to bed down in a private corner of concrete in the heart of the city — a shadowy doorway, a dark niche beneath a viaduct, a cold hard spot in the recesses of a parking garage.

We settled for a parking garage on downtown's south end. But Trombone, a toothless Vietnam veteran and the ramrod of the group, was uneasy. The garage had been a recent find that had proven perfect for bedding down at night. Why jeopardize it by entering during daylight? he wondered aloud.

His friends weren't listening. Not John, who was big and tipsy. Not John's tiny girlfriend with the trembling hands — the one who coughed up phlegm and sported a purple shiner. Not the stocky, grandfatherly gent called Silver Eagle.

We slipped into a corner of the garage next to warm heating pipes, trying to maintain secrecy.

We talked in hushed tones, passing around cigarettes and Thunderbird wine. I will never forget how Silver Eagle unfolded the blankets and delicately draped them around our shoulders. Or how I recoiled at this loving gesture because the bedding reeked of urine. It reminded me that I was a tourist in the homeless world, that while I was *with* them, I was not one of them.

We had been largely ignored by the business people who shuttled in and out of the garage.

But it didn't last long.

A smartly dressed 50-ish woman parked her car, watched us for a few minutes, then marched 20 indignant yards to where we sat.

"You can't stay here," she spat, her eyes hard as she looked down at us. "You have to leave."

The confrontation struck an emotional chord. The heat of her demand felt like racism — blind rejections small and large that I first felt as a Texas schoolboy and still experience at times today. No one made eye contact. Nothing was said. We simply rose and folded the blankets. Trombone and I helped John struggle to his feet and propped him up as we shuffled from the gray bunker like refugees cast adrift.

The five of us struggled two blocks through foul-smelling alleys littered with broken glass before allowing John and his girlfriend to plop down on the sidewalk in front of an office building. It was still cold, but at least they were sitting on the sunny side of the street.

REPRINTS of The Times series 'On the Street' will be available beginning Tuesday, March 17, at the front reception desk at The Times, John Street at Fairview Avenue. For bulk orders, call 464-2461.

Gold Award
THE SEATTLE TIMES
Seattle, Washington
Celeste Ericsson,
Marian Wachter

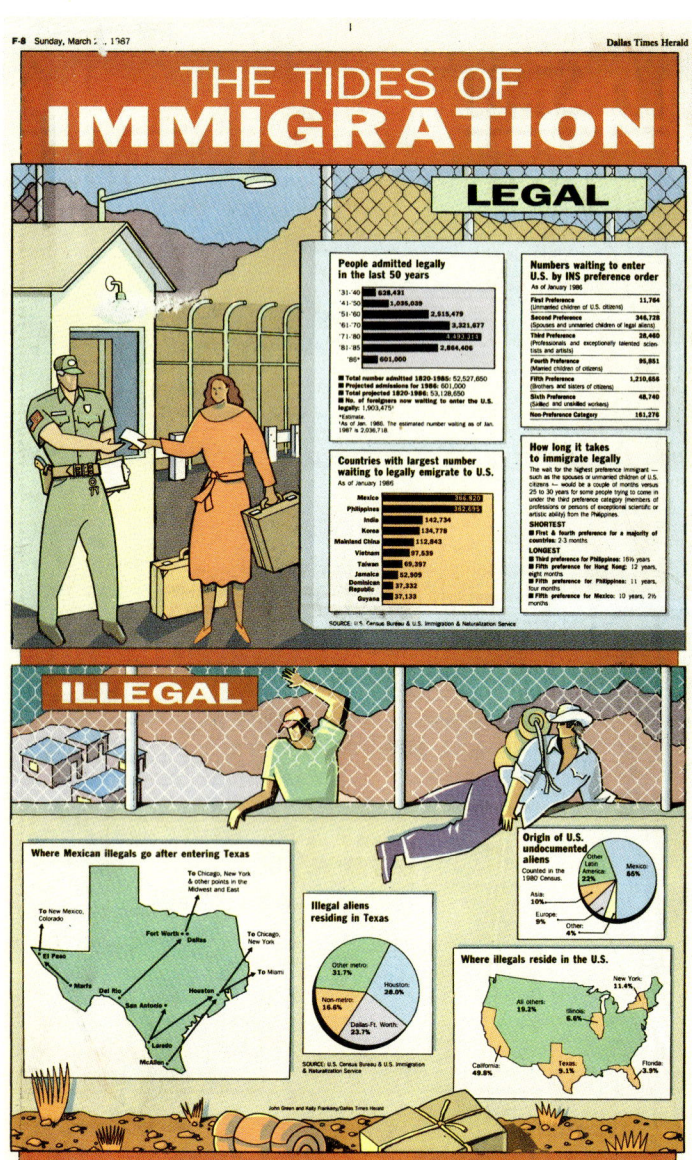

Award of Excellence
THE HARTFORD COURANT
Hartford, Connecticut
Randy Cox

Award of Excellence
DALLAS TIMES HERALD
Dallas, Texas
Dallas Times Herald staff

Special Sections

Silver Award
THE ORANGE COUNTY REGISTER
Santa Ana, California
Pam Marshak

Silver Award
USA TODAY
Arlington, Virginia
USA Today staff

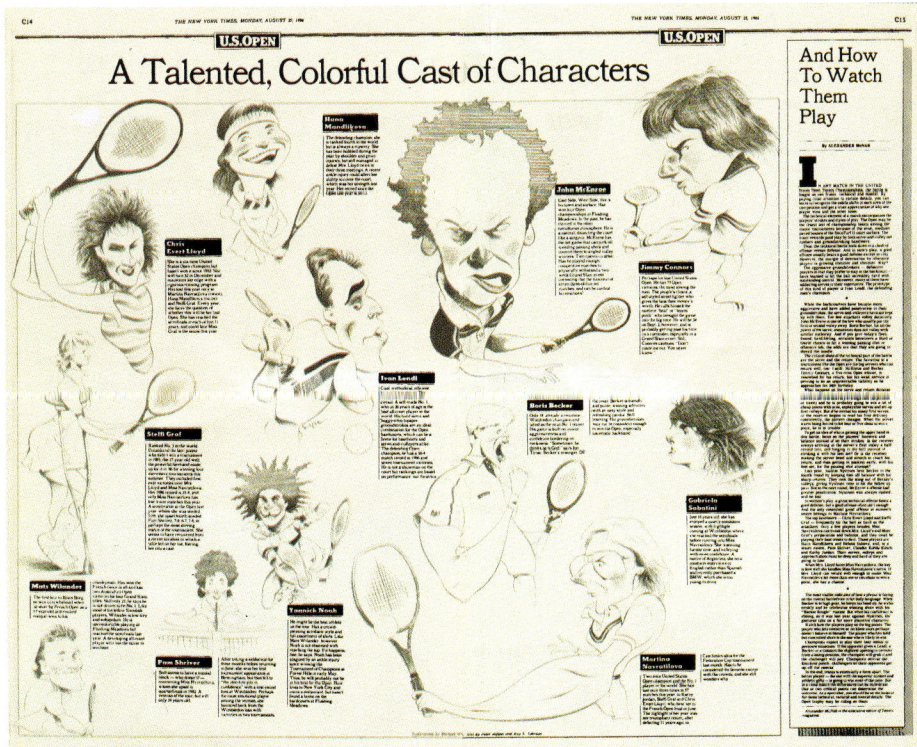

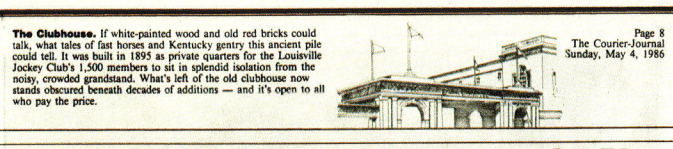

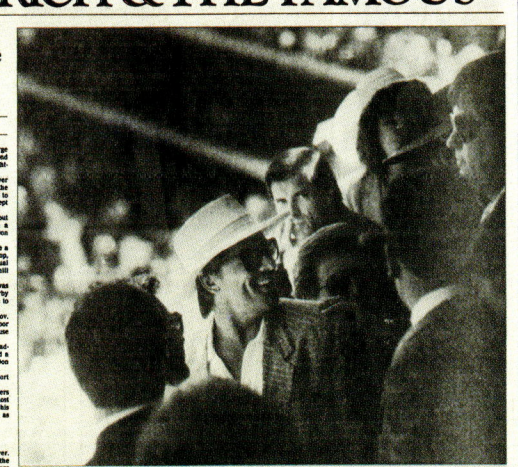

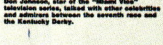

Award of Excellence
THE COMMERCIAL APPEAL
Memphis, Tennessee
Robert L. Wilson

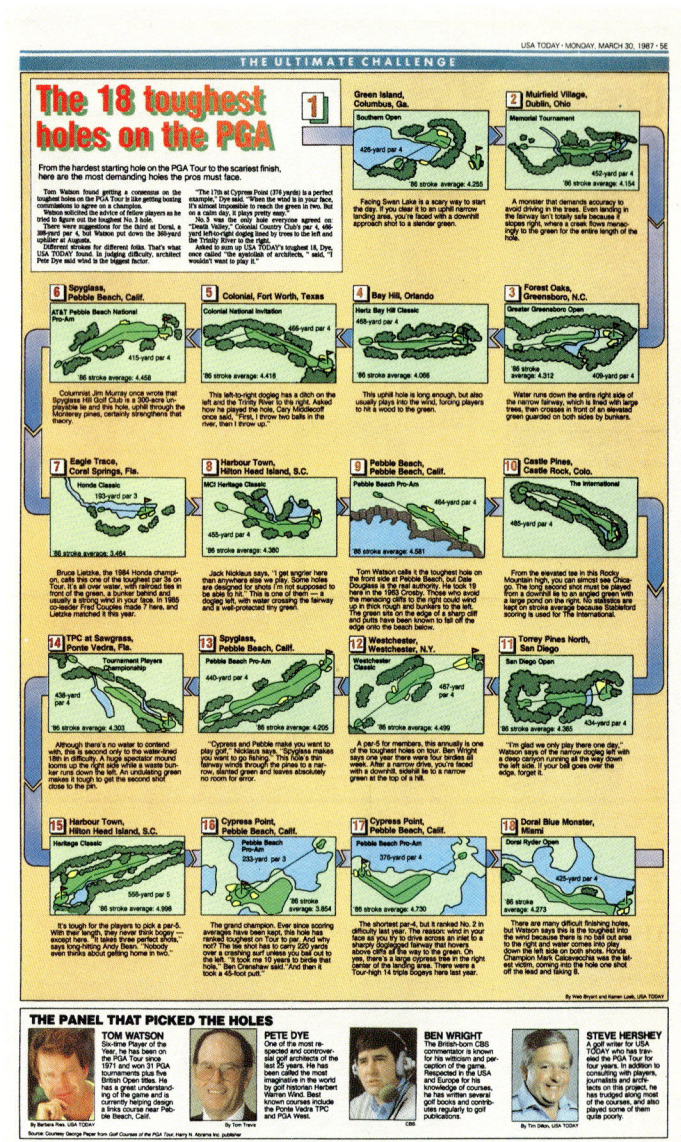

Award of Excellence
USA TODAY
Arlington, Virginia
USA Today staff

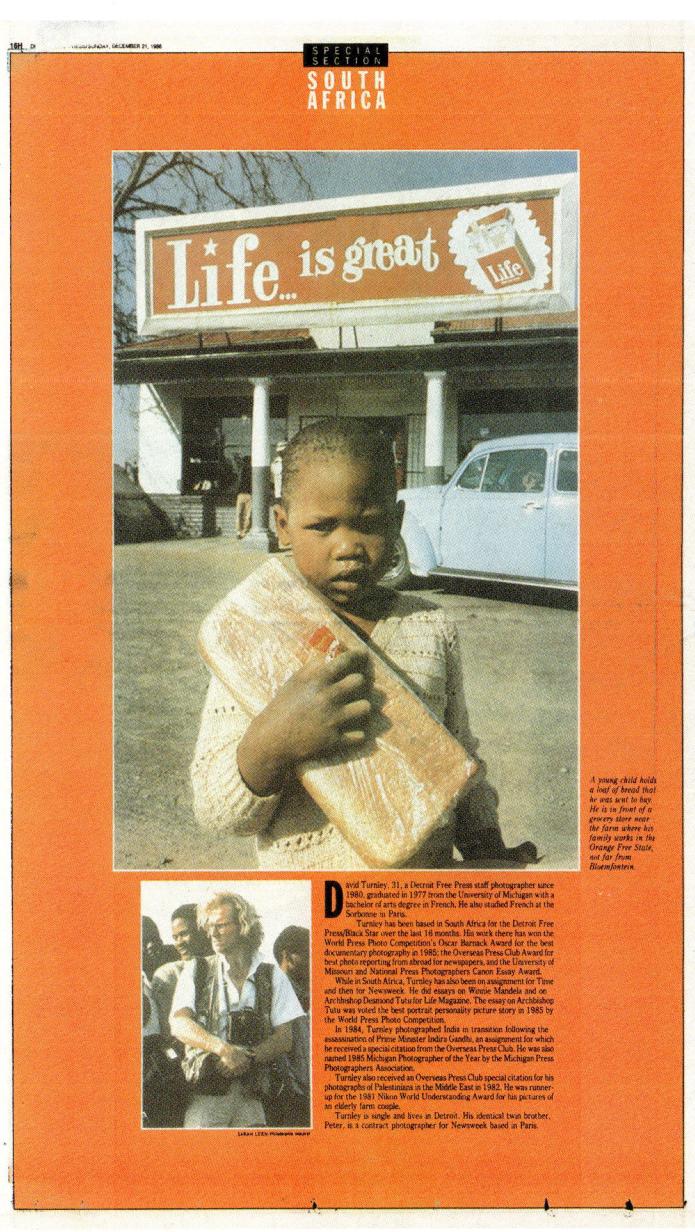

Beach Blanket Book Bag

THE PATIENT HAS THE FLOOR
By Alistair Cooke.
304 pp. New York: Alfred A. Knopf. $16.95.

By Bernard Avishai

EVERYBODY knows Alistair Cooke. He's that cordial English gentleman who guides us weekly through the polished parlors (and equally polished sentences) of the British upper classes. Were it not for Mr. Cooke, would we appreciate the stiffness of a lady's gown or the delicacy of her gossip? Would we assume a link between good literature and good leather or admire a Scotsman who knows his place? At the same time, Mr. Cooke has brought us his masterly television series, "Alistair Cooke's America," in which he seemed to know all about the huddled masses who came to the United States from such places as Latvia and Italy. Yet he told their stories so compassionately it was hard to discern whether he actually believed in the American dream or was simply fascinated by it.

Mr. Cooke, the son of a metalworker, first met Yanks when they were billeted with his family in Blackpool during World War I ("All their ranks had identical table manners"). He arrived in this country in 1932, in the middle of F.D.R.'s first campaign for the Presidency; he became a citizen in 1941, the year of the London blitz. His weekly BBC radio broadcast, "Letter From America," a celebration of the American commonwealth of equality, jazz and land ownership, marked its 40th anniversary last March. And if there were ever any doubts about how seriously he has taken his citizenship during this time, "The Patient Has the Floor" ought to dispel them.

Mr. Cooke emerges from this selection of speeches delivered over the last 20 years as a champion of the Emersonian desire for classlessness, of the Constitu- *Continued on page 49*

Bernard Avishai, an associate professor in the Massachusetts Institute of Technology's writing program, is the author of "The Tragedy of Zionism."

ENTER TALKING
By Joan Rivers with Richard Meryman.
Illustrated. 398 pp. New York:
Delacorte Press. $17.95.

By Max Wilk

ENTER talking? In this era of the hype, Joan Rivers's title wins hands down as the year's greatest understatement. She does not merely talk, she takes aim, begins to fire and rakes her audience — 373 pages plus index, acknowledgements, and last but far from least, a heartfelt dedication "To Edgar [her husband] who made this book happen, and to Johnny Carson, who made it all happen."

Years ago, while investigating what made great comedians tick, I interviewed the great "Perfect Fool," Ed Wynn. He had a simple formula for success. "I come out and in the first couple of minutes I make friends with the audience," he said. "After that, I can do anything with them, and they'll accept and love me."

Today's gospel according to Joan Rivers is entirely revisionist. "I have to be the toughest one in the room or they will talk right through me," she warns us. "They have to know I am like a lion tamer who says, 'If you come near me, I'll kill you.'" And in dealing with the improbable business of being a stand-up comedian, she has that calling remarkably well figured out. "You must want it so badly you will suffer anything, anything, just to get on a stage in front of people — be willing, again and again, to pick yourself up and keep going after you have been hit on the head by a sledgehammer. ... We are all crazy and crazed."

No argument. Miss Rivers has been there, and she certainly knows of what she speaks. The trouble is that she continues to speak, on and on, in what must be the longest stand-up monologue ever recorded on tape. It was arranged for print by a collaborator, Richard Meryman. And, as they used to say in the days when Miss Rivers was battling her way upward through Second City, the Chicago comedy troupe, and Greenwich Village boîtes and assorted joints, she lets it all hang out. All of it, from Day One. We are treated to her early life as chubby middle-class Joan Molinsky, who was starved for affection. ("Comedy is power. We can be in *Continued on page 33*

Max Wilk is the author of "A Tough Act to Follow" and the forthcoming "And Did You Once See Sidney Plain," a memoir of S. J. Perelman.

THE CHARACTER FACTORY
Baden-Powell and the Origins of the Boy Scout Movement.
By Michael Rosenthal.
Illustrated. 335 pp. New York:
Pantheon Books. $22.95.

By Jonathan Gathorne-Hardy

PERHAPS unfairly, I've always found scouting faintly ludicrous. My only two personal experiences of it were a bit odd and not really conducive to respect. Also, I can remember as a boy those photographs of King George VI — ridiculous, like all adult Scouts, in baggy shorts and wide-brimmed hat — looking as if he couldn't tie a knot to save his life.

Robert Stephenson Smyth Baden-Powell, first Baron Baden-Powell, the subject of Michael Rosenthal's new study, could tie knots. Born in 1857, he went to Charterhouse school in 1870. Typical of his period, he despised work — "often sleeps in class" — and loved games. Two hints of the future: he was a successful schoolboy actor; he was a solitary, who loved creeping about the Godalming countryside having fantasies that he was an American Indian or a trapper. School was followed by the army, in India and Africa.

Baden-Powell served until 1910 — 34 years. The youngest Major General, the hero of the siege of Mafeking by the Boers in 1899-1900, a figure in Madame Tussaud's wax museum — superficially his career seems brilliant. Actually, he was a military disaster. For many years he saw no active service at all. When he eventually did, in Afghanistan, he became overexcited and shot himself in the leg.

Mafeking should never have taken place. Baden-Powell was supposed to remain mobile and harass the Boers. He holed up in the obscure corrugated-iron out- *Continued on page 47*

Jonathan Gathorne-Hardy's most recent books are a collection of short stories, "The Centre of the Universe is 18 Baedekerstrasse," and the forthcoming novel, "The City Beneath the Skin."

THE FUNERAL MAKERS
By Cathie Pelletier.
247 pp. New York:
Macmillan Publishing Company. $16.95.

By Susan Kenney

A BLURB on the back cover of this latest in a growing number of wild and crazy novels from Maine claims this may "well be the first Northern Southern Novel." It has been suggested before that there is a similarity between recent Maine fiction and the tough and earthy, often sensational yet sensitive, fiction known as Southern Gothic written

Susan Kenney teaches at Colby College in Maine. Her most recent book is "Graves in Academe."

from the 1930's on by such authors as William Faulkner, Erskine Caldwell, James Dickey and Flannery O'Connor. Last year "The Beans of Egypt, Maine," Carolyn Chute's popular first novel, was compared to (among other novels) Faulkner's chronicles of the Snopeses, and there are other, lesser-known Maine writers such as Lucy Honig, Willis Johnston, Fred Bonnie and S. T. Colby who have produced fine fiction that includes elements of the regional grotesque. The similarity should really come as no surprise; even though "Tobacco Road" and "God's Little Acre" are set in the South, folks around here have speculated for some time that Mr. Caldwell may have gleaned a lot of his local color from the area around Mount Vernon, Me., where he lived from 1925 to 1932. Local legend also has it that the actual setting of Mr. Dickey's 1970 novel "Deliverance" was South Solon, Me., the river the upper Kennebec.

But none of these novels is as completely dominated by a specific region as Cathie Pelletier's fine first novel, "The Funeral Makers." Though she has renamed the setting Mattagash, both her stunning descriptions of the particular physical and social geography of the place and her reference to it by name in the touching dedication to her forebears make it clear that the story takes place in Allagash country in northern Maine. In this book geography is a character and place is destiny. Even if you live in Maine, it's hard to imagine exactly how remote Mattagash and its real-life counterpart are, so tune in the weather news on television or get out your road atlases. If New England looks like a bare right leg stuck up in the air after it's kicked a 60-yard field goal, then Allagash is between the first and second toes, in what is known as the Valley, where the rivers flow, as opposed to the County (Aroostook), where the potatoes grow. It takes as long to drive from Portland, Me., to Fort Kent, the largest town in the area (pop. 4,826), as it does from Portland to New York City. Allagash, 29 miles upstream, has fewer than 450 inhabitants. The fictional Mattagash has even fewer. It is the *Continued on page 19*

THE NEW YORK TIMES BOOK REVIEW 7

A SPECIAL REPORT
The Dallas Morning News

By David Tarrant
Staff Writer of The News
© 1986, The Dallas Morning News

HUNGRY AND HOMELESS

■ Single mothers ■ Mentally ill ■ Families ■ Elderly ■ Alcoholics

Even before freezing temperatures seize Dallas in earnest, unprecedented numbers of hungry and homeless have packed shelters, creating a crisis that relief officials say will test the mettle of the city.

The prognosis is grim.

Today, the city's 4,000 homeless people already are competing each night for 1,400 shelter beds while shelves at some food pantries are bare.

Tomorrow, a worst-case scenario of weather and economics could slam the door, leaving many of the homeless out in the cold.

"A lot of people are going to suffer," said Lori Palmer, a Dallas City Council member and director of the North Texas Food Bank. "More people are going to be without shelter, more people are going to be without food, more people are going to be without adequate health care."

Thousands of others, meanwhile, are living at street's edge, only a rent check away from losing their homes. Relief agencies that traditionally have come up with emergency rent money have been assaulted in such numbers that they are turning people away.

Continued on Page 2.

Top photo: Megan Roberts, 3, watches a slow-moving food line on a recent Sunday morning at the corner of Harwood and Cadiz streets.
Above: Megan approaches a businessman on his way home from work to ask for money.
Above right: Megan and her brother Joshua sleep on the hood of their family's car near the Austin Street Shelter.

Reprints

THE GREATEST

RICK MACLEISH / CHUCK BEDNARIK / JULIUS ERVING / HAROLD JENSEN / TUG MCGRAW

THE 50s

The damaged Hawaiian Pilot limping past Alcatraz after a collision with another freighter. *1953.*
Gordon Peters
Sea gulls landing on an ice-covered pond in Golden Gate Park. *1950.*
Ken McLaughlin

54

THE 50s

An irate Sadie Case of Emeryville offering her glasses to the umpire
during a Mother's Day game at Seals Stadium. *1953.*
Bob Campbell

55

Award of Excellence
SAN FRANCISCO CHRONICLE
San Francisco, California
Howard Finberg

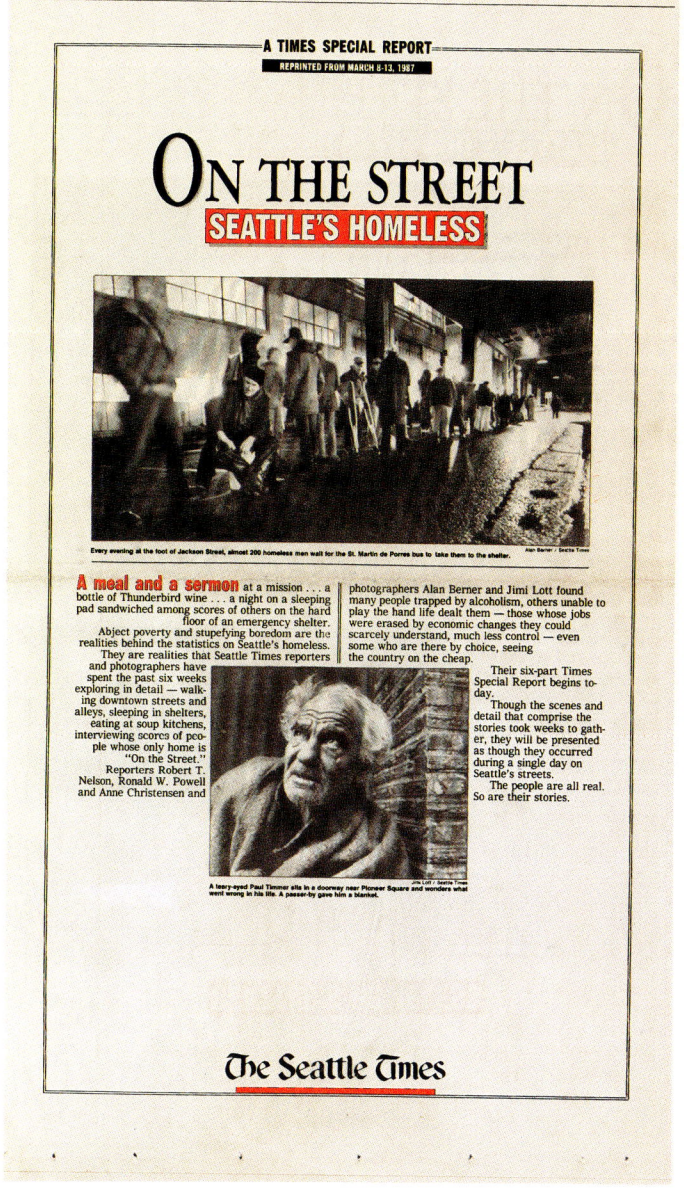

SPECIAL REPORT

DETROIT FREE PRESS
December, 1986

WASTED LIVES

John and Vera Rucker still look for an answer in the slaying of their 18-year-old daughter, Melody, below left.   John COLLIER/Great Free Press

"I KNOW MELODY IS IN HEAVEN AND SHE CAN'T BE HURT. I JUST WORRY ABOUT ALL THE KIDS OUT HERE WHO CAN BE HURT."

—Vera Rucker, Melody's mother

Detroit a sad leader in children shot dead

By BARBARA STANTON
Free Press Staff Writer

Detroit, a city long inured to bullets and body counts, has one more sad statistic to contemplate as 1986 draws to a close: Its children are being killed by gunfire at a rate apparently unmatched in other major cities.

Thirty-three youngsters 16 and under had been shot to death as of Saturday. Eight other children were killed by gunfire, either apparent suicides or accidents. Of the 41 fatalities, 33 were boys and eight

were girls; one was white, the rest were black.

A record murder rate is nothing new to Detroit, which led the nation's 10 largest cities in homicides per capita in 1985 and racked up 536 slayings from January to the end of October this year, according to the most recent police figures.

But the homicide epidemic, for years the leading cause of death among black males 18 to 24, now is seeping downward to claim their younger brothers and sisters. On the city's meanest streets, a deadly conjunction of

kids, drugs and guns is taking its toll of youth.

No other city for which figures are available seems to match Detroit's rate of child slaughter. Houston came closest, with 26 deaths, but that figure includes at least six child abuse cases. Detroit's toll of 41 dead by firearms does not include child abuse cases or deaths by other weapons. In Chicago, the toll for 1986 is 15, excluding child abuse and arson deaths.

And in 1986, with 41 fatalities and another 317

See KIDS, Page 16

Award of Excellence

DETROIT FREE PRESS
Detroit, Michigan
John Goecke,
Suzanne Yeager

A TIMES SPECIAL REPORT
REPRINTED FROM MARCH 8-13, 1987

ON THE STREET
SEATTLE'S HOMELESS

Every evening at the foot of Jackson Street, almost 200 homeless men wait for the St. Martin de Porres bus to take them to the shelter.   Alan Berner / Seattle Times

A meal and a sermon at a mission . . . a bottle of Thunderbird wine . . . a night on a sleeping pad sandwiched among scores of others on the hard floor of an emergency shelter.

Abject poverty and stupefying boredom are the realities behind the statistics on Seattle's homeless.

They are realities that Seattle Times reporters and photographers have spent the past six weeks exploring in detail — walking downtown streets and alleys, sleeping in shelters, eating at soup kitchens, interviewing scores of people whose only home is "On the Street."

Reporters Robert T. Nelson, Ronald W. Powell and Anne Christensen and

photographers Alan Berner and Jimi Lott found many people trapped by alcoholism, others unable to play the hand life dealt them — those whose jobs were erased by economic changes they could scarcely understand, much less control — even some who are there by choice, seeing the country on the cheap.

Their six-part Times Special Report begins today.

Though the scenes and detail that comprise the stories took weeks to gather, they will be presented as though they occurred during a single day on Seattle's streets.

The people are all real. So are their stories.

A teary-eyed Paul Timmer sits in a doorway near Pioneer Square and wonders what went wrong in his life. A passer-by gave him a blanket.   Jimi Lott / Seattle Times

The Seattle Times

Award of Excellence

THE SEATTLE TIMES
Seattle, Washington
Celeste Ericsson,
Marian Wachter,
Cole Porter

Overall Design

Gold Award
CHANDLER ARIZONAN TRIBUNE
Mesa, Arizona
Alan Crabtree, Gary Markstein,
Art Moore, Michelle Wise

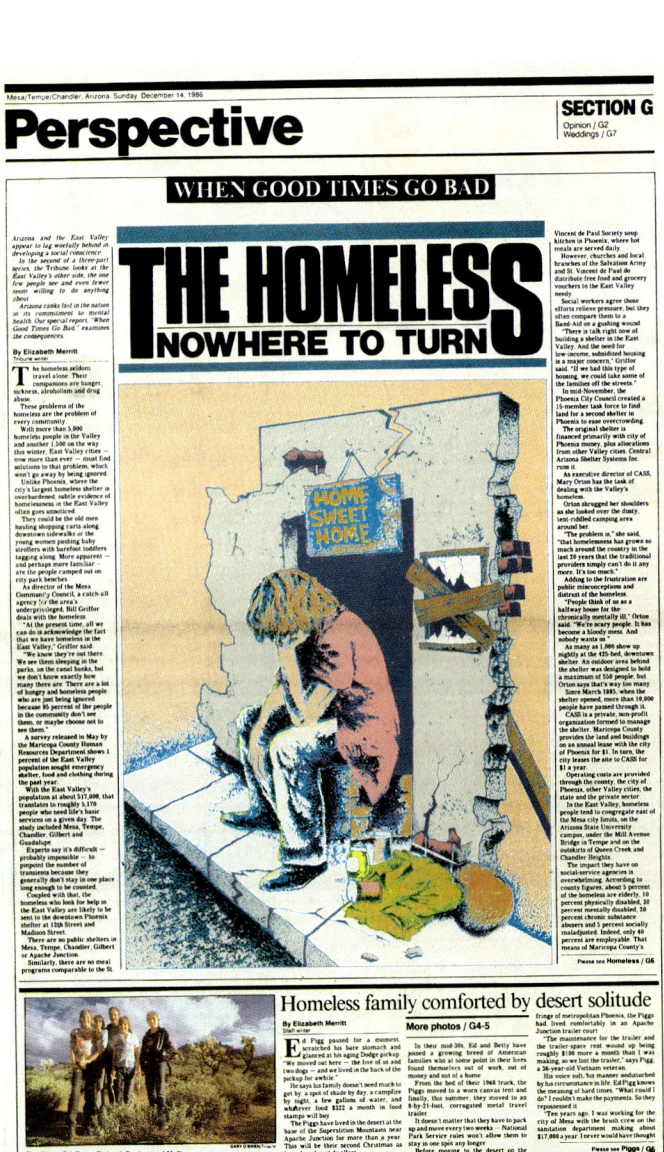

Circulation 75,000-150,000

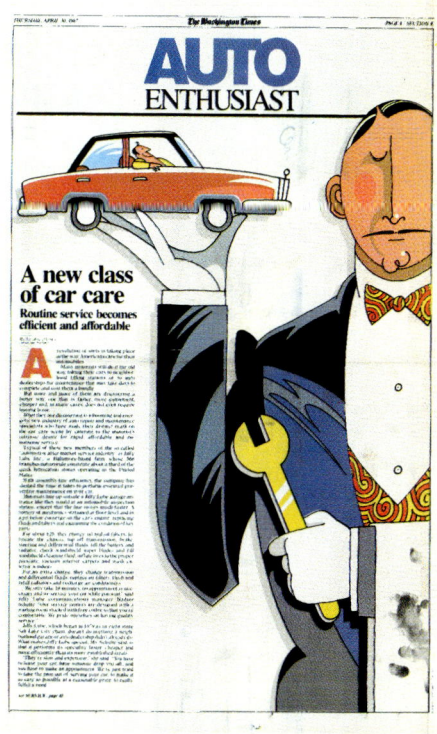

Award of Excellence
THE WASHINGTON TIMES
Washington, D.C.
Joe Scopin, Gil Roschuni,
staff

Circulation Above 150,000

Award of Excellence
HELSINGIN SANOMAT
Helsinki, Finland
Carl Henning,
Petri Enarvi

Award of Excellence
THE SEATTLE TIMES
Seattle, Washington

CHAPTER 4
Magazines

"Too many entries nuked the news, showing us only the noise, the cacophony of stuff on a page. We've all had our wild thing with color. Now we have to get back to our real job, which is presenting information. The winners were the pages that communicated, that helped the reader understand what was going on on the page."

JOHN BODETTE

Overall Design

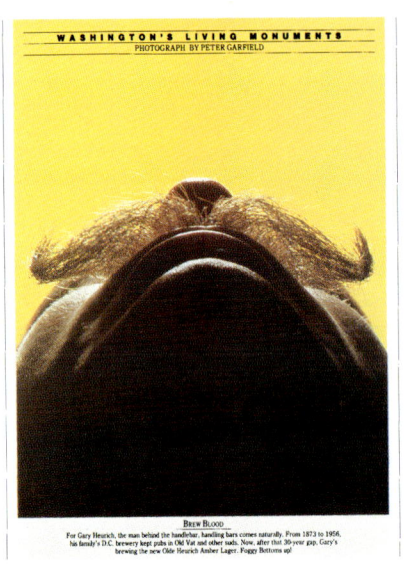

Nicholas Goes for Baroque

Silver Award
THE WASHINGTON POST
Washington, D.C.
Brian Noyes

Award of Excellence
THE PLAIN DEALER MAGAZINE
Cleveland, Ohio
Gerard Sealy

Award of Excellence
LOS ANGELES TIMES
Los Angeles, California
Michael Parrish,
Nancy Duckworth

Special Sections

Silver Award
THE NEW YORK TIMES
New York, New York
Susan Slover

Silver Award
DETROIT NEWS
Detroit,
Michigan
Stephen Cvengros,
Felix Grabowski,
Mike Ban,
Joseph Lippincott,
Ken Raniere,
Robert Gallagher

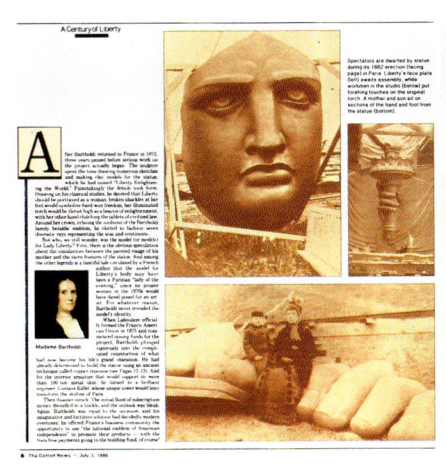

On the road...
with the kids

Cruising Canada with four children

BY LOUISE ERDRICH
AND MICHAEL DORRIS

Distance on a long car trip can be measured in various ways. If you're alone, your journey may last through a count of half-hourly newscasts or add up to the total of conversationless hours between cups of coffee. If you're with a friend or lover, it may amount to the number of high school stories exchanged, the tally of songs to which you've both forgotten the words, or the accumulated recriminations over enticing rest stops passed by in favor of "let's try the next one." If

LOUISE ERDRICH IS THE AUTHOR OF *THE BEET QUEEN* AND *LOVE MEDICINE*. MICHAEL DORRIS' NOVEL *A YELLOW RAFT IN BLUE WATER* WILL BE PUBLISHED BY HOLT IN THE SPRING. THEY LIVE WITH THEIR CHILDREN IN RURAL NEW HAMPSHIRE.

you're traveling as a family, as we did last June with four of our five children, from the Pacific Northwest and west to east across Canada, it often boils down to the number of license plates spotted, the hours until the next affordable motel with a kidney-shaped pool, or the maximum proportion of snacks to sit-down, nutritious food one can tolerate.

Canada is a big country. It takes four large packages of powdered milk to keep two babies marginally content in their car seats from British Columbia to Ontario, and at least one water slide a day to subdue older children gone stir-crazy in their futile attempts to complete travel bingo cards. There are stretches of hundreds of miles in British Columbia, Alberta, Saskatchewan and Manitoba with nary a dry cleaner shop, a moving *Continued on page 39*

Award of Excellence
THE BOSTON GLOBE
Boston, Massachusetts
Lucy Bartholomay

Silver Award
THE NEW YORK TIMES
New York, New York
Susan Slover

Loose-fitting shorts are the
comfortable foundation for
a variety of casual summer looks.

Far left: Rubberized flax jacket and cotton shorts from Ideas by Massimo Osti for C. P. Company of Italy. Jacket, $350. At Macy's, Louis, Boston. Shorts, $85. At Mario's, Seattle. Marshall Field's, Chicago. Woman's knit rayon top from Byblos. Silk scarf wrapped around waist by Katharine Hamnett. Hat by Matsuda. Center, from left: Plaid cotton shirt, $200, and shorts, $175, by Giorgio Armani. At Giorgio Armani Boutique, 815 Madison Avenue, Ultimo Ltd., Chicago. Stonewashed cotton shirt by Henry Grethel, $60. At Bonwit Teller, The Loft, 313 Amsterdam Avenue. James Campion, Hanover, N.H. Cotton shorts from Jantzen, $27. At Emporium-Capwell, San Francisco. Joslins, Denver. Woman's linen shirt and Bermuda shorts from Kikit. Hat by Patricia Underwood. Near left: Cotton and silk hand-knit sweater by Joseph Abboud, $375. At Bergdorf Goodman. Louis, Boston. Polo shirt from Perry Ellis Men. Chambray shorts from British Khaki by Robert Lighton, $46. At Church Creek Clothiers and Outfitters, Charleston, S.C. H. Gross & Company Outfitters, Princeton, N.J. Cotton sweatshirt, $34. From J. Crew Outfitters, 1 Ivy Crescent, Lynchburg, Va. 24506-1001. Striped cotton shorts from WilliWear by Willi Smith, $40. At Bloomingdale's. Burdines, Miami. Bottom left: Sunglasses from Ray-Ban by Bausch & Lomb, $106. At Sunglass Hut, Herald Center, 1 Herald Square; Atlanta, Houston and Miami.

Cover Designs

Black and White, One Color

Award of Excellence
THE WALL STREET JOURNAL
New York, New York
Greg Leeds

Award of Excellence
THE NEW YORK TIMES
New York, New York
Beth Williams

Award of Excellence
MINNEAPOLIS STAR AND TRIBUNE
Minneapolis, Minnesota
Todd Grande

Award of Excellence
THE WALL STREET JOURNAL
New York, New York
Joe Dizney, Greg Leeds

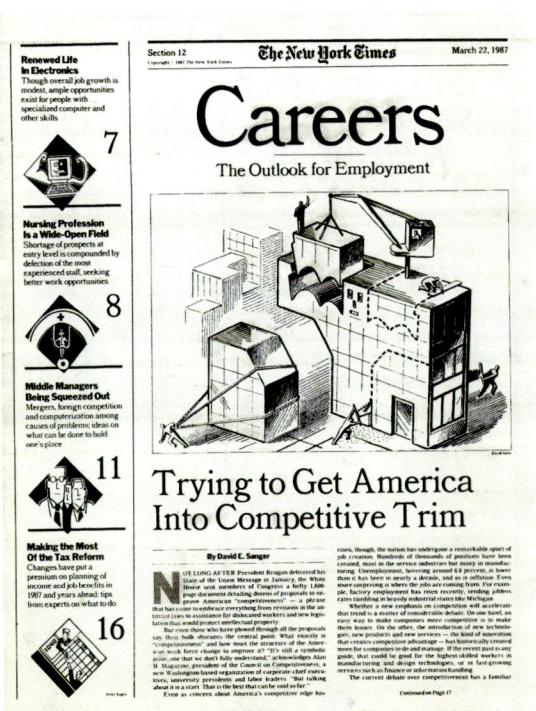

Silver Award
THE NEW YORK TIMES
New York, New York
Richard Weigand

Award of Excellence
THE BOSTON GLOBE
Boston, Massachusetts
Lucy Bartholomay

The Boston Globe
MARCH 15, 1987

Adventures in
T R A V E L

Award of Excellence
THE BOSTON GLOBE
Boston, Massachusetts
Lucy Bartholomay

Old-fashioned and elegant, Gramercy Park soothes a harried traveler   **B**urgundy commemorates the visit of Thomas Jefferson 200 years ago   **T**he joys and travails of traveling across Canada in a car full of kids   **A** camper gets face to face with the wilds of Alaska   **T**he enigma of the elaborate Indian ruins of Chaco Canyon is unraveled   **W**ind Star combines the luxury of a cruise with the romance of a sailing ship

THE BOSTON GLOBE · NOVEMBER 9, 1986

"Cry for us and
our children."

DRUGS
IN
OUR
LIVES

Award of Excellence
THE BOSTON GLOBE
Boston, Massachusetts
Lucy Bartholomay

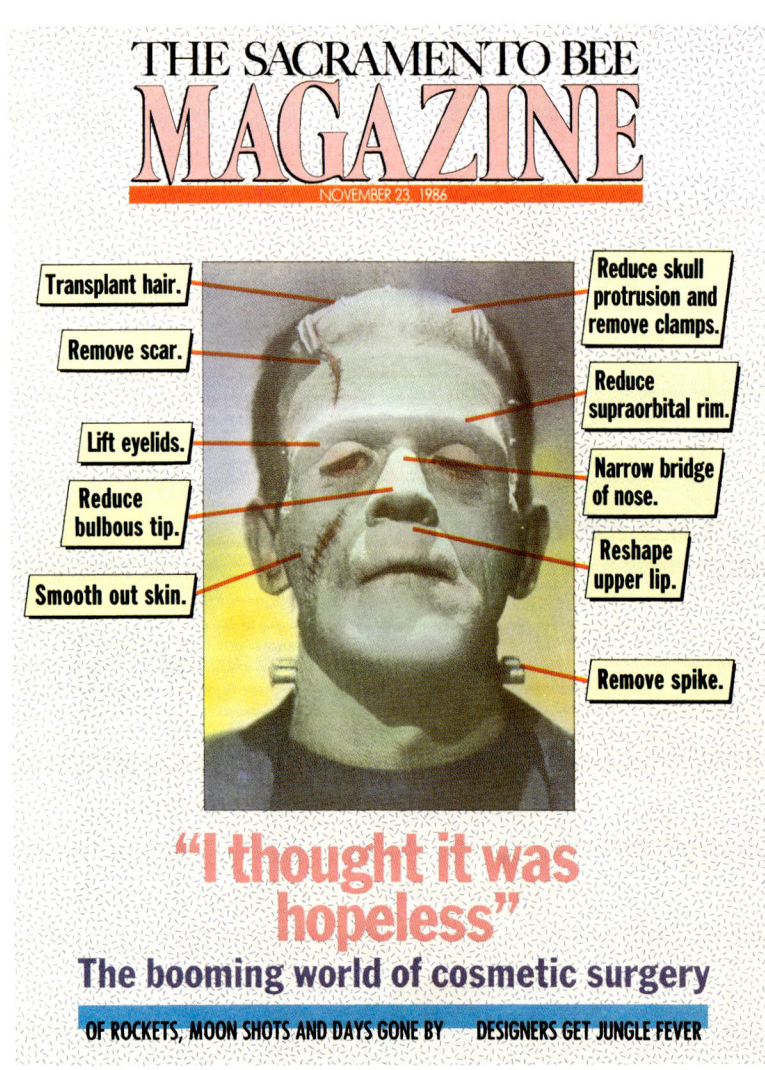

Two or More Pages

Silver Award
THE NEW YORK TIMES
New York, New York
Ken Kendrick

Award of Excellence
THE NEW YORK TIMES
New York, New York
Diana LaGuardia,
Art Director;
Audrey Satterwhite,
Designer

R
a two-piece hound's-tooth check suit reminiscent of the 1950s with baggy, pleated trousers. Worn with suspenders and a cotton T-shirt, he definitely looks cool. Karen's leather and tulle skirt, worn with the wool turtleneck bodysuit, is another unusual option from Paul Cornish for holiday festivities. The pearl, ruby and gold necklace and earrings are by Cartier. Makeup: Prescriptives.

IT TAKES TWO... TO JIVE

TABLE HOPPING

BY SHIRLEY GREGORY

Photography by Nigel Dickson

54   DECEMBER 1986   TORONTO

Award of Excellence
THE GLOBE AND MAIL, TORONTO MAGAZINE
Toronto, Ontario, Canada
Toronto Magazine staff

Award of Excellence
THE NEW YORK TIMES
New York, New York
Ken Kendrick,
Art Director;
Richard Samperi,
Designer

SICILY AND THE MAFIA

By Roberto Suro

"My crime was to have been born and bred in a family of Mafia traditions, and to have lived in a society where all are Mafiosi. For this they are respected, while those who are not are scorned."

Written in a rough scribble, those words were part of a confession offered by a man named Leonardo Vitale, who walked into Palermo's police headquarters in March 1973 and volunteered a tale of murder and extortion. A fit of conscience, apparently, moved Vitale to describe in detail the workings of several Mafia clans in Sicily.

Although the authorities already suspected some of the men he implicated, no crime was taken against them. Vitale was declared mentally ill, and all his accusations were dismissed. He did, however, earn himself a jail term for his trouble. And a few months after he was released, in 1984, Vitale was shot to death on his way home from church one Sunday morning.

To denounce the Mafia in Sicily in 1973 was madness. Now 15 years later, several of the men fingered by Vitale are among the 456 defendants in the largest criminal trial ever conducted in Italy — the so-called maxi-trial, now in its fourth month in Palermo. Important evidence for the prosecution has come from another informer, Tommaso Buscetta, who like Vitale grew sick of being "a man of honor."

Instead of getting locked up and declared insane, Buscetta became the subject of complex agreements between officials in Sicily and New York that offered him American citizenship, a home, a lifetime stipend and many bodyguards in return for detailed testimony about his 30 years as a Mafia member. Information provided by Buscetta has also been used as evidence in the prosecution of 20 alleged Mafia members in the United States — part of a broad crackdown, coordinated...

ing 11 important trials in the New York area alone, that American authorities hope will have a major impact on Mafia ties between the United States and Sicily.

The distance between Vitale and Buscetta marks a period of brisk change in Sicily — change in the Mafia, in law enforcement and in politics. Over the last decade, the Mafia's growing involvement in international drug trafficking has sharply altered the traditional role of Sicilian crime, helped using the atmosphere of public tolerance and official neglect it has long enjoyed. For several years, rival clans engaged in a bloody competition for dominance, and declared a virtual open hunting season on public officials who dared to intervene.

Now the state has begun to fight back. The Mafia had a tradition of collaborating with the state in a mediating and stabilizing role — so long as its interests were respected, of course," notes Pino Arlacchi, a sociologist whose book "The Mafia Business" is widely regarded as a classic text. "Now important sectors of the state are trying to declare the Mafia a foreign body and expel it." Leading the anti-Mafia fight is a cadre of young Sicilian officials who, an enormous personal risk, are trying to undo not just a criminal organization but an entire social structure.

Roberto Suro is a correspondent in The New York Times's Rome bureau.

A portfolio of photographs depicting the Mafia's role in Sicily — and efforts to curb it — begins on the following page.

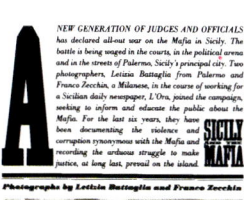

A NEW GENERATION OF JUDGES AND OFFICIALS has declared all-out war on the Mafia in Sicily. The battle is being waged in the courts, in the political arena and in the streets of Palermo, Sicily's principal city. Two photographers, Letizia Battaglia from Palermo and Franco Zecchin, a Milanese, in the course of working for a Sicilian daily newspaper, L'Ora, joined the campaign, seeking to inform and educate the public about the Mafia. For the last six years, they have been documenting the violence and corruption synonymous with the Mafia and recording the arduous struggle to make justice, at long last, prevail on the island.

Photographs by Letizia Battaglia and Franco Zecchin

Award of Excellence
ANCHORAGE DAILY NEWS
Anchorage, Alaska
Peter Dunlap-Shohl

Award of Excellence
THE BOSTON GLOBE
Boston, Massachusetts
Lucy Bartholomay

Single Page

FOOD

by Caroline Maupin

The Best of the Bush League

T

he Beatles yearned for *Strawberry Fields Forever.* Walt Whitman said "the running blackberry would adorn the parlors of heaven." And, of course, Fats Domino got his thrill on *Blueberry Hill.*

With their jewel-like beauty and luscious flavor, berries are almost everyone's favorite fruit — particularly in summer, when locally grown berries are in season. Somehow the strawberries and raspberries of summer make winter's seem pallid, in both color and flavor. Seasonal prices are better, too, so we can enjoy them more often.

And there are many ways to enjoy berries. They are tempting straight from the vine; in homemade ice cream or as a topping for ice cream or yogurt; in pies, shortcakes, cobblers and tarts. But besides these traditional dishes, you will want to try new ways to take full advantage of summer's plethora.

To please everyone, make a fresh salad of all the various berries. Some diners will want (Continued on page 25)

PHOTOGRAPHY: LON COOPER. BERRIES COURTESY OF AMERICAN PRODUCE

Pick your favorites: the berries of summer include raspberries, strawberries, blueberries, blackberries and gooseberries.

JULY 27, 1986   DALLAS LIFE MAGAZINE   23

Portfolios of Work

CATTLE COUNTRY

Don't try to understand 'em, just rope, throw and brand 'em

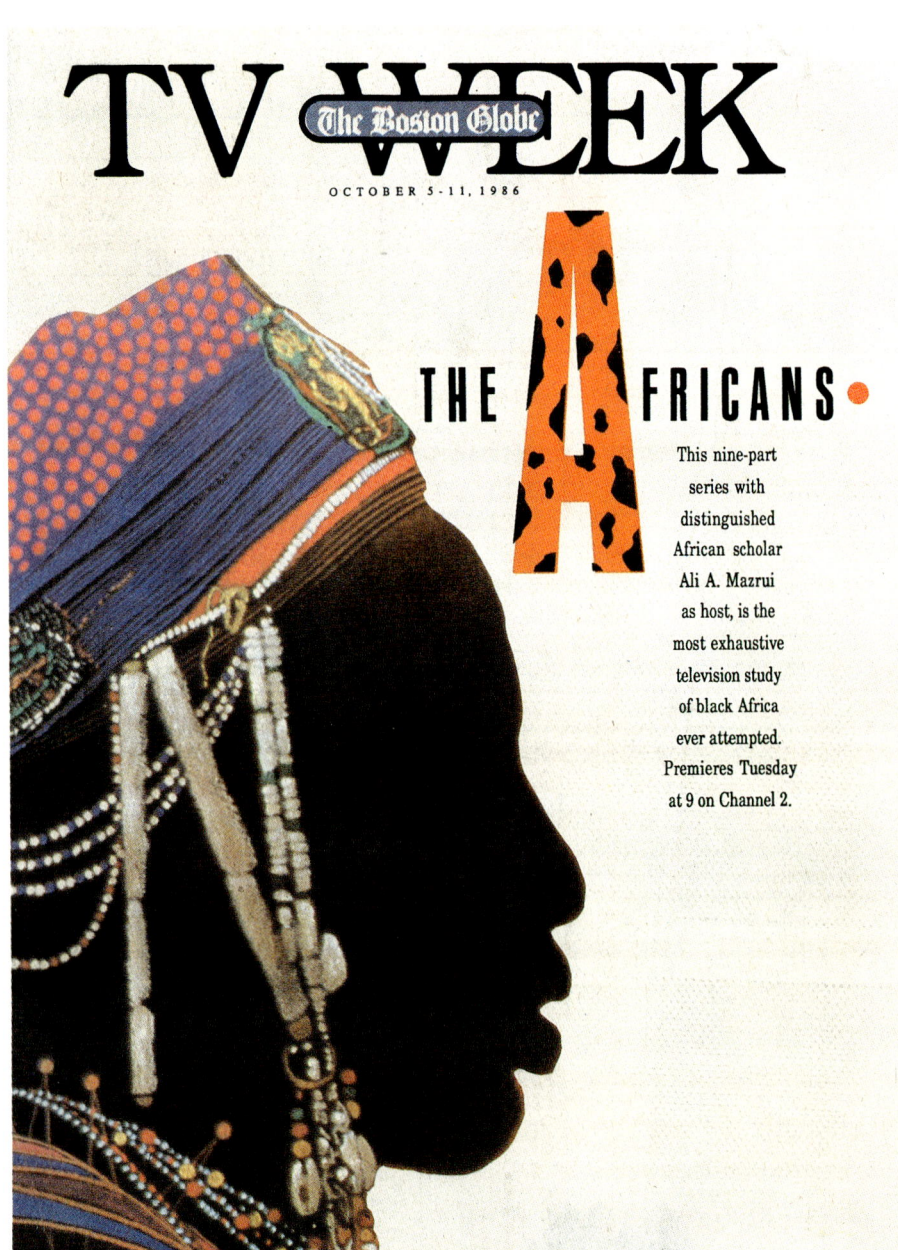

TV WEEK

The Boston Globe

OCTOBER 5-11, 1986

THE AFRICANS

This nine-part series with distinguished African scholar Ali A. Mazrui as host, is the most exhaustive television study of black Africa ever attempted. Premieres Tuesday at 9 on Channel 2.

GREYHOUND

Greyhound Bus Station
New York Avenue between 11th and 12th streets NW
Now hidden behind a modern facade

INSIDE/OUT
PHOTOGRAPHS BY PAUL FEINBERG

DISAPPEARING D.C.

Parts of downtown "dee cee" once had the feeling of a small town gone to seed—rundown, yet charming in its decline. As the large gray office buildings, luxury hotels and tinted-glass apartment complexes replace the colorful holes-in-the-wall of old, we pause to honor the visual treasures of a Washington that used to be.

JANUARY 4, 1987   19

Award of Excellence
THE WASHINGTON POST
Washington, D.C.
Brian Noyes

Award of Excellence
THE GLOBE AND MAIN, DESTINATIONS MAGAZINE
Toronto, Ontario, Canada
James Ireland

CHAPTER 5
Art and Photos

"The next phase for photojournalism is to learn how to use color in a documentary way. We do feature fronts with color and that's it—we're into glitzy color, huge bands of color, bombastic color. Just a few papers have learned to get beyond that, and we'll have to convince ourselves that color is a valid documentary approach."

C. THOMAS HARDIN

"Nice photos and beautiful landscapes don't move me, but put a human being in a landscape and I'll be interested. Outstanding photographs depicting the human condition will always move people deeply—a love story can be told thousands of times, but it will still make me cry."

SARAH GIOVANITTI

"I saw hardly any real news graphics among the entries. There were lots of colored maps, but editors who want informational graphics to explain, need to know what language to use—graphic, photographic, typographic. Every story has within it informational parts, but most stories are left waiting in the wings, anticipating journalists predeterining which of the languages should be used. I've yet to see a good diagram of how an Exocet missle works, for example. True informational graphics require a great deal of hard work, from writers, editors and designers."

EDWIN TAYLOR

Black and White, One Color

Silver Award
THE WASHINGTON POST
Washington, D.C.
Marty Barrick,
Joe Teodorescu

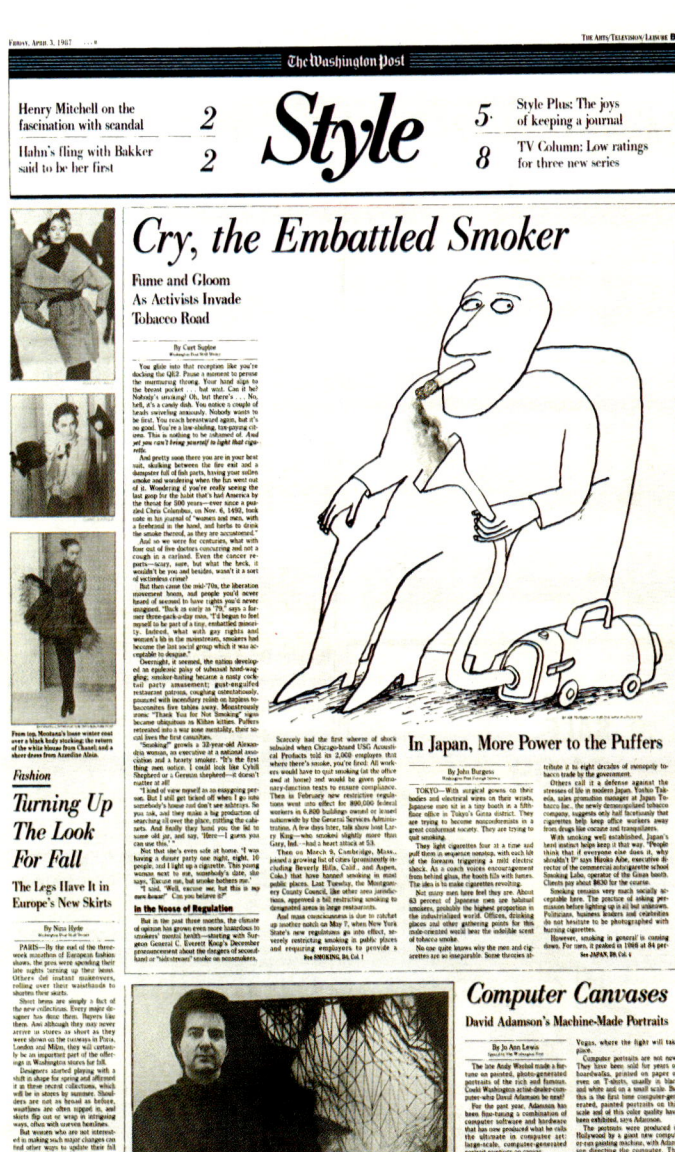

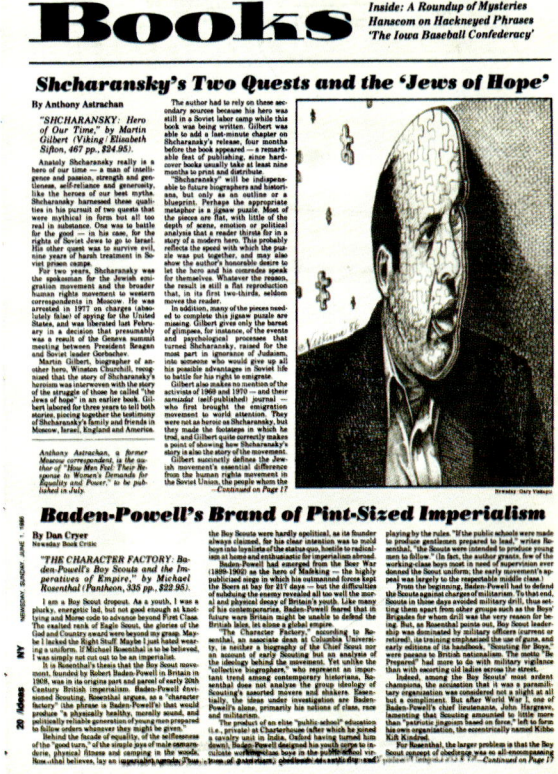

Award of Excellence
NEWSDAY
Melville,
New York
Gary Viskupic

Award of Excellence

EL NUEVO DIA
San Juan,
Puerto Rico
Jose L. Diaz de Villegas, Sr.

Award of Excellence

THE WALL STREET JOURNAL
New York, New York
Barbara Kelley

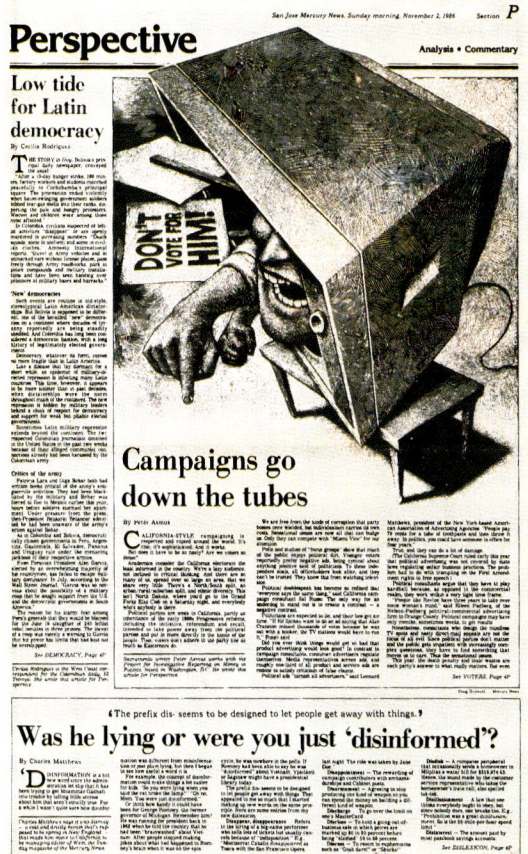

Award of Excellence
NEWSDAY
Melville,
New York
Ned Levine

Part III

Real Estate

Saturday   **Newsday**   September 27, 1986

Pulling Money From Thin Air

By Sara Lessley

ON EAST 52ND STREET, a four-story rental apartment building is undergoing conversion. On its roof, a separate six-unit condominium has just been constructed.

Instead of building on a vacant lot or adding on a few floors — costly undertakings in crowded Manhattan — a legally separate residence was created *on top of* the existing structure.

Two factors explain this first-of-its-kind "lollipop condo," says John Donohoe, a Manhattan attorney for the conversion sponsors. There's less red tape with new construction, but equally as significant: the unused air space above the old building is valuable enough to make the difficult development worthwhile.

It's just the latest example of using air as a kind of raw material in residential construction. "Underutilized" air space — above buildings that don't reach the allowed zoning height — can be skimmed off and sold. Developers buy these —Continued on Page 35

Over-55 Exemption / Home Sellers Weigh Heavier Tax Load. Page 7

Living In / Sands Point: Discovering the Stuff of Legends. Pages 32 33

Award of Excellence

THE MIAMI HERALD
Miami, Florida
Randy Stano,
Art Director;
Sean Kelly,
Illustrator

por PACO VILLON

Cómo COMPRAR BUENOS VINOS sin tener que HIPOTECAR la CASA

EN GRANDE hizo un recorrido por las principales tiendas que venden vinos al detalle y hace unas buenas recomendaciones para los días de las fiestas

Award of Excellence
EL NUEVO DIA
San Juan,
Puerto Rico
Enrique Agramonte

BOOKS/7C
EDITORIALS/2C
LETTERS/2C

Viewpoint

Sunday, April 19, 1987   The Miami Herald **Section C**

PLAYING FOR KEEPS: SHULTZ WINS

By negotiating the same way he plays golf, George Shultz scored his greatest triumph.

by JAMES McCARTNEY

3 cases tested free press

By MARTIN MERZER

School integration

Everyone benefits; let's find way to do it more fairly

By CHARLES WILLIE

A reporter's life: It's a lonely world

By FRED GRIMM

Fred Grimm

Award of Excellence

THE MIAMI HERALD
Miami, Florida
Randy Stano,
Art Director;
Rich Bard, Editor
Sean Kelly,
Illustrator

Art and Photos 121

Two or More Colors

Silver Award
THE NEW YORK TIMES
New York, New York
Tom Bodkin,
Art Director;
Barton Lidice Benes,
Illustrator

Award of Excellence
SAN JOSE MERCURY NEWS, WEST MAGAZINE
San Jose, California
Bambi Lee Nicklen, Art Director; Sidney Fischer,
Illustrator

SPRING CAREERS

THE SUN   Job market '87   SUNDAY, APRIL 26, 1987

THE GUIDE
Good things to see, hear and do / 14D

CLASSIFIED/21D
MOVIE TIMES/4D
COMICS/18D

Weekend

Friday, June 20, 1986   The Miami Herald   Section D

Robert Redford and Debra Winger:
Admirable acting.

Star power, wit make 'Eagles' fly

By CHRISTINE ARNOLD
Herald Arts Writer

Why do so many critics hate *Legal Eagles?* Because producer-director Ivan Reitman, who did *Ghostbusters* and *Animal House* and *Stripes,* tried to go grown-up? Because Robert Redford, who normally exudes as much warmth as a wooden Indian, is trying to be funny? Because Debra Winger looks dowdy? Because the plot, which would like to emulate and gently spoof movies like *Adam's Rib,* has its share of course.

Movie Review

Legal Eagles (PG) ★★★

Maybe it's just a case of terminal pickiness. Because *Legal Eagles,* torts and all, is fun and entertaining. What more should a summer movie be?

In their flawed but serviceable screenplay, Jim Cash and Jack Epps Jr. (authors of *Top Gun*) combine murder, the courtroom and the New York art world. *Legal Eagles* begins with the 1968 murder of artist Sebastian Deardon, who has just commemorated her with a signed painting. One of his,

Fast forward to today, with gangly Chelsea having metamorphosed into the ravishing Daryl Hannah. The grown-up Chelsea has just been arrested for trying to steal one of her daddy's paintings. She's being defended by the spunky Laura Kelly (Winger), whose novel attempts at getting clients off the hook have included putting a dog on the stand.

Laura's legal nemesis is also a guy who raises

Please turn to EAGLES / 9D

'Karate Kid II' missing magic

By RYAN P. MURPHY
Herald Writer

'Columbia Pictures' *The Karate Kid Part II* re-teams Ralph Macchio and Pat Morita in their smash hit roles!" bellows the press release. "The story is focused, expanded and made even more dramatic than the original."

Movie Review

The Karate Kid Part II
(PG) ★

Let's get two things straight here. First of all, the person who wrote that exultant release needs to take a sedative.

Secondly, he obviously hasn't seen the movie he's whining about. *Karate Kid II* is not focused. It is a rambling tale revolving around Daniel (Macchio) and his mentor Miyagi (Morita) as they travel to the old master's homeland of Okinawa to see his dying father. Bad supporting actors flounder around aimlessly, clueless as to where they're going or what they will do once they get there.

Kid II is not comparable to its predecessor. It is

Please turn to KARATE / 7D

There are plenty of ways to play it cool during the Florida summer. All it takes is a little imagination.

By LINDA R. THORNTON
Arts Writer

Egad, it's here. Summertime.

June showers have cheated the heat until now, but between raindrops, the sun is mean. Air conditioners are working overtime. School let out in most of South Florida this week. And, as if we needed the calendar to remind us, summer officially begins Saturday.

How to make it through September? You could hide inside your air-conditioned home, car or office. But that wouldn't be much fun, would it?

There are plenty of places to play it cool this summer in Dade, Broward and Palm Beach counties. Many are indoors, where air condi-

BEAT THE HEAT

INDOORS

Ice skating

Make believe it's winter. The temperature rarely rises above 50 degrees in the few remaining ice skating rinks in South Florida.

● At the **Miami Beach Youth Center,** nonmembers can skate for $3 ($1 center admission, $1 rink admission and $1 skate rental). Skating times vary each day; 2700 Sheridan Ave., Miami Beach; call 673-7767 for more information.

● The **Sunrise Ice Skating Center,** at 3363 Pine Island Rd., Sunrise boasts an Olympic-size rink. Admission ranges from $3.50 to $6.50 (plus $1 skate rental), depending on time and day. Call 755-0011.

Work up a cold sweat

Get a part- or full-time summer job in an ice-packing plant. With demand for ice cubes and blocks at a seasonal high, some ice manufacturers in South Florida, among them Royal Palm Ice in Miami, Reddy Ice in Fort Lauder-

tioning provides blessed relief from the humidity outside. Others are right under the sun's fire-red nose, with the wind and the water acting as natural coolers.

Here are some suggestions on how to beat the heat.

Museums, galleries

Soak up culture instead of rays this summer at any of the many indoor (and air-conditioned) museums, art galleries and libraries in the area. Here is some of what's available. Remember that exhibitions may change during the season.

● **Bass Museum** of Art, 2121 Park Ave., Miami Beach, 673-7530: *Miami Color,* photographs of Miami and Miami Beach, through July 6; admission Wednesday-Sundays $2 adults, free to children under 18; admission by donation on Tuesdays.

● **Historical Museum of Southern Florida,** Metro-Dade Cultural Center, 101 W. Flagler St., Miami, 375-1492: The exhibition *M.A.S.H. Binding Up the Wounds,* comes from the Smithsonian in Washington and opens July 4. It includes stage sets and props from the *M.A.S.H.* television series. Other exhibits include walk-through South Florida history, shipwreck gold and cannons and Audubon bird prints. Admission is $3 for adults, $2 for children ages 6-12.

● **Mitchell Wolfson Jr. Collection,** Miami-

Please turn to COOL / 10D

dale and Artic Ice in Deerfield Beach, are hiring extra hands to stack and pack the cold stuff. The wages are modest ($4-$6 an hour), but the job will keep you cool.

SEAN KELLY / Miami Herald Staff

SHORT SUBJECTS

■ **THE COLORS WERE BOLD IN NORTH AMERICA** at the turn of the century, and so were the artists responsible for "The Advent of Modernism." The Center for the Fine Arts puts a sample of their work on exhibit beginning Saturday. See Art / 15D.

■ **HE'S GONE SOLO,** but that doesn't mean he won't have the *Rhythm of the Night* on his side. El Debarge, the leader of the family pop-soul group, appears Saturday at the Knight Center. He'll perform works from his just-released solo debut album. See Concerts / 14D.

■ **ROCKERS BLUE OYSTER CULT** will turn the Atlantis Water Theme Park into Club Ninja, after their recent LP by the same name. They'll do hits like *Don't Fear the Reaper* and *The Last Days of May,* as well as selections from *Club Ninja.* See Concerts / 14D.

■ **REMEMBER 'CATCH THE WIND,' 'COLOURS'** and 'Sunshine Superman'? Singer/songwriter Donovan brings his brand of flower power into the '80s. Listen to his mellow music Saturday at the Musicians Exchange in Fort Lauderdale. See Concerts / 14D.

■ **BAGS, BEEHIVES AND BASKETS,** an exhibit exploring the art of natural and artificial containers, is the first exhibit at Miami Youth Museum in its new location. See Potpourri / 16D. ■ **LOVERS OF LATIN MUSIC** could hardly hope for a better week: Singer Celia Cruz heats up Casanova's, crooner Jose Jose is at the Dade County Auditorium and Brazilian Nelson Ned performs at Les Violins. See Concerts / 14D.

Art and Photos 123

Award of Excellence
THE MIAMI HERALD
Miami, Florida
Randy Stano,
Art Director;
Rhonda Prast,
Designer;
Sean Kelly,
Illustrator

Award of Excellence
SAN JOSE MERCURY NEWS, WEST MAGAZINE
San Jose, California
Bambi Lee Nicklen, Art Director; Ken Coffelt,
Illustrator

Award of Excellence
EL NUEVO DIA
San Juan,
Puerto Rico
Jose L. Diaz de Villegas, Jr.

Award of Excellence
SAN JOSE MERCURY NEWS
San Jose, California
Sidney Fischer

Award of Excellence
THE NEW YORK TIMES
New York, New York
Richard Weigand,
Art Director;
Maris Bishofs,
Illustrator

Silver Award
THE HARTFORD COURANT, NORTHEAST MAGAZINE
Hartford, Connecticut
Lane Smith, Roxanne Stachelek

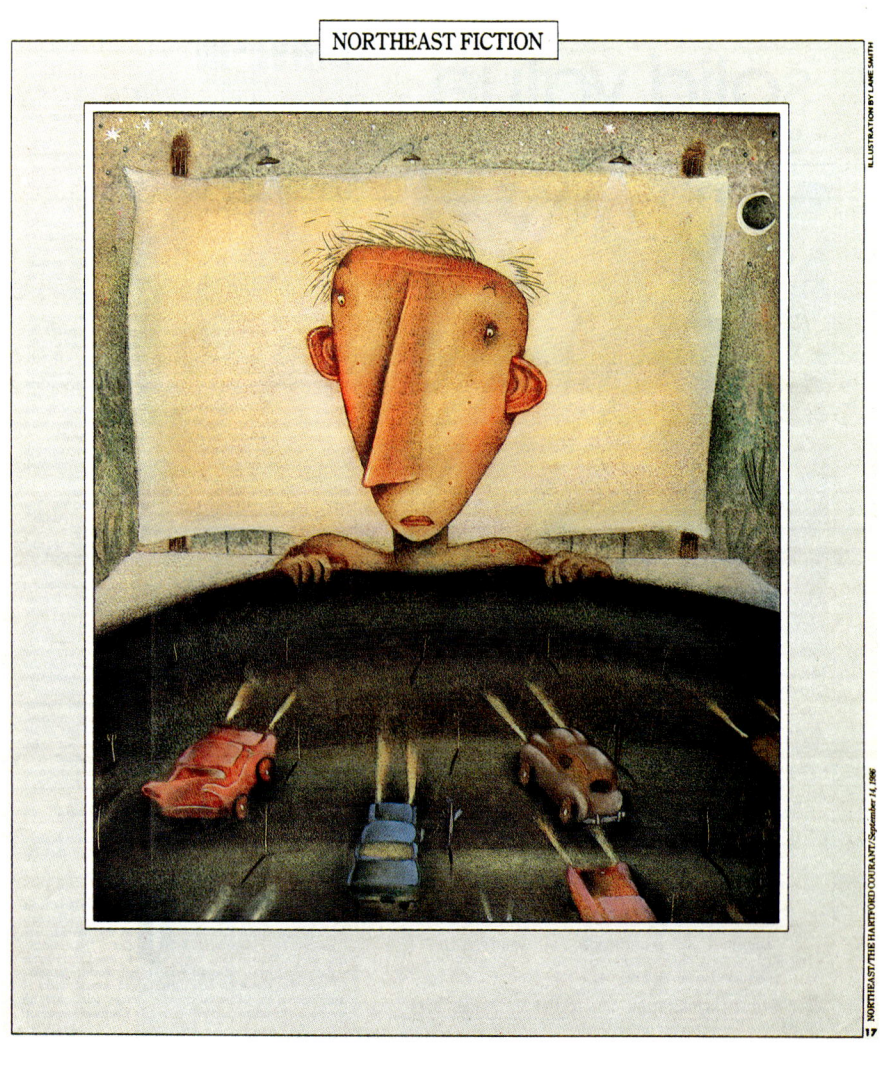

Illustration by Kerry Meyer

Award of Excellence
KANSAS CITY STAR
Kansas City, Missouri
Kerry Meyer

Award of Excellence
THE DALLAS MORNING NEWS
Dallas, Texas
Karen Blessen

Award of Excellence
NEWS/SUN-SENTINEL, SUNSHINE MAGAZINE
Fort Lauderdale, Florida
Kent Barton

The Hartford Courant

TRAVEL

SECTION F
SUNDAY
MARCH 1, 1987

Get down to business of cruise fun

By JAY CLARKE
Knight-Ridder Newspapers

Ahoy there, landlubbers, it's time to think cruising!

No, we don't mean industry trends, passenger counts, dock fees and all that sort of deep-think jazz. We're talking about fun stuff, because that's what cruising is about.

Sure, the front-office folks at the cruise lines worry about bookings and such, because January and February are the two biggest months for making cruise reservations. In fact, Royal Caribbean Cruise Line officials have found that the first Monday after New Year's Day is an industry barometer. They call that Monday Wave Day, and if sales are good that day, their year will be good; if sales are so-so, so will be the year.

This year, you might like to know, Wave Day was a record-breaker.

But you don't have to fuss with this, or anything else, when you're thinking cruise. Forget about the office, your overdue bills and the widening split between your wife and your mother. Do check on fare deals, ambiance and amenities on the ship of your choice.

Then set sail and make like the Love Boat, even though nobody can live up to the television image. Shoot for the moon on your next cruise, but settle for the attainable:

• **Eat like a bear that's just come out of hibernation:** They serve so many meals on cruise ships that you probably *can* eat like a hungry bear, but chances are you'll dine more moderately and certainly with better manners. So plan on three good meals a day but don't expect gourmet quality — I've never yet seen a restaurant that can serve 1,000 people three times a day and maintain that kind of level. Hungry between meals? Usually you can get hot dogs or hamburgers out by the pool, and the midnight buffet is popular with the late crowd.

• **Hobnob with famous folks so you can drop names at your next party:** Film, television and sports stars like to cruise, too, especially when they get paid for it. You'll find scads of them doing personal appearances at sea this year. On my last two or three cruises, I have a.) chewed the fat with Stewart Granger at the bar, b.) discussed upcoming novels with James Michener, c.) exchanged jokes with Bernie Kopell, and d.) chatted about the rigors of acting with Linda Purl. Some of the stars booked for cruises this year include Patricia Neal and Dick Shawn (the Stella Solaris), Phyllis Diller and Hank Aaron (the Norway), Vincent Price (Royal Princess), and Todd Christensen of the Los Angeles Raiders (Island Princess).

• **Go on a cruise nobody's done before:** Several first-time and one-and-only cruises are planned this year. The Britannis, for instance, is planning the only circumnavigation of the South American continent, if that's your kind of thing. The Sea Cloud will retrace the South Pacific itinerary of Captain Cook. The World Discoverer will call for the first time ever at the Laccadives Islands in the Arabian Sea.

• **Meet the girl or boy of your dreams and live happily ever after:** Good luck. It's possible, but for heaven's sake don't go on a cruise all starry-eyed and expecting romantic fireworks if you're single. While marriages have resulted from meetings at sea, they are most definitely exceptions.

See Cruises, Page F6

Airlines locked in fare wars

Cut-rate tickets available, but with many restrictions

By STEVE SILK
Courant Travel Writer

Those advertisements for $79 flights to Florida look mighty tempting here on Connecticut's frozen tundra.

But if you're planning to use the new bargain-basement fares to soak up some Florida sunshine, don't pack your beach ball and snorkel yet.

"Right now you're not going to get a 'MaxSaver' fare to Florida," said Wendy Gilmore, a retail travel consultant at Connecticut Travel Services in New Britain. "People don't realize that."

MaxSaver, a term originated by Continental Airlines, refers to new low fares recently introduced by most major domestic carriers.

"I was able to book one guy [on a MaxSaver] to Florida," she said, "but he was real flexible. He wanted to go to Fort Lauderdale any time over a one-month span. There was nothing for Fort Lauderdale, but we finally got him a flight to Tampa."

Gilmore said the airlines set aside a limited number of seats for low fares, but these seats were taken by people who had booked Florida flights last September. They simply dumped their more expensive SuperSaver tickets for MaxSaver rates when these became available.

Though you aren't likely to get to Florida for $79, you might get to most other U.S. destinations for considerably less than you would have paid a few months ago. A round-trip ticket to Los Angeles, for example, can cost as little as $190.

But to guard against one of the major industry bugaboos — no-shows — most airlines have made the purchase and use of these inexpensive tickets rife with restrictions. (Only Pan American Airlines offers its lowest rates without restrictions.) Would-be passengers are forced to run a gauntlet of conditions that might prove daunting to many.

See Fares, Page F4

Illustration by Peter Hoey / The Hartford Courant

Don't be a flying fool: Bone up on the best bargains

If you're hoping to take advantage of the low airline rates:

• When you see new low fares advertised, call your travel agent or the airlines immediately. You have to make a decision quickly. (Because of the volume of calls received by the airlines in response to these offers, it often is easier to make reservations through an agent.)

• Plan as far ahead as possible and make arrangements early. But remember that you won't be able to change or cancel your plans without forfeiting what you paid for the ticket.

• Be flexible. Discounted fares to some destinations may not be available from Bradley International Airport. To take advantage of them, you may have to travel to New York or Boston.

• If you can't get the flight you want, keep trying. If a flight isn't selling seats at the computer-projected higher rate, the airline might elect to offer more seats at discounted rates. But remember, if seats are unavailable at the lowest fares, you cannot be put on a waiting list to take advantage of possible future availability.

• Plan to travel at off-peak times. Most seats are likely to be available on midday flights Mondays through Thursdays and on Saturdays.

• Buy your ticket early. "Underline buy early," says Jay Walpole, an Eastern Airlines shift manager at Bradley. "If you don't buy a ticket, the fare isn't guaranteed." Even if you book your flight six months early, it doesn't mean anything until the ticket is purchased.

• Consider purchasing trip cancellation insurance to cover your ticket costs if illness forces you to cancel a flight. This insurance is available from most travel agents. (At their discretion, some airlines will refund money to passengers who produce a doctor's verification that they canceled for medical reasons.)

• Arrive at the airport early because a missed flight means a worthless ticket. If you are leaving from the Hartford area, remember that Bradley has been redesigned. Allow extra time — airline ticket counters have been relocated and some parking areas are farther from the terminal.

STEVE SILK

Santa Catalina Island is a sparkling jewel off the California coast

By DANIEL B. WOOD
Christian Science Monitor

SANTA CATALINA ISLAND, Calif. — "There's our Safeway grocery; they deliver. There's our post office; they don't," says the shuttle driver, Bob, on the 12 o'clock leg of Santa Catalina Island's "Town of Avalon Tour."

He grinds gears on San Franciscolike hills and wrestles the steering wheel as the bus negotiates hairpin turns on one-way roads lined by palm and eucalyptus trees. Eventually, from a vantage point high above the small harbor, you look down at a square mile of whitewashed bungalows on stilts, Victorian bed-and-breakfast inns and Spanish-style haciendas with glinting cobalt or burnt auburn roofs. This seaside southern California quaintness seems poured over the steep slopes of but one craggy cove of this otherwise untouched island.

Twenty-one miles long and anywhere from ½ to miles wide, Catalina is twice the size of Manhattan but rugged, mountainous and rustic. The only town, Avalon (pop. 2,200, with 800 registered cars), might fit on a large city block. With no buildings more than a few stories high, the town is an architectural mix of rustic Spanish, brightly painted box cottages and funky California ranch houses with highly individualized designs: tile, skylights, gazebos, patios, porches, trellises, gates.

The rest of the island is a geologic monolith of scrubby coastal plants, cactuses, shrubs and contorted hybrid oaks. Ironwood trees grow in the rocky cliff areas, which feature steep drop-offs to inaccessible pebble beaches. Hundreds of bison and thousands of goats, snakes and foxes roam freely with a large population of ravens overhead.

Fourteen bison were brought to Catalina for co-starring roles in "The Vanishing American," filmed in 1924; they have since multipled to about 600. Other Hollywood films were made there, including "Mutiny on the Bounty" (1935), scenes from numerous Old West and South Sea movies, and the opening segment of the "Fantasy Island" television series.

Catalina has the most vegetation and wildlife of the eight channel islands — all formed by wrenching faults 25 million years ago. Eight plants are endemic and unique to the island — the Catalina cherry tree and St. Catherine's lace among them — and tour guides liken the island to the rest of southern California before development. Back in town, guides also play up what Avalon doesn't have: traffic lights, fast-food franchises and portable stereos (the latter are illegal).

It was the Portuguese explorer Juan Rodriguez Cabrillo, sailing from Spain, who first claimed the island in 1542, naming it San Salvador. Sixty years later, another Spaniard named the island Santa Catalina for St. Catherine of Alexandria.

Chewing-gum magnate William Wrigley is credited with beginning Catalina's rise as a world-renowned playground. After purchasing the controlling interest in the Santa Catalina Island Co., which owned all the property in 1919, Wrigley invested huge sums of money to attract visitors. Projects included an enormous ballroom casino — the first round structure in southern California. There was also a bird park with "the largest bird cage in the world." Wrigley added thousands of extraordinary birds and invited the public, free. He also set up a baseball field, where his Chicago Cubs trained each spring. Catalina soon became a favorite vacation spot for stars, and not long thereafter became accessible to the public.

Today, construction on the island is severely restricted by the Santa Catalina Island Conservancy, which owns 86 percent of the island and seeks to preserve its natural wonder. Housing is so scarce that government-financed developments had to be built to accommodate government employees.

The number of daily cruise ships visiting Catalina from three mainland ports — Long Beach, San Pedro, and Newport — has increased in recent years, according to the Chamber of Commerce. This reflects a general boom in which the populace grew by one-third since the early 1970s, along with a host of condominium

See Santa Catalina, Page F3

Award of Excellence
THE HARTFORD COURANT
Hartford, Connecticut
Peter Hoey

128 *Art and Photos*

Award of Excellence
KANSAS CITY STAR/TIMES
Kansas City, Missouri
Kerry Meyer

Kerry Meyer

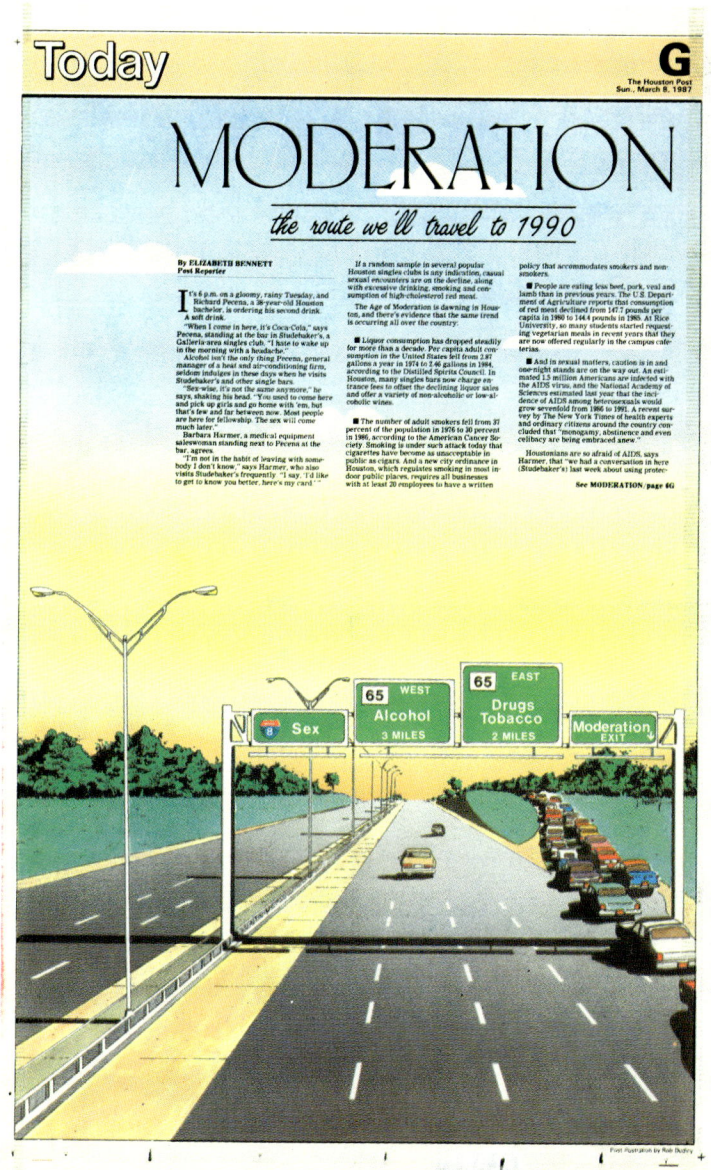

Award of Excellence
THE HOUSTON POST
Houston, Texas
Rob Dudley

Sunday Democrat and Chronicle
December 21, 1986

Award of Excellence
DEMOCRAT AND CHRONICLE, UPSTATE MAGAZINE
Rochester, New York
Kate Weisskopf, Art Director; David Cowles, Illustrator

Award of Excellence
THE WASHINGTON POST
Washington, D.C.
Peggy Robertson,
Art Director;
Becky Heavner,
Illustrator

Award of Excellence
THE CHRISTIAN SCIENCE MONITOR
Boston, Massachusetts
Susan B. Tyner

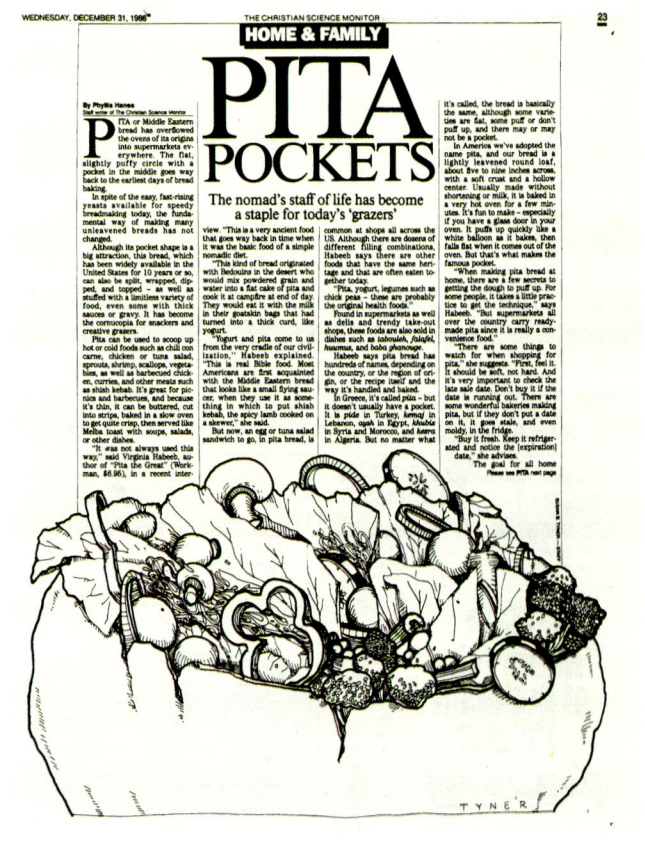

Photojournalism

Spot-News

Award of Excellence
THE TAMPA TRIBUNE
Tampa, Florida
Bob Westenhouser

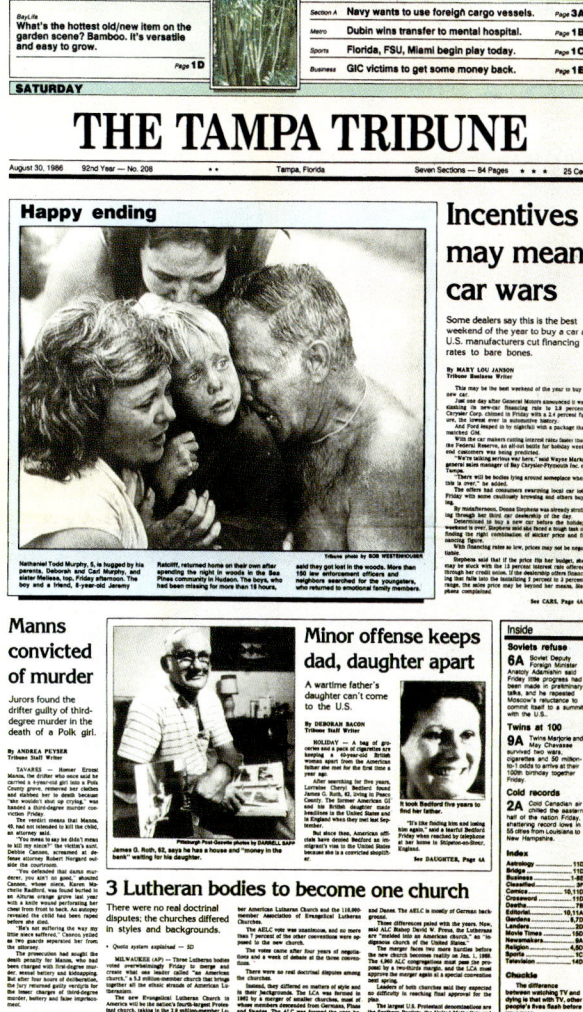

Award of Excellence
DETROIT FREE PRESS
Detroit, Michigan
Detroit Free Press staff

PALM BAY DEATH: A victim lies shot to death next to a car in the Palm Bay Shopping Center Thursday. Medical crews checked this person and moved on to help those still alive.

Pat Jarrell, FLORIDA TODAY

Award of Excellence
FLORIDA TODAY
Melbourne,
Florida
Pat Jarrell

Eyewitness account:

'He was shooting anything that moved. He shot at the parking lot, shot at K mart, shot anything he saw'

FLORIDA TODAY

Joe Carnevale of Palm Bay went to Publix early Thursday evening to buy beer. His quick trip to the store turned into a nightmare as he heard gunfire, followed by loud screams, from within.

"I heard this pop, pop, pop," Carnevale, 34, said shortly after he and about eight other people ran out the back of the store at 4711 Babcock St. N.E. into nearby woods.

"I wasn't sure what happened until everyone started screaming and people started falling. Then I just started running toward the back, figuring he was coming this way. And he kept firing."

Carnevale said he and the other people who had run out of the store with him stayed in the woods for about five minutes and then ran across the street to an apartment complex.

"Some people wanted to stay there (in the woods)," he said. "We were out in the woods and we could still hear him shooting. Even when he went across the street we could still hear him shooting."

"There were so many shots. It sounded like there might be two people."

George Luhrs, of Instant Images, in the same shopping center as Publix, gave this account from himself and the manager of Publix.

An elderly man barreled down the entrance of the center near K mart in a white Toyota. He squealed his tires and made a right turn and then pointed a gun at a woman who worked at the supermarket.

He didn't shoot her but then slapped the car and shot four people, one at gunpoint in the stomach. He hit one man in the left temple and then shot him again in the neck.

The man then careened around in the car to Luhrs, another store in the Publix center, and shot an elderly woman in a car. He then moved across the street to the Winn Dixie in the Sabal Palm Shopping Center and started shooting inside

STAYING CLEAR: Police officer takes cover under a truck.

Pat Jarrell, FLORIDA TODAY

Photographer: Scene like 'war zone'

When FLORIDA TODAY photographer Pat Jarrell arrived at Publix in Palm Bay early Thursday evening she had no idea of the spectacle awaiting her.

"I just assumed it was going to be more of a routine crime scene. I had no idea it was going to be like this."

Jarrell arrived at Publix before the area was roped off by police. As she took pictures,

Jarrell observed a man's body lying near a car.

"I walked up and saw the body lying there and it was real eerie because no one was shooting around it.

"I felt like I was in a war zone. I failed to understand how it could be happening here in our own neighborhood."

Reported by FLORIDA TODAY Staff Writer Alice Moynihan.

the store.

Other witnesses told similar tales.

Gerard Franklin of Pet Palace of Palm Bay Inc., another store in the Publix shopping center, said he saw an old man with white hair and a beard driving a white Toyota.

The shots sounded like they were from a shotgun or automatic weapon, he said. "I didn't stay out to see the rest. All I know is he killed one person in front of the Publix."

Babcock Street and the shopping centers were crawling with police. But at 6:35 p.m., he said. "It looks calm now, but I still see people running for their cars."

Stephanie Call, of Allen's Hallmark Card and Gift Shop in the center, said she first saw the man in front of Ricford Drugs, next to the Hallmark store.

"I could hear the gunshots, like an automatic pistol. He shot out the windows on a blue Ford Fairmont. It seems like there was more than one involved because I heard shooting at Publix and then at the Winn Dixie."

Witnesses said some people fled in their cars while others ran to various stores in the center.

The suspect was wearing camouflage clothing and a military-style cap and carrying a high-powered

rifle, said Bob Jones, 20, the son of the manager of Lunn's Supermarket in the Publix shopping center. The 5-foot-11 man was standing behind a tree in front of Publix when he opened fire at random, he said.

Then got into a small brown car and drove across the street to Winn Dixie. "Like he just didn't care. Like he owned the damn place."

"There were so many kids and old people walking around that I was concerned about getting them out of the way."

"It's just been a nightmare."

Wayne Landry, 29, warehouse manager of Lunn's in Publix shopping center, said the man was about 6 feet tall with a medium build, gray hair and a beard. He was wearing a brown shirt and gray slacks and was 50 to 55 years old.

"He was shooting anything that moved. He shot at the parking lot, shot at K mart, shot anything he saw."

Another witness, Sandy Sharpe, an employee of the Movie Market near Publix, said. "I just saw him shooting and we ducked and came around the counter and called the police. I finally got up and locked the door. I am very scared right now."

Shirley Bunker of Palm Bay was going to work out at the Cosmopolitan Spa near Winn Dixie when the shooting occurred. "I was scared to death. The first thing that came to mind was the McDonald's thing" in California.

Bunker said she was just pulling into the parking lot when she asked someone what was going on. She saw people hiding behind their cars and heard a man screaming, "Get down."

She went across the parking lot to the Burger King and was hiding out with some people there, looking for a safe place.

Looking around, she said she saw a bullet hole in a nearby car and some guy lying near it. Then the ambulance came and took everyone in, she said. She jumped in the ambulance.

"It's shocking, it really is. You don't think it's going to happen to you. I just hope they get him."

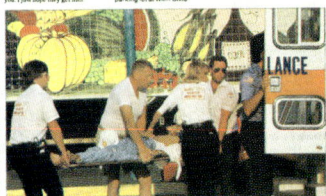

TENSE VIGIL: Law enforcement officers stand ready to act in the parking lot at Winn Dixie.

Pat Jarrell, FLORIDA TODAY

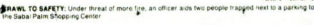

CRAWL TO SAFETY: Under threat of more fire, an officer aids two people trapped next to a parking lot at the Sabal Palm Shopping Center.

TO THE RESCUE: Harbor City Volunteer Ambulance workers and a passer-by aid an unidentified gunshot victim outside the Publix supermarket. Crews tended victims throughout the night.

Pat Jarrell, FLORIDA TODAY

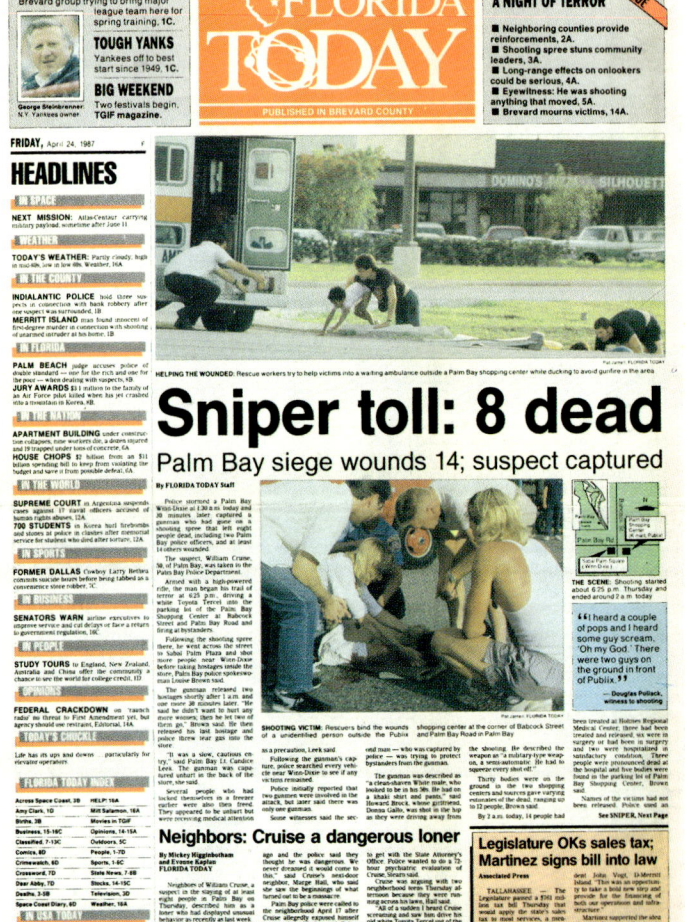

Award of Excellence

THE HARTFORD COURANT
Hartford, Connecticut
Cloe Poisson

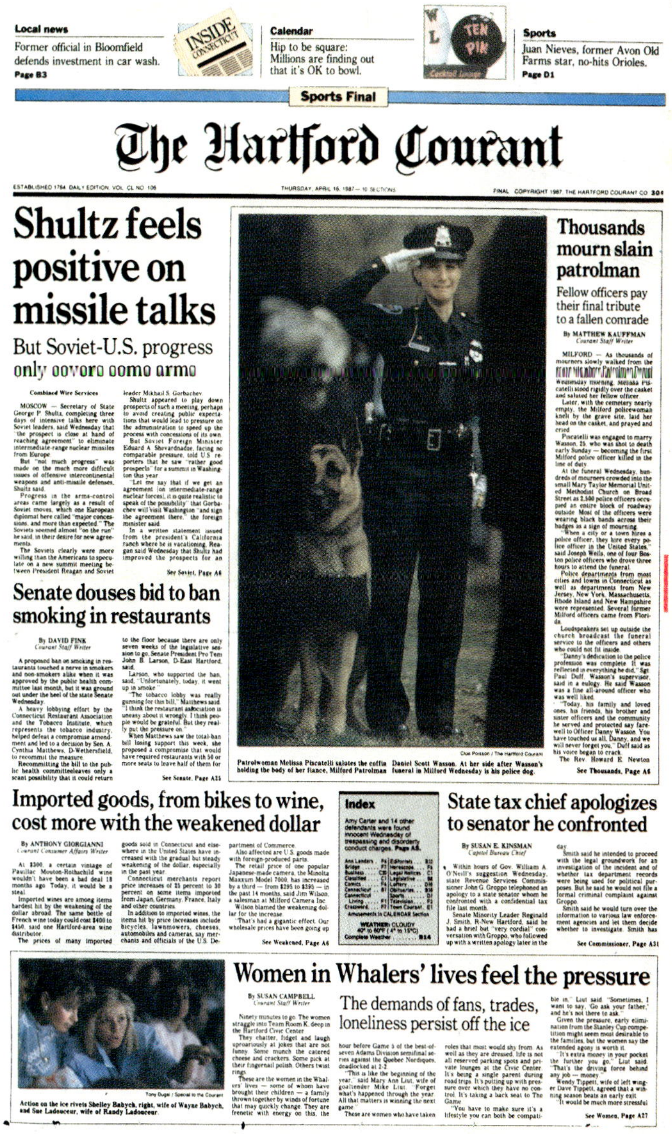

Local news
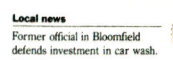
Former official in Bloomfield defends investment in car wash.
Page B3

Calendar
Hip to be square:
Millions are finding out that it's OK to bowl.

Sports
Juan Nieves, former Avon Old Farms star, no-hits Orioles.
Page D1

Sports Final

The Hartford Courant

ESTABLISHED 1764 DAILY EDITION, VOL. CL NO. 106 — THURSDAY, APRIL 16, 1987 — 10 SECTIONS — FINAL COPYRIGHT 1987, THE HARTFORD COURANT CO 30¢

Shultz feels positive on missile talks

But Soviet-U.S. progress only covers some arms

Combined Wire Services

MOSCOW — Secretary of State George P. Shultz, completing three days of intensive talks here with Soviet leaders, said Wednesday that "the prospect is close at hand of reaching agreement" to eliminate intermediate-range nuclear missiles from Europe.

But "real much progress" was made on the more difficult issues of offensive intercontinental weapons and anti-missile defenses, Shultz said.

Progress in the arms-control areas came largely as a result of Soviet moves, while one European diplomat here called "major concessions, and more than expected." The Soviets seemed almost "on the run" he said, in their desire for new agreements.

The Soviets clearly were more willing than the Americans to speculate on a new summit meeting between President Reagan and Soviet

leader Mikhail S. Gorbachev.

Shultz appeared to play down prospects of such a meeting, perhaps to avoid creating public expectations that would lead to pressure on the administration to speed up the process with concessions of its own.

But Soviet Foreign Minister Eduard A. Shevardnadze, facing no comparable pressure, told U.S. reporters that he saw "rather good prospects" for a summit in Washington this year.

"Let me say that if we get an agreement (on intermediate-range nuclear forces), it is quite realistic to speak of the possibility" that Gorbachev will visit Washington "and sign the agreement there," the foreign minister said.

In a written statement issued from the president's California ranch where he is vacationing, Reagan said Wednesday that Shultz had improved the prospects for an

See Soviet, Page A6

Senate douses bid to ban smoking in restaurants

By DAVID FINK
Courant Staff Writer

A proposal ban on smoking in restaurants touched a nerve in smokers and non-smokers alike when it was approved by the public health committee last month, but it was ground out under the heel of the state Senate Wednesday.

A heavy lobbying effort by the Connecticut Restaurant Association and the Tobacco Institute, which represents the tobacco industry, helped defeat a compromise amendment and led to a decision by Sen. A. Cynthia Matthews, D-Wethersfield, to recommit the measure.

Recommitting the bill to the public health committee means only a scant possibility that action will return

to the floor because there are only three weeks of the legislative session to go. Senate President Pro Tem John B. Larson, D-East Hartford, said.

Larson, who supported the ban, said, "Unfortunately, today, it went up in smoke."

The tobacco lobby was really gunning for this bill," Matthews said. "I think the restaurant association is uneasy about it wrongly. I think people would be grateful. But they really put the pressure on.

When Matthews saw the health ban bill losing support this week, she proposed a compromise that would have required restaurants with 50 or more seats to leave half of them for

See Senate, Page A21

Patrolwoman Melissa Piscatelli salutes the coffin holding the body of her fiance, Milford Patrolman Daniel Scott Wasson. At her side after Wasson's funeral in Milford Wednesday is his police dog.

Cloe Poisson / The Hartford Courant

Thousands mourn slain patrolman

Fellow officers pay their final tribute to a fallen comrade

By MATTHEW KAUFFMAN
Courant Staff Writer

MILFORD — As thousands of mourners slowly walked from the [...] Wednesday morning, Melissa Piscatelli stood rigidly over the casket and saluted her fellow officer.

Later, with the cemetery nearly empty, the Milford policewoman knelt by the grave site, laid her head on the casket, and prayed and cried.

Piscatelli was engaged to marry Wasson, 25, who was shot to death early Sunday — becoming the first Milford police officer killed in the line of duty.

At the funeral Wednesday, hundreds of mourners crowded into the small Mary Taylor Memorial United Methodist Church on Broad Street as 2,500 police officers occupied an entire block of roadway outside. Most of the officers were wearing black bands across their badges as a sign of mourning.

"When a city or a town loses a police officer, they lose every police officer in the United States," said Joseph Wells, one of four Boston police officers who drove three hours to attend the funeral.

Police departments from most cities and towns in Connecticut as well as departments from New Jersey, New York, Massachusetts, Rhode Island and New Hampshire were represented. Several former Milford officers came from Florida.

Loudspeakers set up outside the church broadcast the funeral service to the officers and others who could not fit inside.

Danny's dedication to the police profession was complete. It was reflected in everything he did," Sgt. Paul Duff, Wasson's supervisor, said in a eulogy. He said Wasson was a line all-around officer who was well liked.

"Today, his family and loved ones, his friends, his brother and sister officers and the community he served and protected say farewell to Officer Danny Wasson. You have touched us all, Danny, and we will never forget you. Duff said as his voice began to crack.

See Thousands, Page A6

Imported goods, from bikes to wine, cost more with the weakened dollar

By ANTHONY GIORGIANNI
Courant Consumer Affairs Writer

At $300, a certain vintage of Pauillac Mouton-Rothschild wine wouldn't have been a bad deal 18 months ago. Today, it would be a steal.

Imported wines are among items hardest hit by the weakening of the dollar abroad. The same bottle of French wine today could cost $400 to $450, said one Hartford-area wine distributor.

The prices of many imported

goods sold in Connecticut and elsewhere in the United States have increased with the gradual but steady weakening of the dollar against foreign currencies.

Connecticut merchants report price increases of 15 percent to 30 percent on some items imported from Japan, Germany, France, Italy and other countries.

In addition to imported wines, the items hit by price increases include bicycles, lawnmowers, cheeses, automobiles and cameras, say merchants and officials of the U.S. De-

partment of Commerce.

Also affected are U.S. goods made with foreign-produced parts.

The retail price of one popular Japanese-made camera, the Minolta Maxxum Model 7000, has increased by a third — from $295 to $395 — in the past 14 months, said Jim Wilson, a salesman at Milford Camera Inc. Wilson blamed the weakening dollar for the increase.

That's had a gigantic effect. Our wholesale prices have been going up

See Weekbend, Page A6

Index

Ann Landers	F6
Bridge	F7
Business	E1
Classified	F11
Comics	F8
Connecticut	B1
Courant 3	
Crossword	F7
Editorials	D10

Editorials	B10
Horoscope	F6
Legal Notices	E11
Lottery	A4
Movies	D6
Obituaries	B6
Sports	D1
Stocks	E2
Town Courant	E11

Amy Carter and 14 other defendants were found innocent Wednesday of trespassing and disorderly conduct charges. Page A6.

Amusements in CALENDAR Section

WEATHER: CLOUDY
40° to 60°F (4° to 15°C)
Complete Weather B14

State tax chief apologizes to senator he confronted

By SUSAN E. KINSMAN
Capitol Bureau Chief

Within hours of Gov. William A. O'Neill's suggestion Wednesday, state Revenue Services Commissioner John G. Groppo telephoned an apology to a state senator with he had confronted with a confidential tax file last month.

Senate Minority Leader Reginald J. Smith, R-New Hartford, said he had a brief but "very cordial" conversation with Groppo, who followed up with a written apology later in the

day.

Smith said he intended to proceed with the legal groundwork for an investigation of the incident and of whether tax department records were being used for political purposes. But he said he would not file a formal criminal complaint against Groppo.

Smith said he would turn over the information to various law enforcement agencies and let them decide whether to investigate. Smith has

See Commissioner, Page A21

Women in Whalers' lives feel the pressure

The demands of fans, trades, loneliness persist off the ice

By SUSAN CAMPBELL
Courant Staff Writer

Ninety minutes to go. The women struggle into Team Room K, deep in the Hartford Civic Center.

They chatter, fidget and laugh operationally at jokes that are not funny. Some munch the catered cheese and crackers. Some pick at their fingernail polish. Others twist rings.

These are the women in the Whalers' lives — some of whom have brought their children — a family thrown together by winds of fortune that may quickly change. They are frenetic with energy on this, the

hour before Game 5 of the best-of-seven Adams Division semifinal series against the Quebec Nordiques, deadlocked at 2-2.

"This is like the beginning of the year," said Mary Ann List, wife of goaltender Mike List. Forget what's happened through the year. All that matters is winning the next game.

These are women who have taken

roles that must would shy from. As well as they are dressed, life is not all reserved parking spots and private lounges at the Civic Center. It's being a single parent during road trips. It's putting up with pressure over which they have no control. It's taking a back seat to The Game.

"You have to make sure it's a lifestyle you can both be compati-

ble in," List said. "Sometimes, I want to say, 'Go ask your father,' and he's not there to ask."

Given the pressure, early elimination might seem most desirable to the families, but the women say the extended agony is worth it.

"It's extra money in your pocket — or it's not," List said.

That's the driving force behind any job — money.

Wendy Tippett, wife of left wing-er Dave Tippett, agreed that a winning season beats an early exit.

"It would be much more stressful

See Women, Page A27

Action on the ice rivets Shelley Babych, right, wife of Wayne Babych, and Sue Ladouceur, wife of Randy Ladouceur.

Tony Bugas / Special to the Courant

Cloudy
see weather, page 3A

Cardinals edge Seminoles – 1D

Lindley on people watching people at the ball – 1B

Tallahassee Democrat
Florida's Capital Newspaper
Home

82nd Year, No. 8   Thursday, Jan. 8, 1987   25 Cents

Martinez makes hiring freeze official

By Dave Bruns
Democrat Capital Bureau

Gov. Bob Martinez on Wednesday asked Cabinet members to halt hiring for long-vacant jobs in their state agencies. He also formally announced his plan to freeze hiring for about 2,000 positions in the 10 state agencies controlled by him.

Also, Martinez acknowledged an error in meeting privately with senior Republican lawmakers Wednesday. During his campaign, Martinez promised not to meet secretly with lawmakers.

Some Cabinet members said they'd try to cooperate with the governor, but aides to Comptroller Gerald Lewis and Secretary of State George Firestone said

their bosses had no immediate plans to halt hirings.

Martinez said the hiring freeze would affect about 2,000 jobs and could save the state $45.5 million a year appropriated for unfilled jobs. He did not say how long the freeze would last.

He said the freeze would have little effect on state services. State workers not on the job can't be providing services to taxpayers, he noted.

"I have serious doubts about the real need for jobs that have been vacant for more than three months," Martinez said. "There may be good reasons for a prolonged vacancy, but if so, I want to know the reasons."

The new governor added that he planned to count the $45.5 million toward the $800 million in waste that

he's promised to "sweat out" of state government over four years.

"Every drop of perspiration is going to count toward that $800 million," he said.

Under the hiring freeze, ordered into effect Wednesday, Martinez has halted hiring for any jobs that have been open for six months. These jobs cannot be filled without written authorization from the governor's office, Martinez said.

To fill jobs that had been open three to six months, agency managers will have to get the permission of agency heads, Martinez said.

Finally, Martinez said he was asking all agency heads to submit lists of state employees hired since he was elected Nov. 4.

At the same time he ordered the freeze in the governor's agencies, Martinez sent a brief letter to Cabinet members asking them to consider similar action in other state agencies, including their own.

Ten of the 25 state agencies, employing about half of all state workers, report directly to Martinez. The six Cabinet members, each elected independently of Martinez, lead their own agencies.

Another five agencies are run by appointed boards hired by the Cabinet and governor. Martinez asked the Cabinet to consider similar hiring freezes for those agencies. The four remaining agencies are run by independent commissions.

See MARTINEZ, 2A

Firefighter James Allen checks for pulse on pilot Wednesday

Phil Sears, Democrat

a.m.

Bomb hurts former Lebanese president, kills four

BEIRUT, Lebanon — Assassins wounded former Lebanese President Camille Chamoun and 40 other people and killed three bodyguards and a passer-by with a remote-controlled car bomb as his motorcade drove through Beirut on Wednesday.

Chamoun, 86, a Christian who was the architect of the first U.S. military peace-keeping mission in the Mid-east and now serves as Lebanon's finance minister, suffered minor shrapnel wounds in the face and both hands, police said.

The morning blast tore out a hole 6 feet deep and 14 feet wide and hurled Chamoun's bullet-proof Mercedes Benz about 60 feet off the road in the Mariahen industrial district of Christian East Beirut.

"But if (Chamoun's car) miraculously landed on its wheels and he survived along with his driver," said a police representative.

It was the fifth time in 19 years that assassins attempted to kill Chamoun, a respected political figure to whom Christian government officials and militia commanders turn for advice in times of crises.

"God is protecting us," Chamoun said in an interview broadcast by the Christian Voice of Lebanon radio.

He made no accusations, and no group claimed responsibility for the bombing.

The station taped the interview after Chamoun left N-tal-Deu hospital, where his wounds were bandaged.

Police said a Peugeot 504 car laden with 165 pounds of explosives blew up as Chamoun's motorcade, en route to a meeting of the Lebanese Front, passed. The front is a coalition of Christian groups involved in Lebanon's civil war, now in its 12th year.

Commission tries, tries again

KINGWOOD, W.Va. — After three days and 264 ballots, the Preston County Commission remained deadlocked 4-4 Wednesday in voting for a commission president.

Bills aren't being paid, and property-reappraisal hearings are piling up.

"It's past the point of humor," said Nancy Bachart, county clerk since 1975, on Wednesday.

It's traditional in the northern West Virginia county for the clerk to be getting head of the commission while a new president is being elected.

Both men vying for the presidency are Republicans. Ward Thomas, a retired businessman and the incumbent president, has led the commission for more than 10 years. Jesse Jennings, a farmer, has served on the commission since 1984.

Some say the battle is the old vs. the new. Elder members want to keep Thomas, and newer members want a change in leadership.

The commissioners meet again tonight.

Index

Advice	9C	Local/State	1B
Business	5D	Obituaries	2B
Classified	4B	Sports	1D
Comics	10C	Stocks	6D
Editorial	10A	Television	11C
Features	1C	Theaters	9C

If you have a story or photo idea, please call the Democrat between 9 a.m. and midnight at 599-2151.

Plane crash kills one

By Mark Pankowski
Democrat staff writer

A single-engine plane crashed into the Ochlockonee River shortly after takeoff Wednesday, killing the pilot and slightly injuring a passenger.

Pilot Benjamin Brown, 78, of Tallahassee, was found dead inside the partially submerged plane, said Leon County sheriff's spokesman Dick Simpson.

James Edwards, the six-seater plane's only passenger, said he survived by bailing out right below the plane crashed.

"Before we hit, I opened the door" and jumped out, said the 31-year-old Tallahasseean.

Simpson said the 1966 Cessna 210 crashed shortly before 11:45 a.m. about a half-mile north of the Tallahassee Commercial Airport where it took off.

Before crashing, the plane clipped two major power lines, each carrying 115,000 volts of electricity, Simpson said. The wires were freed but did not snap.

Edwards, whose left arm was slightly injured, said the Cessna 210 stalled after taking off.

"The plane sounded" just like a car that needed a tuneup," he said. "It kept cutting off and going down."

See CRASH, 9A

Do presidents have right to keep illness under wraps?

WASHINGTON — On a 75-ton yacht cruising through Long Island Sound in July 1893, doctors removed a large part of President Grover Cleveland's jaw in the apparently mistaken belief he had cancer. The operation and the seriousness of the disease was — was kept secret for 10 years. The public was told only that the president had a couple of teeth pulled.

It was not a good political moment for the president to appear disabled. Economic depression was spreading, the Philadelphia and Reading Railroad had gone bankrupt, unemployment was rising and 500 banks had bellicine on his status.

The cover-up was carefully orchestrated. In a show of strength, Cleveland, just before

his operation, called a special session of Congress to meet later in the summer. By that time, he had been fitted with an artificial jaw, and despite a press report that the president was "critically ill with a malignancy," The New York Times proclaimed that his speech to Congress "removed every lingering doubt of his entire soundness of body."

Almost a century later, a medical cover-up of this magnitude is unthinkable — or is it?

Certainly President Reagan's health problems appear to have been well reported in the media. As he recovers from the surgery to remove part of his prostate, the White House has issued daily bulletins on his status.

On Wednesday, Reagan's doctor said "things could not be

See PRESIDENTS, 2A

James Garfield
Democrat Files

Spent tax refund leads to arrest of local bar owner

By Soneni Bryant
Democrat staff writer

Tallahassee tavern owner Scott W. Shaffer was arrested Wednesday by the Florida Department of Law Enforcement and charged with grand theft of a $32,520 unauthorized tax refund he received in 1984.

The arrest was the result of a joint investigation by FDLE and the Florida Department of Revenue, following a Tallahassee Democrat inquiry into business tax refunds.

The FDLE also is investigating whether Department of Revenue employees may have been involved in the refund transaction.

Shaffer, 33, was released on a $2,500 bond late Wednesday. He could not be reached for comment.

According to the FDLE warrant for Shaffer's arrest, the Department of Revenue mailed Shaffer a check for $32,520 in January 1984.

The check, issued by the Comptroller's Office, was paid from the state general revenue fund to Shaffer

See REFUND, 9A

Award of Excellence

TALLAHASSEE DEMOCRAT
Tallahassee, Florida
Phil Sears

Art and Photos 133

Eva Calloway, 87, can remember sitting with her family when she was so young her legs couldn't touch the ground. Now there are other little girls—like 4-year-old Chere Boone, for whom the church seems a mammoth place.

Award of Excellence
THE WASHINGTON POST MAGAZINE
Washington, D.C.
Brian Noyes, Art Director;
Maria Stenzel, Photographer

Award of Excellence
THE WASHINGTON TIMES
Washington, D.C.
Kevin Gilbert

Award of Excellence

THE NEW YORK TIMES
New York, New York
Diana LaGuardia,
Art Director;
Kevin McPhee,
Designer;
Michael O'Neill,
Photographer

VENUS
GROWING UP ON SKID ROW

La tensión

Quienes se congregaron en las proximidades del DuPont Plaza presenciaron muestras extraordinarias de valor, colectivo e individual, de la Policía, los bomberos y las cuadrillas de rescate de la Defensa Civil. Con gran arrojo y desprecio por los peligros, se entregaron al rescate de los huéspedes, subiendo por livianas escaleras de aluminio, de un piso a otro, buscando afectados por el denso humo, atentos al drama y a la gran tensión, siempre apercibidos de la urgencia de su función de samaritanos.

Silver Award
EL NUEVO DIA
San Juan, Puerto Rico
Jose I. Fernandez,
Luis Ramos,
Ramon Korff,
Gary Williams

Award of Excellence
THE DENVER POST
Denver, Colorado
Dennis Chamberlin

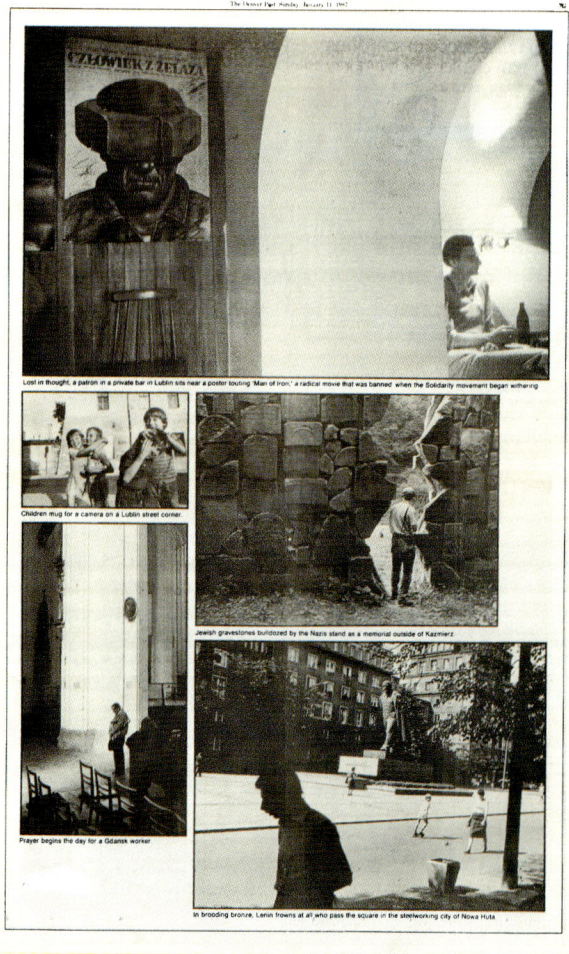

Urban MOSAIC

Informational Graphics

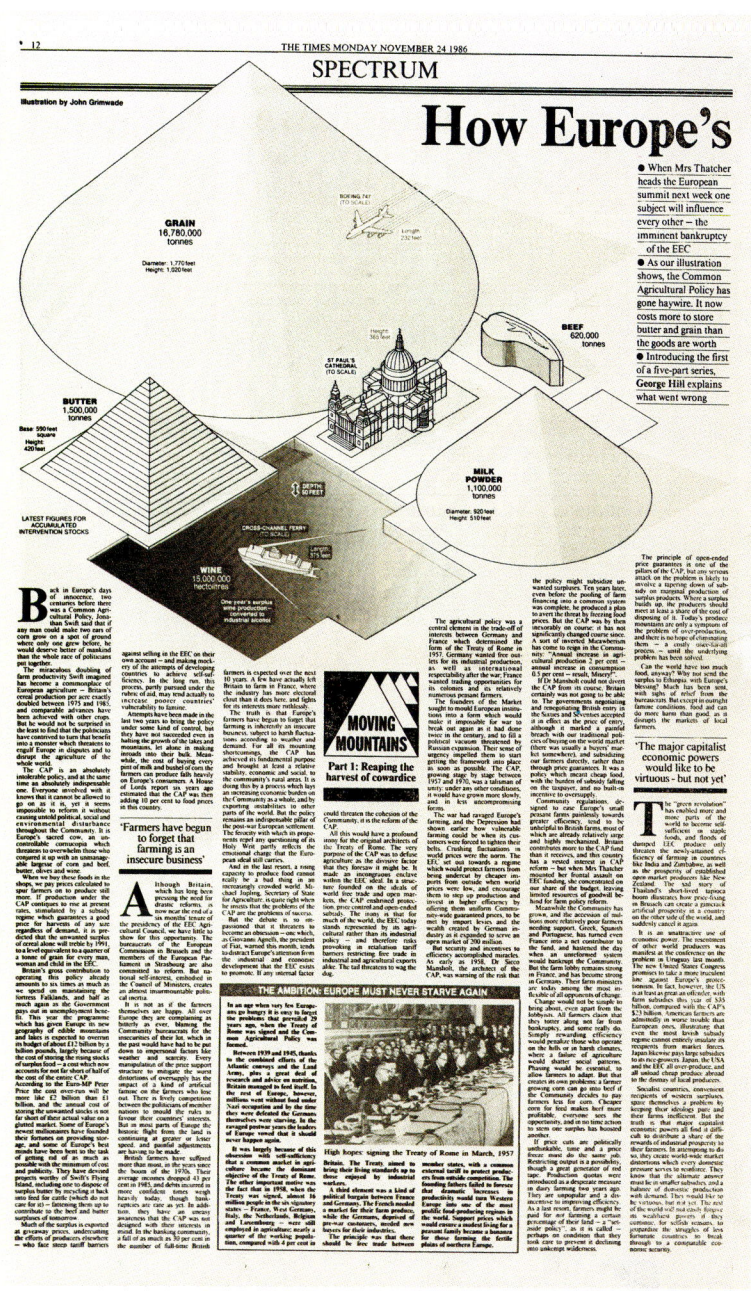

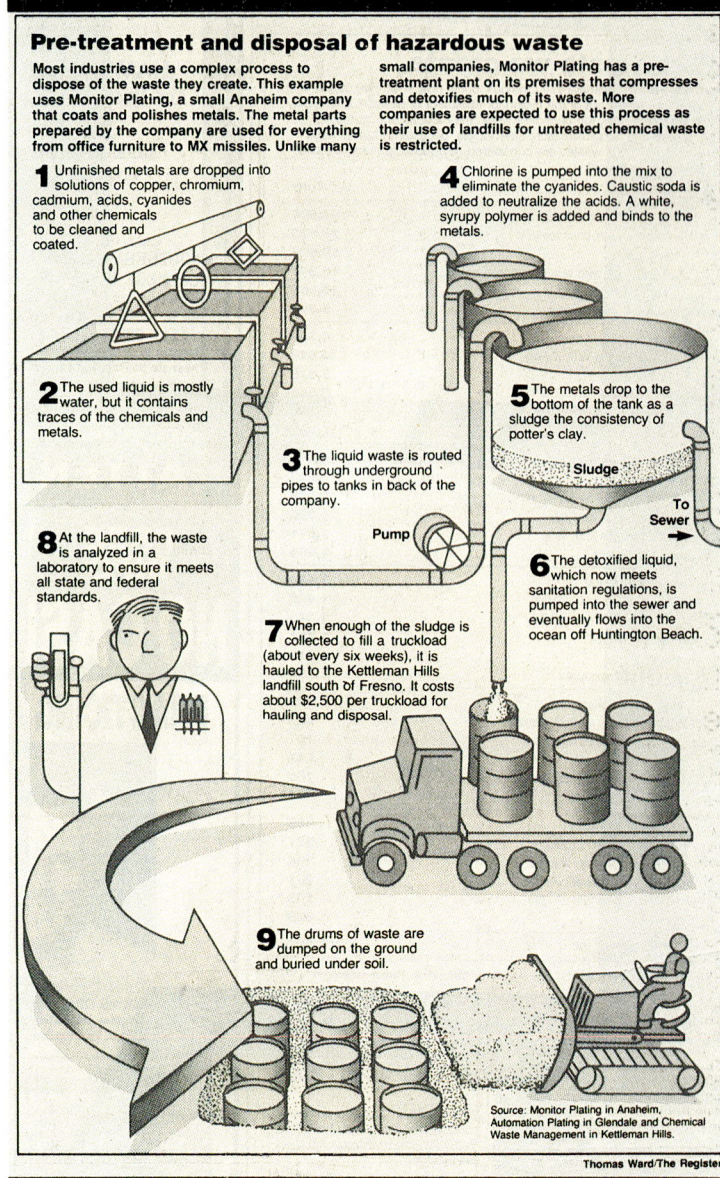

Pre-treatment and disposal of hazardous waste

Most industries use a complex process to dispose of the waste they create. This example uses Monitor Plating, a small Anaheim company that coats and polishes metals. The metal parts prepared by the company are used for everything from office furniture to MX missiles. Unlike many small companies, Monitor Plating has a pre-treatment plant on its premises that compresses and detoxifies much of its waste. More companies are expected to use this process as their use of landfills for untreated chemical waste is restricted.

1 Unfinished metals are dropped into solutions of copper, chromium, cadmium, acids, cyanides and other chemicals to be cleaned and coated.

2 The used liquid is mostly water, but it contains traces of the chemicals and metals.

3 The liquid waste is routed through underground pipes to tanks in back of the company.

4 Chlorine is pumped into the mix to eliminate the cyanides. Caustic soda is added to neutralize the acids. A white, syrupy polymer is added and binds to the metals.

5 The metals drop to the bottom of the tank as a sludge the consistency of potter's clay.

Sludge

Pump

To Sewer

6 The detoxified liquid, which now meets sanitation regulations, is pumped into the sewer and eventually flows into the ocean off Huntington Beach.

7 When enough of the sludge is collected to fill a truckload (about every six weeks), it is hauled to the Kettleman Hills landfill south of Fresno. It costs about $2,500 per truckload for hauling and disposal.

8 At the landfill, the waste is analyzed in a laboratory to ensure it meets all state and federal standards.

9 The drums of waste are dumped on the ground and buried under soil.

Source: Monitor Plating in Anaheim, Automation Plating in Glendale and Chemical Waste Management in Kettleman Hills.

Thomas Ward/The Register

Award of Excellence
THE ORANGE COUNTY REGISTER
Santa Ana, California
Thomas Ward

Award of Excellence
CLEVELAND PLAIN DEALER
Cleveland, Ohio
John Backderf

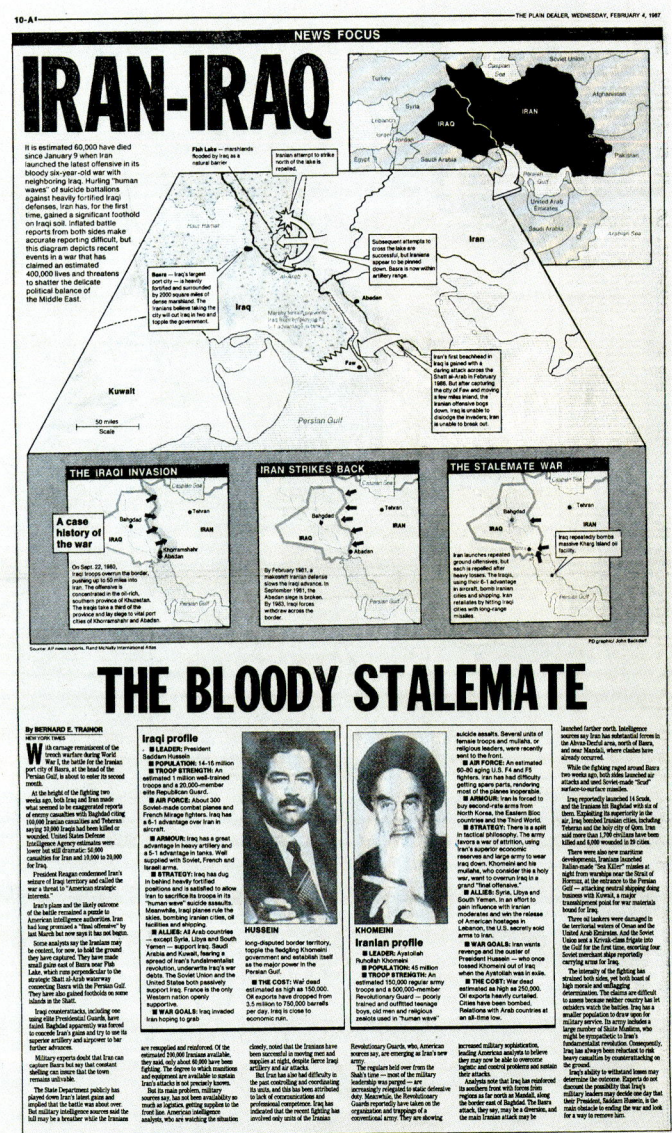

THE PLAIN DEALER, WEDNESDAY, FEBRUARY 4, 1987

NEWS FOCUS

IRAN-IRAQ

THE BLOODY STALEMATE

By BERNARD E. TRAINOR
NEW YORK TIMES

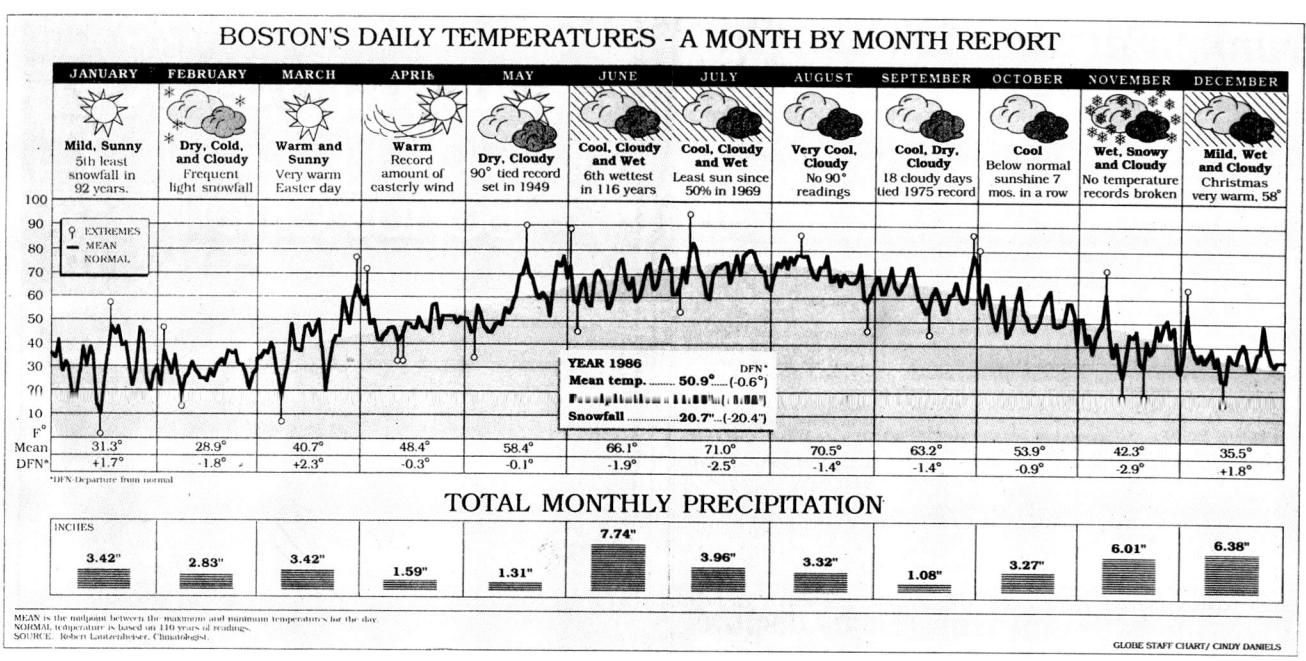

Award of Excellence
THE BOSTON GLOBE
Boston, Massachusetts
Cindy Daniels

Award of Excellence
THE BOSTON GLOBE
Boston, Massachusetts
Cindy Daniels

SIX INCHES PER MINUTE
Capt Walenkamp's long, slow haul to right the Herald of Free Enterprise

Hans Walenkamp: we can never forget this ship is a grave for so many people

On Monday, weather permitting, the operation to salvage the sunken Townsend Thoresen car ferry swings into action. BOB GRAHAM meets the man at the helm

THE FOGHORN voice of Captain Hans Walenkamp bellows with mock rage when he is called the Red Adair of the High Seas.

"Ha, it's what you British want to call me," he roars. "Me? I'm just a sailor, a man of the sea." It is the only time this giant Dutchman has smiled in more than three weeks.

Walenkamp is the man in charge of the operation to rescue the stricken Townsend Thoresen car ferry, the Herald of Free Enterprise. It is more than just a capsized ship – it is a tomb for as many as 200 people.

He is a man who treats the oceans as a mistress – to be loved, but with the caution that she can turn as quickly as a polecat.

Walenkamp retains the love he felt as a boy who spent his summers messing around in boats along the coastline of his home near Rotterdam. And that is remarkable, for he, more than most, has witnessed the full wrath of the seas.

For the past 15 years, he has been part of the operation to salvage the team. He is the master of the Smit Tak salvage fleet – an immense armada of specialised vessels and crew which constantly patrols the world's oceans. His job is simple – to raise ships that have sunk, capsized or been abandoned anywhere on the oceans. He cashes in on the tragic spoils of the seas.

Pressing reasons for working day and night

THIS job, more than any other he has been involved in, holds a special place in his heart. As a young man, he sailed many times in and out of Zeebrugge. He knows only too well the idiosyncrasies of the North Sea.

There is intense pressure on Walenkamp to bring the Herald back to Zeebrugge where it started its fateful journey three weeks ago.

"We can never forget that this ship is more than one that has capsized; it is a grave for so many people," he says.

He understands well that for many relatives of those still missing, the pain will only begin to diminish when the bodies are brought out and identified.

His deep voice raises a shade when he says: "Time is always important with a salvage operation. But this time there is a very special reason for the people who still have someone missing.

"I know that for them there are pressing reasons why we should work day and night. For those people who wait at home to know the truth of whether their relative is on board or not, we can never be quick enough.

"For all of them, the process of learning to live with the pain they now feel, of beginning to forget, can only begin when I have done my job."

This enormous raw-boned sea captain dismisses talk of heroics. To him it is a job. He admits there are dangers, but then, he points out, there are in almost every job and walk of life.

The dangers of the Herald of Free Enterprise are minimal compared with those he has faced. There were the supertankers he pulled out of the Persian Gulf, the legacy of the Iran-Iraq conflict. "I suppose they were the most dangerous," he concedes. "I think I did about 15 of those. There was the constant risk of explosion and being badly burned.

"But on all jobs we are advised by people who know precisely what they are talking about, engineers and fire-fighting experts. I let them assess the risks, and if they tell me the job can be done, then I do it."

When Walenkamp talks of courage there is no trace of irony. "In my book the true heroes are the people who hold down nine-to-five office jobs. Sometimes I am in the office for two weeks at a time, and I can't stand it."

The Smit Tak Action team – the maritime equivalent of the motorway breakdown men – is ready to sail anywhere in the world, at any time, to rescue a stricken vessel.

"The team is between 40 and 50 strong. In Zeebrugge it is strengthened by salvage experts from two local Belgian firms. There are divers – 'the finest in the world,'" says Walenkamp – welders, engineers, ship construction experts and fire fighters.

Throughout the high seas there is a Smit Tak vessel patrolling, ready and waiting. There is, after all, big money at stake.

"We don't look forward to a shipping disaster, particularly when there is loss of life," says Walenkamp. "But each new job we hear of is a fresh challenge."

The sea-going emergency men, the majority of whom have families at home in Holland, spend five months at a stretch at sea. Until two years ago, 48 year-old Walenkamp spent eight months of every year patrolling the oceans. Then he was appointed master of the Smit Tak fleet and it has cut his travelling by half.

They have been called the "Vultures of the Seas". It is a term that Walenkamp dismisses with a shake of his head.

When the Herald of Free Enterprise capsized on the fateful night of

The scene at Zeebrugge this week
The scene at Zeebrugge this week: Smit Tak barges take up position for the operation to 'roll over' the Herald of Free Enterprise

Diagram labels
1. Cables from anchored piles are winched into Takheave barges so shortening cable length and creating pull on ship
2. At the same time, cranes on Taklift barges lift submerged port side
3. How the ship is rotated
4. Take out remaining bodies. Then the pumping operation begins, to float ship (5 - 10 days)

Cables attached to 16 pilings anchored 50 ft into the seabed. Each piling weighs 395 tonnes

Takheave 32 barge

Takheave 31 barge. Pull needed to right ship, 2,000 tonnes per barge; pulling power of each barge, 3,000 tonnes

Cables from Takheave barges to ship remain same length. Cables attached to welded strong-points on ship

Taklift 4 barge Lifting capacity 1600 tonnes

Taklift Norma barge Lifting capacity 400 tonnes

Taklift 5 barge Lifting capacity 1,200 tonnes

Action cable

Point at which reaction cable is attached to ship

Reaction cable

Cables to reaction anchors prevent ship being dragged along seabed by the pulling barges

Herald of Free Enterprise 8,000 tonnes

Deep water channel

Zeebrugge Harbour

NORTH

Herald of

Graphic: ART PHILLIPS

Life-size cross-section of cable used to lift Herald of Free Enterprise.
72-92mm; Total length of cable, 2,655 miles; weight 30 - 42 kilos per metre; load put upon each cable, 250 tonnes

Cables the size of a man's fist

THE three have worked on some of Smit Tak's major rescues – the recovery of the Alexander Keilland oil platform when it capsized in Stavanger Fjord four years ago, the rescue of the giant French tanker the Betelgeuse which exploded in Bantry Bay in 1962, killing 57 crew, and the long list of supertankers pulled out of the Persian Gulf.

But this time, with the Herald of Free Enterprise resting in its shallow grave, a half-mile from the entrance of Zeebrugge harbour, there is an added urgency to their task. If the experts don't get their sums exactly right, they could lose many of the bodies still inside.

March 7, a Smit Tak vessel was alongside within 90 minutes, and played an important role in the rescue of survivors. Thoughts of salvage, says Walenkamp, were secondary at that time.

Walenkamp relies on the expertise of his two best friends – Gerard van Wyk and Hans van Rooy. "In my job I need to trust people, and these two men are the best." All three come from the same district of Rotterdam and went to Maritime School together.

Passengers trapped in the tangled wreckage

ONCE the pulling begins, it is a long, slow process, says Walenkamp. The pulling speed of the two Tak heave barges is a maximum six inches per minute, although it can be much slower. Each step of the way, the pulling will be interrupted for the experts to check progress. Estimates are that the entire operation to roll the ship over into its upright position could take from three hours to a day.

Then begins the grim task for the divers to recover the bodies still missing. The passengers are believed to have been trapped in the tangled wreckage on the A, B and C decks on the submerged port side. Crewmen are thought to be in the engine room areas while a number of truck drivers are believed to be in the cabs of their lorries.

The operation to recover the bodies – they will be unrecognisable – could take up to five days, as divers pick their way through the mass of wreckage.

When all the bodies are thought to have been recovered, Smit Tak will then begin a pumping out operation to re-float the Herald. That could take between five and 10 days, says Walenkamp.

Entire operation will cost £6 million

THE LAST chapter of the salvage of the Herald of Free Enterprise will be as Smit Tak tugs pull it slowly back into Zeebrugge harbour – where the detailed examination to discover what went wrong will begin in earnest.

Smit Tak's contract is one followed by the Lloyd's Open Form of Salvage Arbitration. The ship is insured for £25 million. The entire operation to right it and return it to port is expected to cost about £6 million, the bulk of which goes to Smit Tak.

A spokesman for the firm said that the contract calls for the Herald to be returned "in one piece" to a port. Once returned, said company spokesman Dan Kaakebben, it will be in a state where it can be re-fitted and used again.

But Townsend Thoresen have refused to say if the ship will ever sail again.

SPECTRUM

The race for time and space

Illustration by John Grimwade

SPECTRUM 1

Off into space, economy class

● Passenger flights from London to Sydney in just over an hour? It seemed impossible until a breakthrough in rocket technology breathed fresh life into a British project called HOTOL. Keith Hindley looks at the background of a machine that could shoot us to the front of the space race

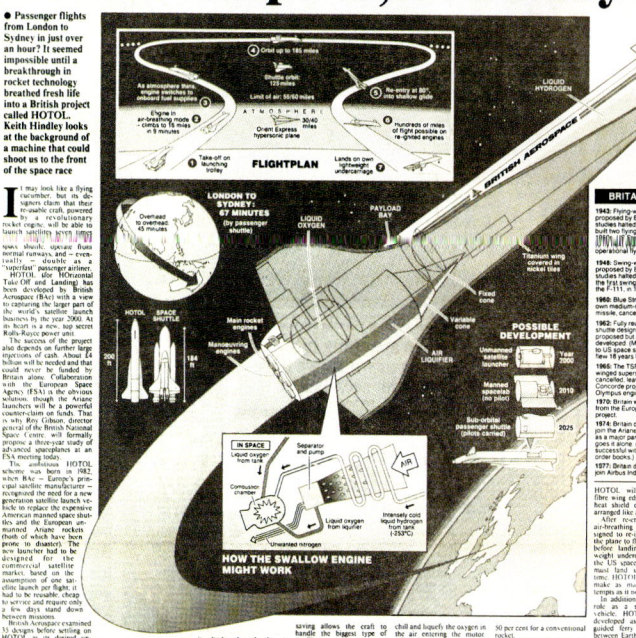

Illustration by John Grimwade

BRITAIN'S MISSED OPPORTUNITIES

SPECTRUM

Into battle with the holy warriors

Illustration by John Grimwade

Today, more talks aimed at ending the Afghan war begin in Geneva. As the diplomats argue, **Sandy Gall**, the veteran ITN newscaster, tells of the most recent of his three visits to Afghanistan, when he saw action alongside Ahmed Shah Masud, the charismatic leader of the mujahidin resistance and a thorn in Kabul's communist side

A MUCH TROUBLED COUNTRY

RESISTANCE: THE MUJAHIDIN

Search for Answers About Osteoporosis
Cases of Crippling Bone Disease Expected to Rise as Baby Boomers Age

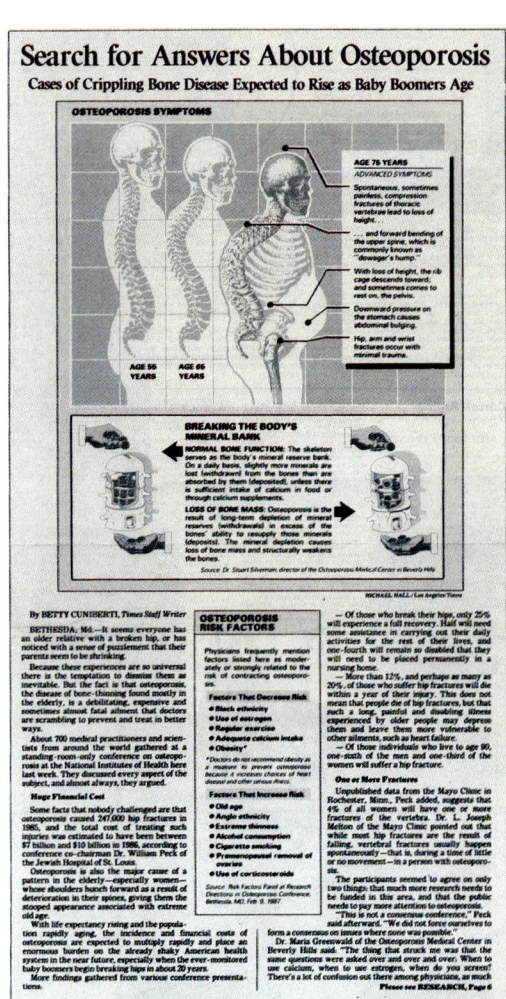

Award of Excellence
LOS ANGELES TIMES
Los Angeles, California
Michael R. Hall,
John Dreyfuss

Award of Excellence
THE TIMES
London, England
John Grimwade

Award of Excellence
LOS ANGELES TIMES
Los Angeles, California
Michael R. Hall,
Terry Schwadron

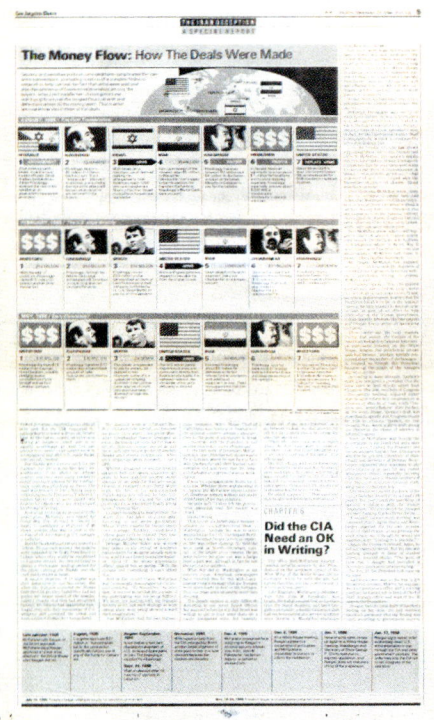

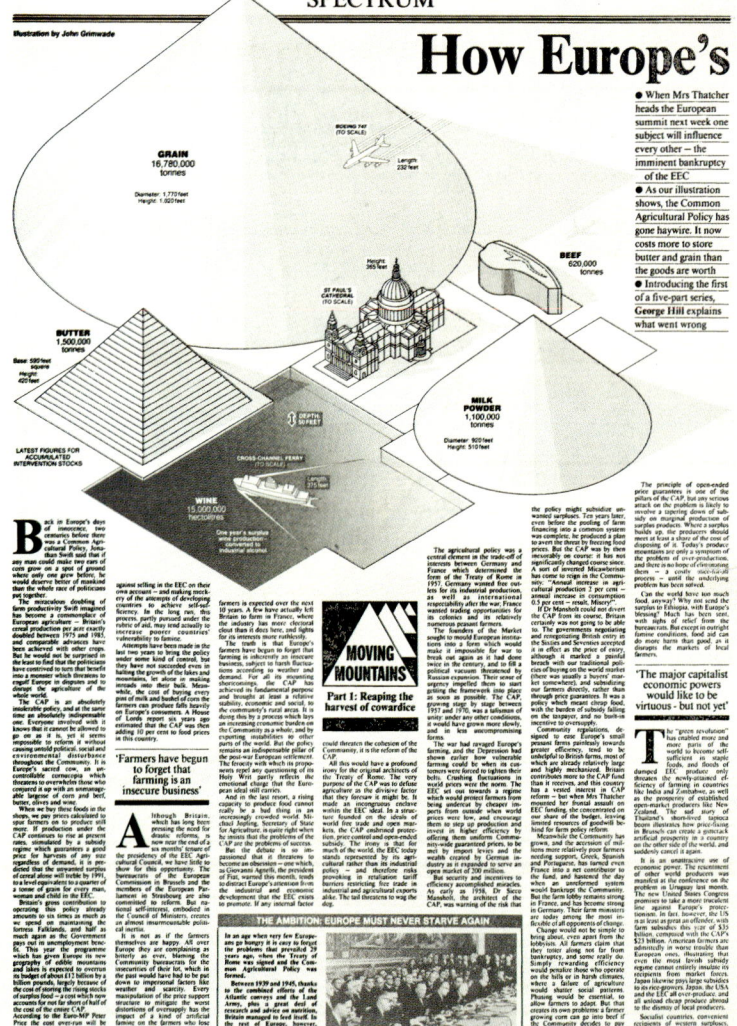

THE TIMES MONDAY NOVEMBER 24 1986

SPECTRUM

How Europe's

- When Mrs Thatcher heads the European summit next week one subject will influence every other — the imminent bankruptcy of the EEC
- As our illustration shows, the Common Agricultural Policy has gone haywire. It now costs more to store butter and grain than the goods are worth
- Introducing the first of a five-part series, George Hill explains what went wrong

MOVING MOUNTAINS
Part 1: Reaping the harvest of cowardice

'Farmers have begun to forget that farming is an insecure business'

'The major capitalist economic powers would like to be virtuous - but not yet'

THE AMBITION: EUROPE MUST NEVER STARVE AGAIN

High hopes: signing the Treaty of Rome in March, 1957

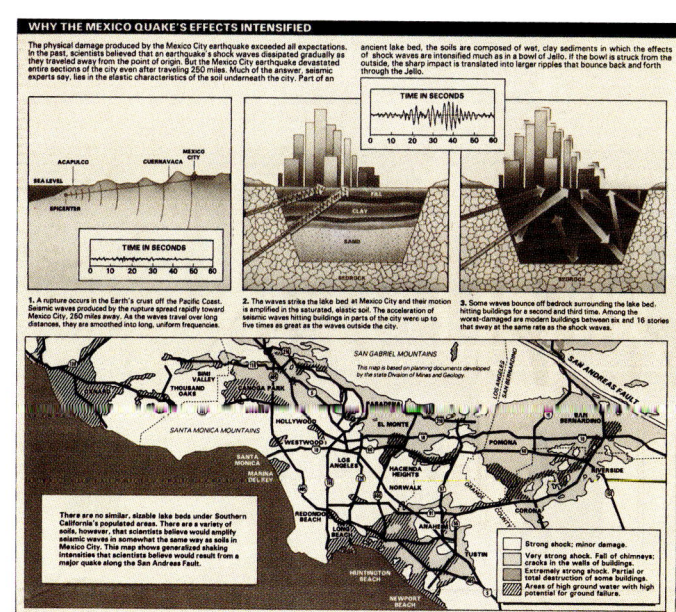

WHY THE MEXICO QUAKE'S EFFECTS INTENSIFIED

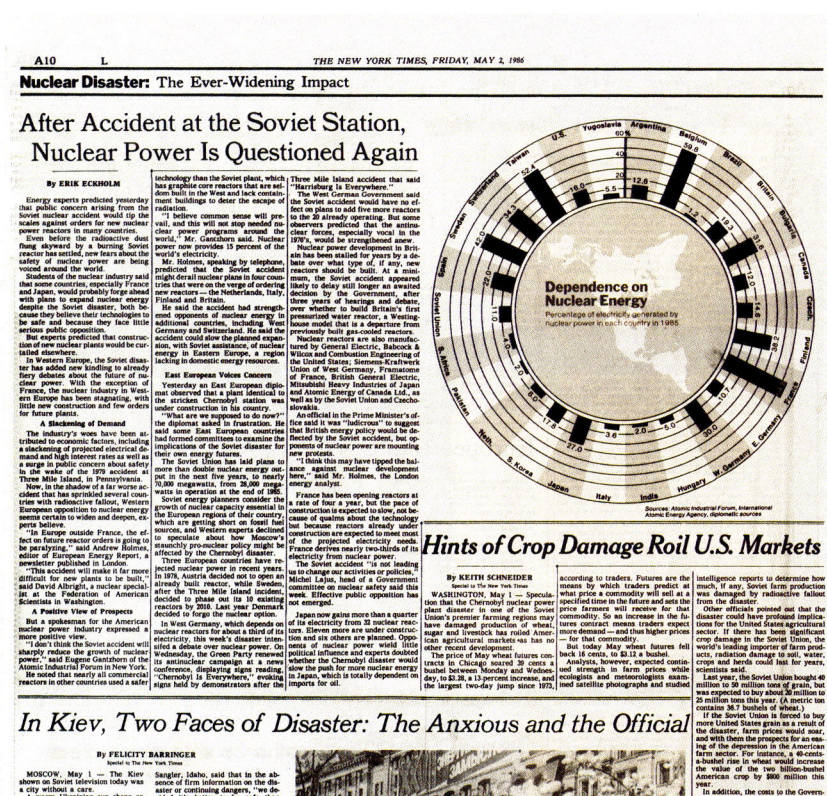

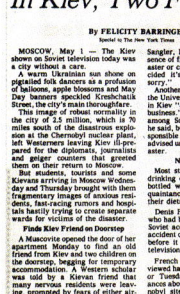

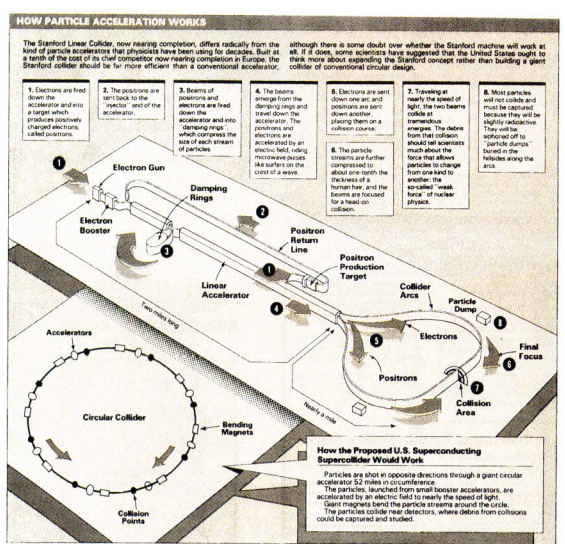

HOW PARTICLE ACCELERATION WORKS

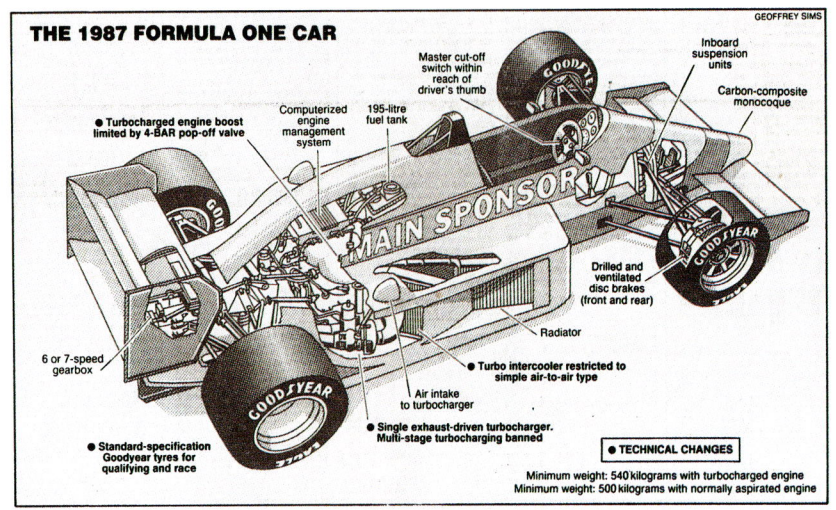

Award of Excellence
THE TIMES
London,
England
Geoffrey Sims

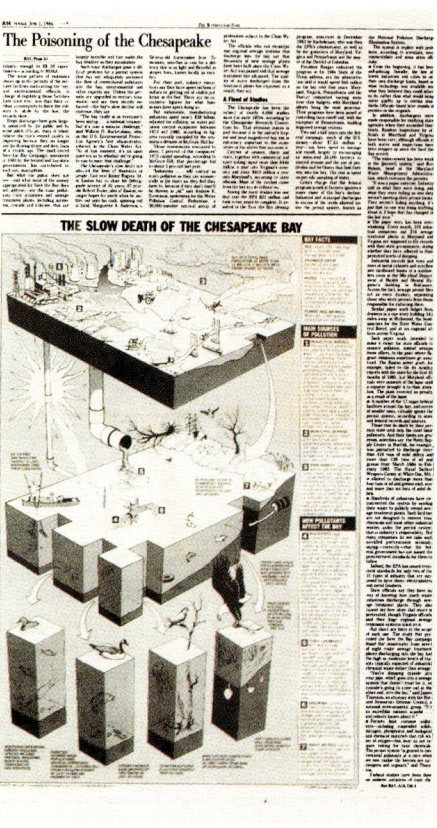

Award of Excellence
THE WASHINGTON POST
Washington, D.C.
Johnstone Quinan

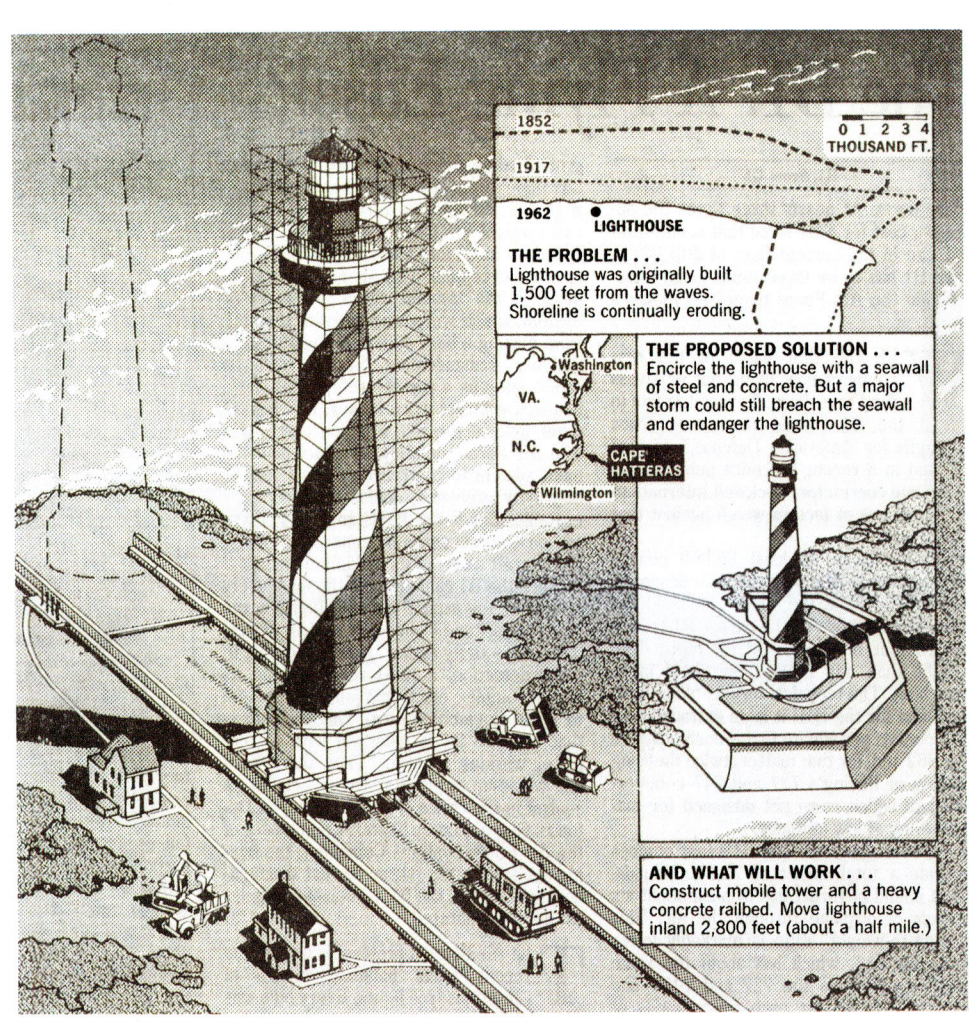

Award of Excellence
THE WASHINGTON POST
Washington, D.C.
Johnstone Quinan

built around a hooked nose, is usually expressionless, showing neither anger nor sadness nor joy. He says little, unless asked.

Martina was a secretary. She wasn't thrilled about that, but it would do until she completed university courses in economics. "I was on my way up," she said. She is the more dynamic of the two, the more expressive. Her broad and clear face can dance with laughter and knot in disapproval. She has blue eyes, vivid red hair and is nearly as big as Achim, with broad shoulders and long legs.

Together, they had a good life. The GDR economy, in fact, is probably the best of the East Bloc states. They had enough money. They had a 1978 Soviet-made car, a color TV, a stereo and an apartment that, compared to those in the sterile highrises that dot East Berlin, had character. It was in an old four-story building on a secluded street, one with nice trees. They had friends and a lot to do, so they were never bored. "Basically, I had it quite well in the GDR," said Martina.

Yet they decided to get out. They decided to shed a life that, by their own admission, was not hell; to risk going to jail for eight years; to risk being shot to death; to gamble the life of Kirsten, Martina's baby by a failed marriage. "Have you been to the GDR?" said Achim. "I've found it very difficult to explain to people who have not been there what it's like."

"People who don't live in the GDR," said Martina, "don't understand my situation."

It was not one thing but many. As a result, they cannot say when it began. There was no searing incident that, in hindsight, they can point to as the first milepost on the road to escape. Instead, grievance slowly piled on grievance. "There's a little bug called a dung bug that rolls dung into balls," Achim said, "and they get bigger and bigger until one day, they're bigger than he is. That's what happened to me. . . . I was fed up."

In a 1985 study of 540 East Germans who had emigrated legally, Professor Volker Ronge of Bergische University in West Germany found that 71 percent had left because of "lack of political freedom" and 66 percent because of "political pressure." (Multiple answers were permitted.)

But Ronge says he distrusts the high totals because he believes many of the East Germans told him what they thought he wanted to hear: that the choice had been made for grand political reasons. In fact, he says, the personal reasons they gave next were probably just as crucial: 56 percent cited a desire to travel, 46 percent complained about the lack of consumer goods in East Germany, 45 percent were upset that the state would not promote them or let them change jobs, 28 percent wanted a new start in life. What they seemed to want in their lives was choice.

"They want what Americans call the right to pursue happiness," said Bernd Wilz, president of a West German refugee association.

The first reasons Achim cites are, in
continued on next page

ILLUSTRATION BY **ROGER HASSLER**

INQUIRER

13

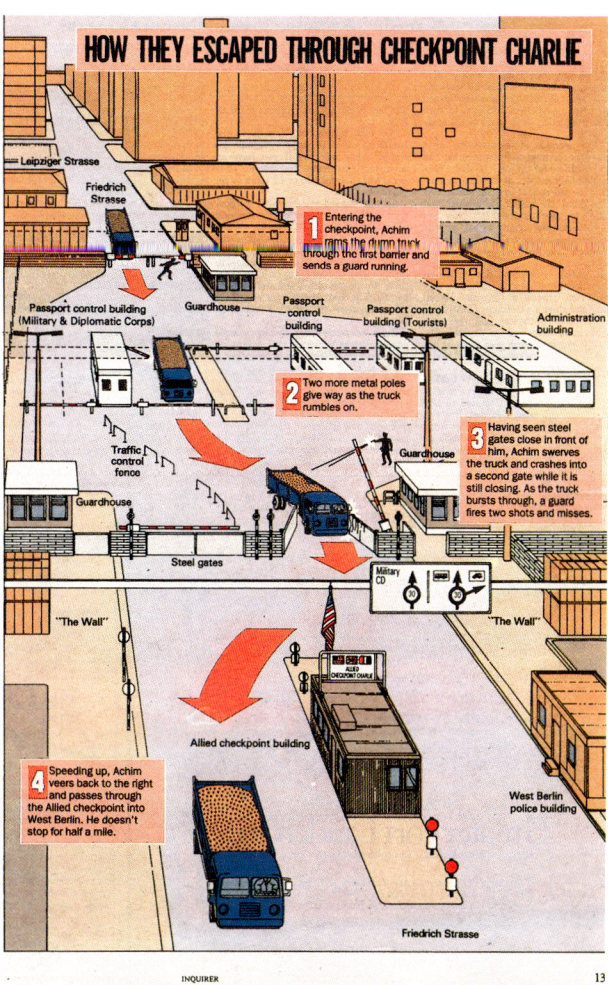

HOW THEY ESCAPED THROUGH CHECKPOINT CHARLIE

Leipziger Strasse

Friedrich Strasse

Passport control building (Military & Diplomatic Corps)

Guardhouse

Passport control building

Passport control building (Tourists)

Administration building

1 Entering the checkpoint, Achim rams the dump truck through the first barrier and sends a guard running.

2 Two more metal poles give way as the truck rumbles on.

3 Having seen steel gates close in front of him, Achim swerves the truck and crashes into a second gate while it is still closing. As the truck bursts through, a guard fires two shots and misses.

Traffic control fence

Guardhouse

Guardhouse

Steel gates

Military CD

"The Wall"

"The Wall"

Allied checkpoint building

4 Speeding up, Achim veers back to the right and passes through the Allied checkpoint into West Berlin. He doesn't stop for half a mile.

West Berlin police building

Friedrich Strasse

Silver Award

PHILADELPHIA INQUIRER
Philadelphia, Pennsylvania
Roger Hassler.

Award of Excellence

THE MIAMI HERALD
Miami, Florida
Randy Stano,
Art Director;
Rick Brownlee,
Graphic Artist

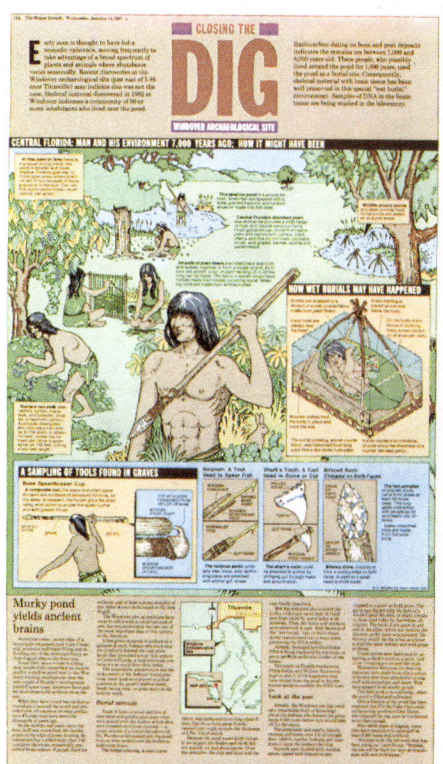

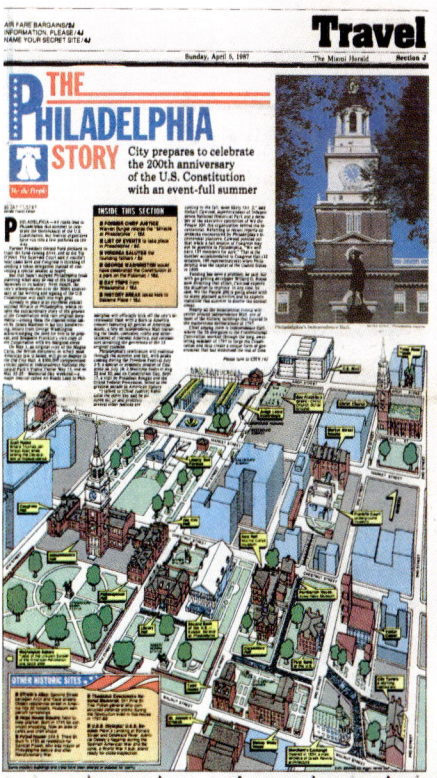

Award of Excellence

THE MIAMI HERALD
Miami, Florida
Randy Stano,
Art Director;
Rick Brownlee,
Graphic Artist

Award of Excellence
USA TODAY
Arlington,
Virginia
Heidi Capousis

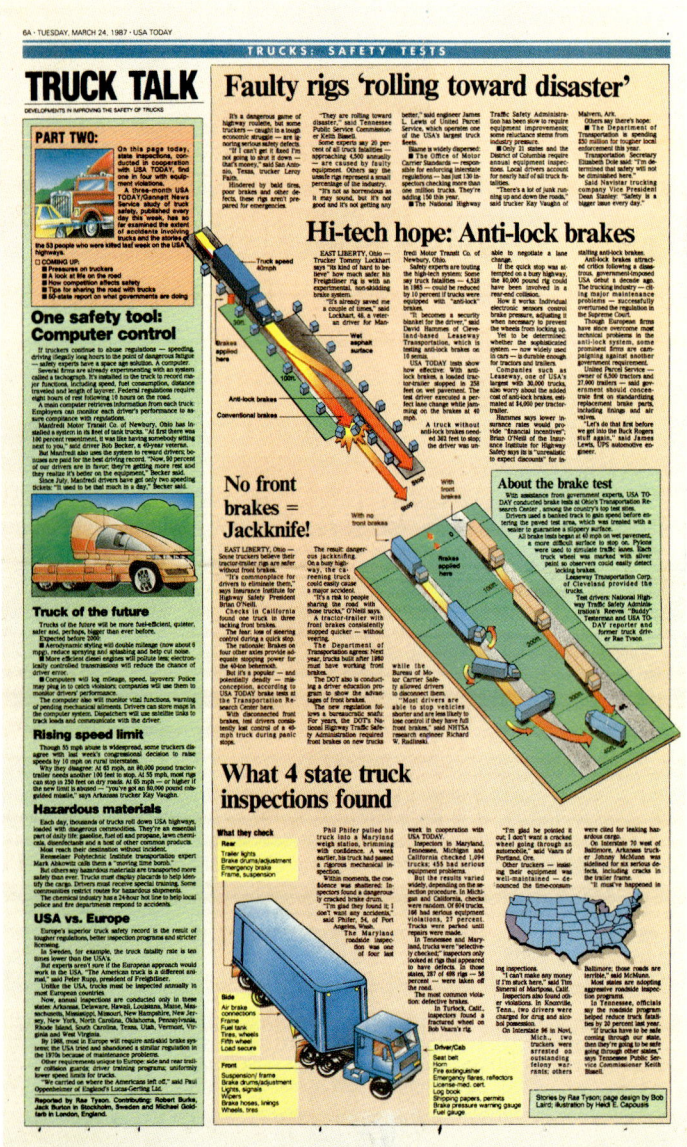

Award of Excellence
THE MIAMI HERALD
Miami, Florida
Randy Stano,
Art Director;
Phil Flanders,
Graphic Artist

The Three-Fingered Mai Tai, developed through experiments with mangoes in Vietnam, drops sharply just six inches before the plate thanks to the irregular rotation imparted by using the thumb to make it squirt off the heel of the hand.

THROWING THE THREE-FINGERED MAI TAI

reject that. I think you should practice using heavier weights. Tom House has the Texas pitchers warm up by throwing footballs on the sidelines. Our mangoes are seven to nine ounces heavier than a baseball. Granted, it's a little wet and sticky for the catchers. But it's the only way to faithfully teach the pitch. Anyway, catchers wear masks."

Amsterdam has been working most closely with Danny Broccoli, trying to get Broccoli to visualize the pitch before he throws it. He made an audio tape for Broccoli to listen to in his sleep, combining principles of zen and self-actualization. (The thought was that Broccoli, who tends to be a literalist—and, some might add, a sociopath—would be the least receptive to subliminal persuasion, and if he could learn this way, anyone could.)

"See the mango, Danny," Amsterdam's taped voice intones. "Feel the mango, Danny. It's just like a baseball. You throw it just like a baseball. Imagine the mango in your hands giving you complete mastery over any batter."

Results so far have been inconclusive. After the first night of listening to the tape, Broccoli

ran to the bullpen, grabbed a mango out of the practice bag, severed it with a vicious bite, spit it out, threw the rest against the outfield fence and bayed at Amsterdam, "Are we here to play baseball or [bleep] around with fruit?"

"He had a crush on Chiquita Banana as a kid," outfielder Oscar Madison said from a safe distance. "She didn't return his phone calls, and he never got over it."

There was one celebrated milestone on the trip: Shortstop Tito Mantequilla scored the Senators' first run, in the eighth inning of their fourth game. Mantequilla was on third when designated hitter Bad Dude Harding hit a soft grounder toward first base, which Bill Buckner let pass through his legs. Just as Mantequilla crossed the plate, Moe-Don Dorcas happily dumped a huge bucket of Kirin beer on manager Major Banks' head.

"Why Kirin, Moe-Don?" Banks inquired as he was toweling off.

"Oscar told me to get a brand you drank during the war," Dorcas said.

"Kirin's a Japanese beer. I was in Vietnam."

"Oh, that war." ■

SENATORS STUFF: Chagrined at 0-6 start, owner Tang Ye-lin threatened to cut off post-game buffet. Catcher Tony Cadenza, who owns restaurant in Hyattsville, said, "Big deal. I wouldn't serve these chicken wings to a dog." But designated runner Gabeen (Orson) Mfoom wrote letter to Tang asking him to reconsider . . . Sadir brothers were prevented from entering Disney World after Twins game; detained at main gate waiting for security clearance . . . On "Wake Up Winter Haven" TV talk show, pitcher Tyler Motherwell argued states should drop sales tax on fine wine and luxury automobiles, and double tax on alcoholic beverages bottled with twist-off tops . . . Born-again second baseman Orlando Jones read in local paper of 6-year-old boy who needed pancreas transplant and offered one of his. ■

ILLUSTRATION BY JO ELLEN MURPHY

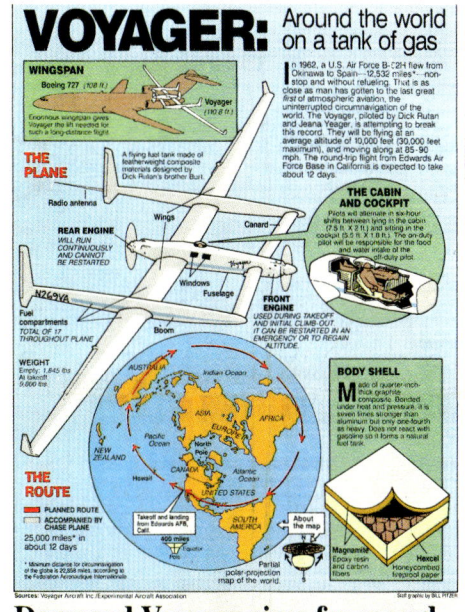

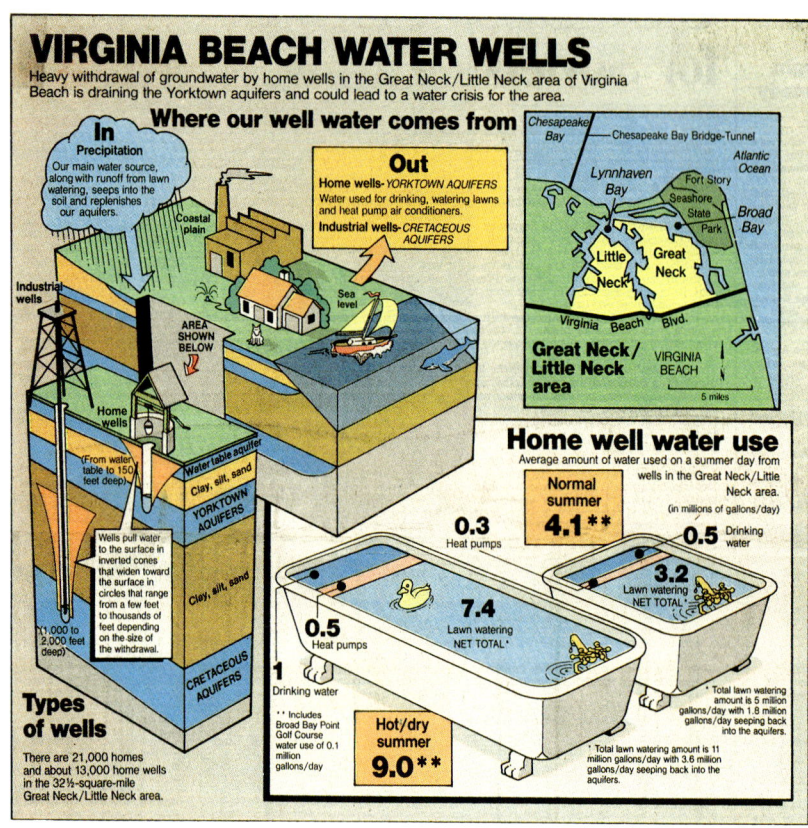

Award of Excellence
THE VIRGINIAN-PILOT/LEDGER-STAR
Norfolk, Virginia
Bill Pitzer

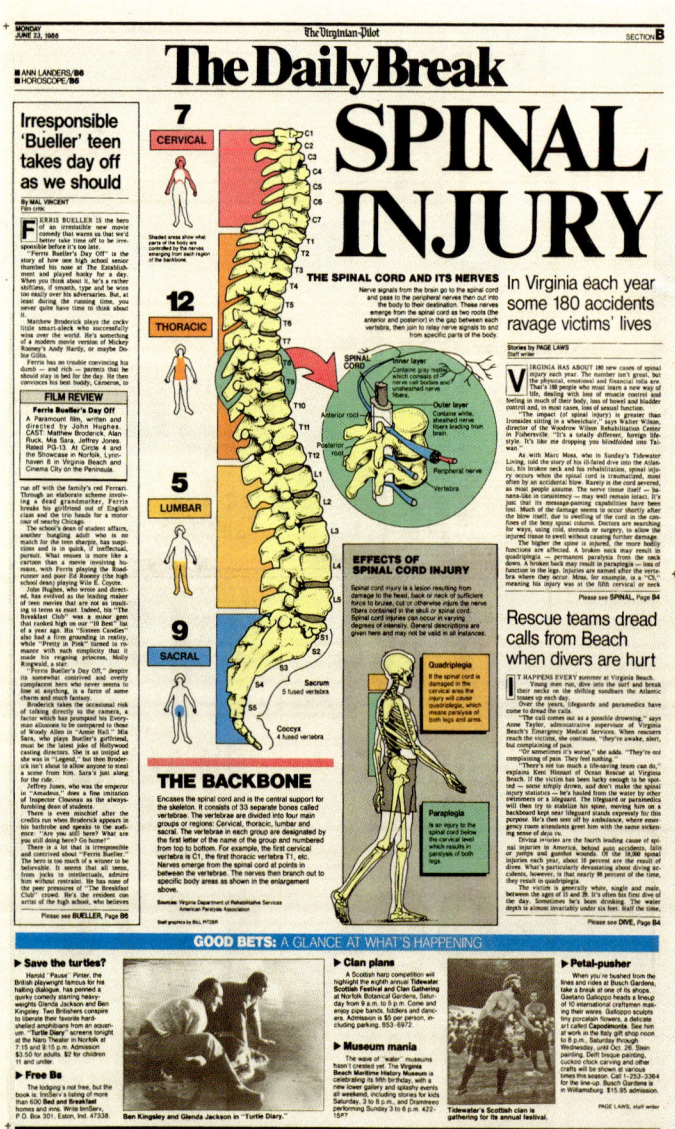

Award of Excellence
THE VIRGINIAN-PILOT/LEDGER-STAR
Norfolk, Virginia
Bill Pitzer

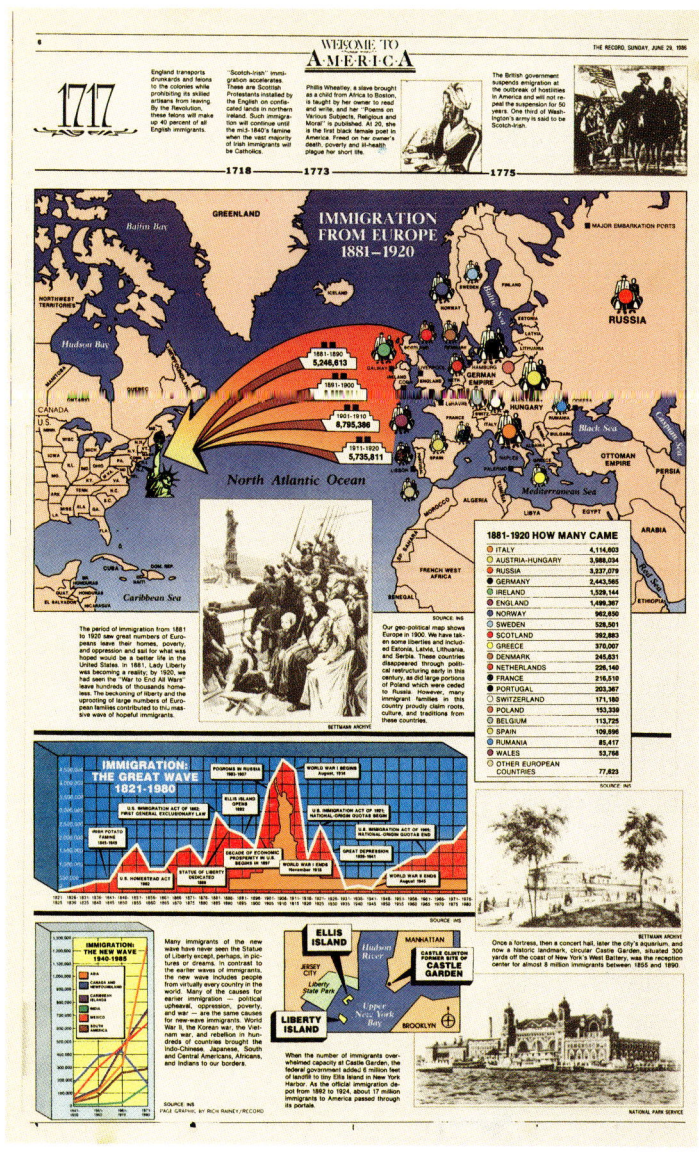

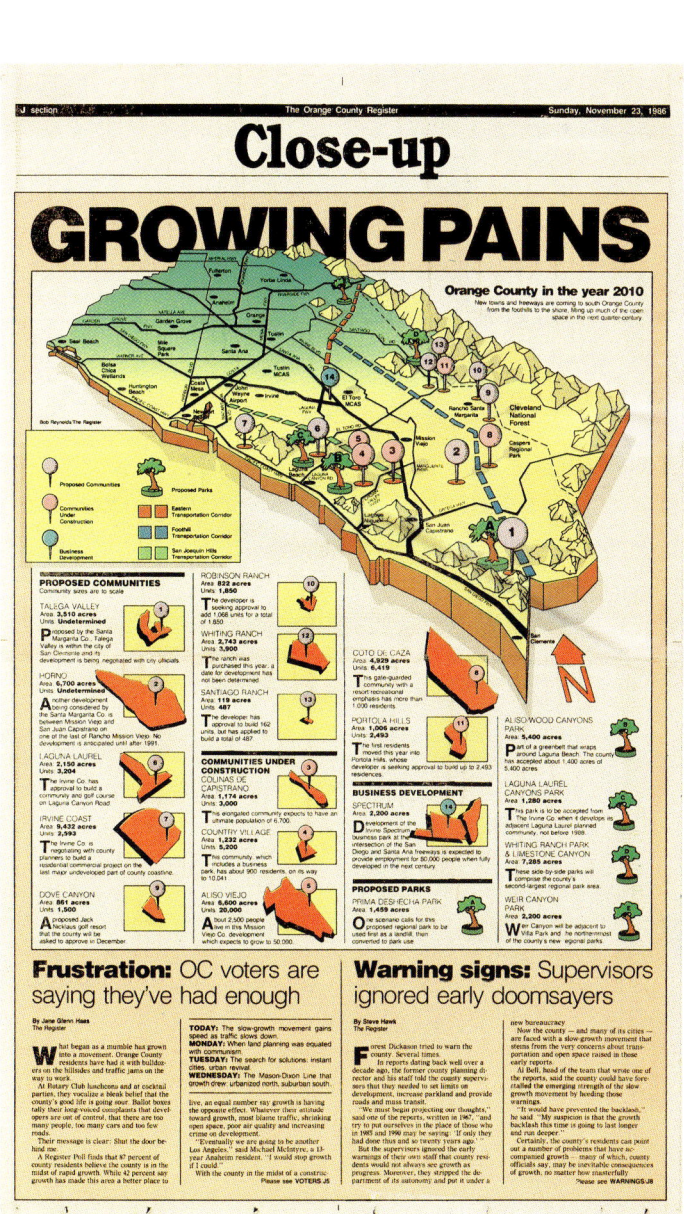

Silver Award

THE VIRGINIAN-PILOT/LEDGER-STAR
Norfolk, Virginia
Bill Pitzer

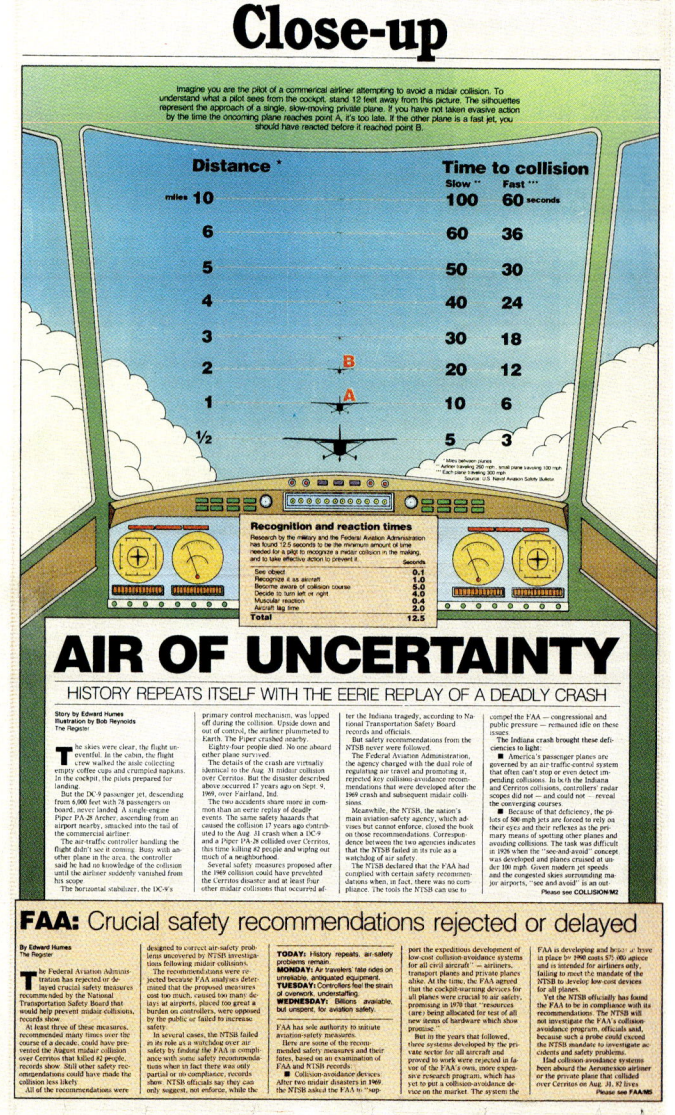

Silver Award

THE ORANGE COUNTY REGISTER
Santa Ana, California
Bob Reynolds

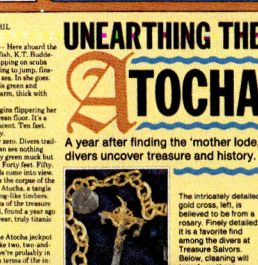

Living Today

Sunday, August 3, 1986   The Miami Herald **Section G**

Simpler life lures many to Ireland

U.S. retirees in search of an idyllic life style are emigrating to the Emerald Isle.

By SONYA ZALUBOWSKI
And BRUCE BARKER
Special to The Herald

George and Kernochan Bowen direct most people who want to see them to Josie's pub. It is easier than describing the unmarked, winding country roads in southwestern Ireland that lead to the retired American couple's cottage.

Besides, everyone at Josie's, a tiny tavern on equally tiny Bandon's main street, knows them and when they might likely stop by.

And on this particular morning, they also knew that the Bowens had been delayed a few hours, rescuing a neighboring widow from a smoky backup in her cottage caused by blackbirds that chose to set up housekeeping in her chimney. George, 66, scrambled to the rooftop to dislodge the unwelcome tenants.

The couple popped into Josie's with big smiles, joking with Jack, the aproned proprietor drawing thick, creamy ales, about what kind of lunchfare he was "foisting" on his crowded establishment.

As the Bowens slipped into a corner booth to chat with their American visitors, it was easy to see that they fit in well with the community where they have lived for a decade.

Like 1930s America

They came seeking the quieter, simpler style of life in Ireland compared by many to the pace and values of 1930s America. Personal relations take top priority in the Emerald Isle, along with the underlying philosophy that the one thing God made plenty of is time to enjoy friends and family.

The Bowens are among an estimated 12,500 American retirees living in Ireland. The U.S. Embassy in Dublin says 7,500 people, among them many Irish nationals returning after working in the United States, receive U.S. benefits checks worth $30 million per year.

The Irish government makes it fairly easy for foreigners to settle in Ireland, but because of persistent economic problems, there is a crucial provision — that immigrants be self-supporting. As a result, the major draw has been retirees, some responding to ethnic ties, others attracted by the lush, idyllic beauty of rural Ireland, and still others, like the Bowens, allured by the peaceful life style.

Unemployment and crime

The government is trying to cope with an unemployment rate near 17 percent, one of the highest in the European Economic Community. The country, from which millions emigrated after the 19th Century famines, saw its population stabilize and begin to grow in the 1960s. More than half the population of three million is now 25 and under, straining a job market and economy that remain rooted in agriculture.

Some of Ireland's unemployed have turned to crime, which, while still rare here compared to many U.S. cities, has become pervasive enough to prompt tourist publications to warn visitors that they should lock their cars and beware of pickpockets.

Burglaries and robberies have increased the most, according to Marjorie Hoban, spokeswoman for the American Women's Club of Dublin. "But life here," she insists, "is relatively safer than anywhere else."

Hoban, whose club helps Americans adjust to

Please turn to IRELAND/3G

More fun facts from Harper's

You may already know that the average person receives 598 pieces of mail a year. But do you know the percentage of Americans who say the United States has never used a nuclear weapon in a war? The episode of Perry Mason in production? Or what Nancy Reagan's hair dresser charges?

The answers are in the August Harper's Magazine Index.

Harper's Index

1. Percentage of Americans who say the United States has never used a nuclear weapon in a war: 11
2. Percentage of cruise-missile test flights that have ended in failure: 38
3. Percentage of the proposed 1986 Star Wars budget that is allocated for "demonstration projects": 56
4. Chances that a family living below the poverty line in 1984 received no public-assistance payments: 2 in 3
5. Percentage increase in the number of blacks living in poverty since 1978: 24
6. In the number of whites living in poverty: 41
7. Number of blacks who left the South between 1960 and 1983: 478,000
8. Number who moved to the South: 528,000
9. Chances that a first-time bride in Kentucky is a teen-ager: 1 in 2
10. Average age of an American nun: 62
11. Chances that an American Catholic is Hispanic: 1 in 4
12. Number of the 173 private religious schools

Please turn to HARPER'S/3G

By MARY VOBORIL
Herald Staff Writer

UNEARTHING THE ATOCHA

A year after finding the 'mother lode,' divers uncover treasure and history.

KEY WEST — Here aboard the M/V Swordfish, K.T. Budde-Jones is strapping on scuba gear, preparing to jump. She first, into the open sea. In she goes. Splash. The water is green and opaque, bathtub warm, thick with pale silt.

Budde-Jones begins flippering her way down to the ocean floor. It's a slow, head-first descent. Ten feet. Twenty feet. Thirty.

Visibility is near zero. Divers trailing Budde-Jones can see nothing through the yellowy green muck but the tips of her fins. Forty feet. Fifty.

Suddenly, boards come into view. Big, big boards. It's the corpse of the Nuestra Señora de Atocha, a tangle of tarry joists and log-like timbers. They're the remains of the treasure galleon's lower hull, found a year ago July 20 after a 16-year, truly titanic search.

Excavation of the Atocha jackpot was supposed to take two, two and-a-half years, "but we're probably in the sixth inning" in terms of the ingot-by-ingot match up with the ship's manifest, says John Durwin, an Atocha scientist.

The archaeological ball game has only just begun; "we're only in the second inning there," Durwin says. When it comes to divvying up the loot, it's the bottom of the ninth. In September, Mel Fisher's Treasure Salvors Inc. will split the treasure among 543 shareholders, investors and employees, including Budde-Jones.

In the underwater fog, Budde-Jones is kneeling in rubble, next to a mass of rounded stones. She has something to say. She reaches into her scuba gear and pulls out an underwater pencil attached to a hard white slate.

"Ballast, 40 tons," she writes on the postcard-size slate. She plucks out a rough-edged triangle of terracotta, writes again: "Pottery." Then something curved and crusty. "Barrel hoop."

She picks up a much smaller, equally curved piece and points at her fins. Bone.

Something else is peg-like, square-edged, black. At first, Budde-Jones is puzzled. She scrapes at it, eyes it closely, writes again. This time she underlines the word, adds punctuation. "Silver!"

Then, "This is the area where 900 silver bars were stacked 5" thick. Keep an eye out for coins." For once, all that glitters is likely to be gold. Depth gauge needles nudge past 55 feet.

Forty tons of silver, 30 tons of copper, 60 tons of ballast. All this pinned the Tot-like cache to the ocean floor. And all this has been exhumed, in 1985 alone: 115 gold bars, bits and disks, 15 gold chains and links; 67 gold coins, 23 other gold items, "like jewelry," says Taffi Fisher Quesada, director of the Treasure Salvors' cursing department. Plus 315 emeralds, 32 silver coin chests, 996 silver bars and more. Much, much more. Quesada reaches into a pants pocket and pulls out a small plastic bag. Inside is a dented gold circlet, engraved with crowns and letters inside and out. "A nun's ring, we think," she says.

In the 17th Century, Spanish bookkeepers were awesomely efficient. One worm-gnawed copy of the Atocha manifest, written on linen paper covered with rolling, curvy script, is on file at the Archive of the Indies in Seville, Spain. It serves as a kind of scorecard, a lost-and-found ledger.

Jim Sinclair, Treasure Salvors conservator, says the "sixth inning" translates into "about 80 percent of the manifest. There are still about 100 gold bars floating around out there somewhere."

Underwater, Budde-Jones drifts along a few more feet, using a thready green rope as a guideline. Visibility isn't improving. It's still like diving in a vat of lukewarm cream of celery soup.

"Area to the south is where pilot's chest, gold ruins & Ali Baba jars were found," Budde-Jones writes. As it

Please turn to ATOCHA/6G

The intricately detailed gold cross, left, is believed to be from a rosary. Finely detailed, it is a favorite find among the divers at Treasure Salvors. Below, cleaning will transform these clumps of silver coins into shining metal.

MAJOR FINDS IN SEQUENCE

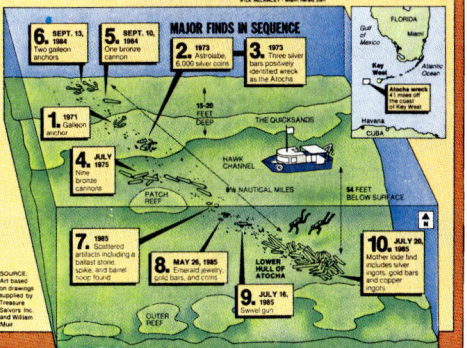

1. **1971** Galleon anchor
2. **1973** Astrolabe, 6,000 silver coins
3. **1973** Three silver bars positively identified wreck as the Atocha
4. **JULY 1975** Nine bronze cannons
5. **SEPT. 10, 1984** One bronze cannon
6. **SEPT. 15, 1984** Two galleon anchors
7. **1985** Scattered artifacts including a ballast stone, spoke, and barrel hoop found
8. **MAY 26, 1985** Emerald jewelry, gold bars and coins
9. **JULY 18, 1985** Swivel gun
10. **JULY 20, 1985** Mother lode find includes silver ingots, gold bars and copper ingots

SOURCE: Art based on drawings supplied by Treasure Salvors Inc. and William Muir

PHIL FLANDERS/Herald Art Staff

THE ORANGE COUNTY Register
Community Edition

LAGUNA BEACH   LAGUNA NIGUEL   SOUTH LAGUNA

August 26, 1986   LB27

DEVELOPMENT COULD BOOST SCHOOL ATTENDANCE

The Laguna Beach Unified School District has suffered declining enrollment since 1977. New housing developments expected to come on line in the future will add an estimated 1,170 students to the district.

Source: Laguna Beach Unified School District

HOUSING PROJECT	Number of dwelling units	Estimated Beginning date	Projected Buildout date	Enrollment K-6	7-8	9-12
1 Laguna Laurel	1536	After 1998	2003	379	129	170
2 Sycamore Hills	661	1985	1987	45	15	47
3 Aliso Viejo	517	1996	2000	127	44	57
4 Irvine Coast	229	1990	1992	10	5	16
5 Irvine Cove	48	1986	unknown	3	1	3
6 Laguna Heights	110	1986	unknown	7	3	8
7 Alta Laguna	36	1986	unknown	3	1	2
8 Laguna Sur	364	1996	1993	26	9	27
9 Monarch Point Ltd.	186	1985	unknown	11	4	12
TOTAL	3687			615	211	343

KEY
△ Existing schools
□ Proposed residential developments
--- City of Laguna Beach

Lisa Ann Mertins/The Register

More homes mean more students

School officials say higher enrollment could lead to an improved curriculum

By Kathleen Lund-Seeden
The Register

New residential development on the horizon in the Laguna Beach area could add as many as 1,200 students to school enrollment by the end of the century.

The influx of new homes — coupled with current high birth rates, which are expected to pour more students into the schools starting in 1990 — could be Laguna Beach Unified's ticket to expanded programs, lower class sizes, renovated school campuses and more and better equipment.

More homes mean more families, and more students translate to additional state

Please see GROWTH/4

INSIDE

Getting the job done: That's the goal of the Laguna Beach Unified School District's new superintendent, Dennis Smith/3

Striving for excellence: The Laguna Beach community wants outstanding education for its children, and the school district is taking steps to make that possible/3

When classes begin: Registration times and starting dates for schools in the area/20

Almanac/25
Tom Murphine/6
Business/13
Food Distribution/26
News Around Town/14
Police Report/27

back TO SCHOOL

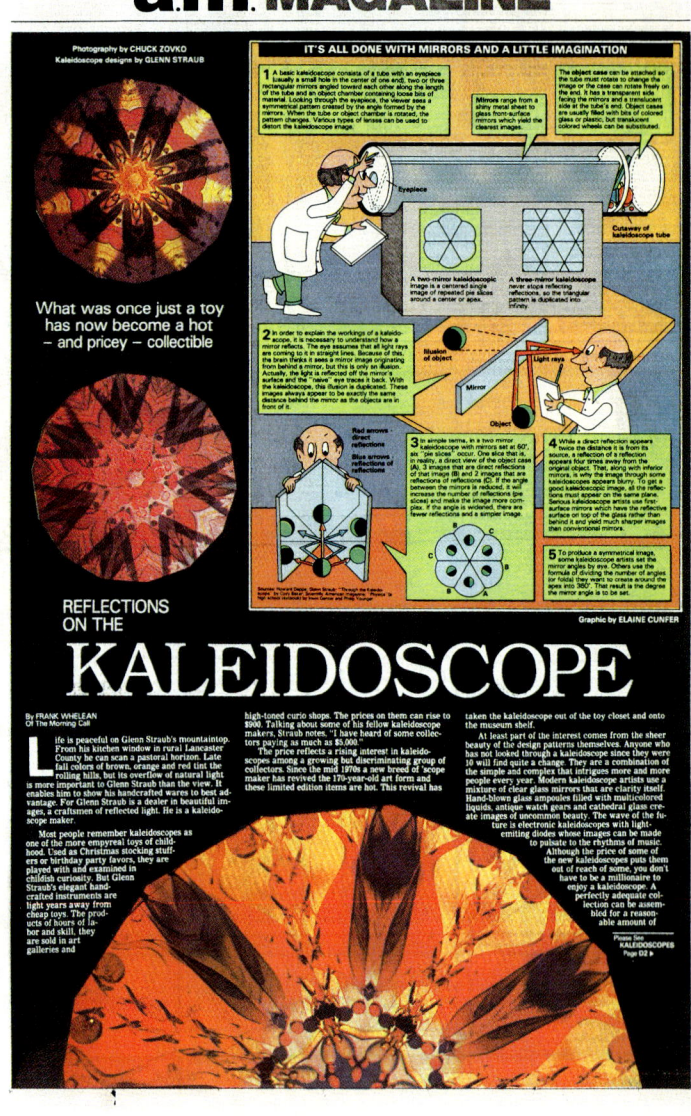

The Morning Call newspaper feature "Reflections on the Kaleidoscope"

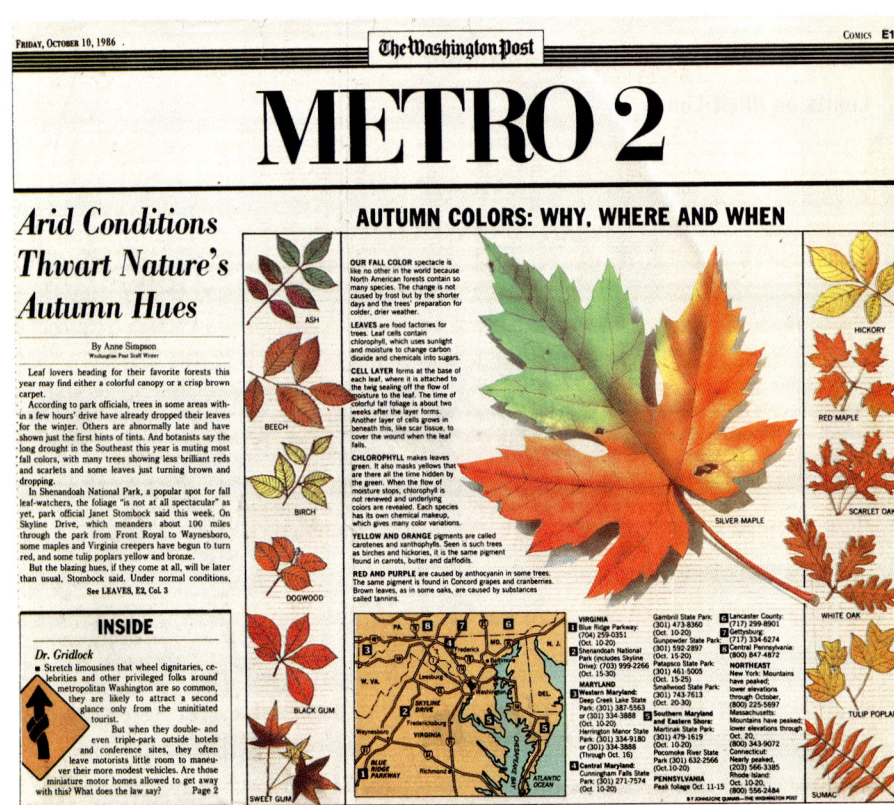

The Washington Post "Metro 2" feature "Autumn Colors: Why, Where and When"

Redesign

THE NEW YORK TIMES, SUNDAY, MARCH 8, 1987

ART

ART VIEW/John Russell

Painting With Fanciful Strokes

Pierre Alechinsky in front of "The Dog King" (1982) at his Guggenheim show.

Many of Alechinsky's creations are conversational in tone, told with relish, and never allowed to go on too long.

Continued on Page 38

GALLERY VIEW / Michael Brenson

Sculpture That Springs From Surrealism

Katie Seiden's show has the humor and energy that helped put the East Village on the art map.

Hanno Ahrens's untitled 1984 wood sculpture in his show at the Sharpe Gallery.

FILM

FILM VIEW / Vincent Canby

Anatomy of an 'R' Rating

After repeated screenings, appeals board members seem to lose touch with the overall film.

THIS WEEK

Two Who Were There View 'Platoon'

The Correspondent   The Marine Officer

Award of Excellence
THE GLOBE AND MAIL
Toronto, Ontario,
Canada
Globe and Mail staff

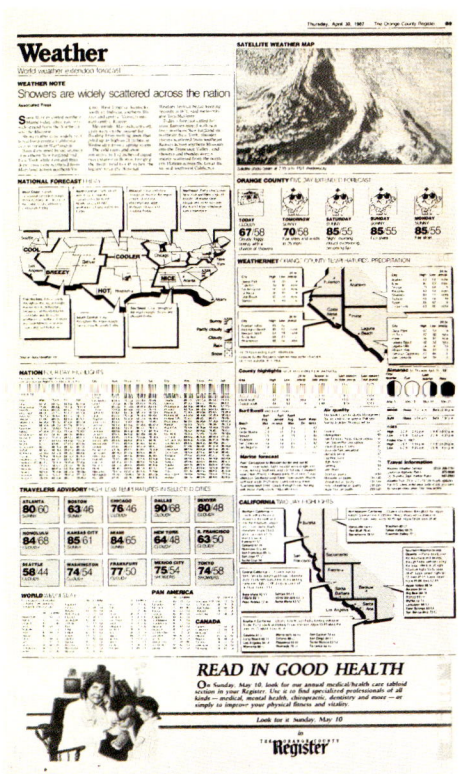

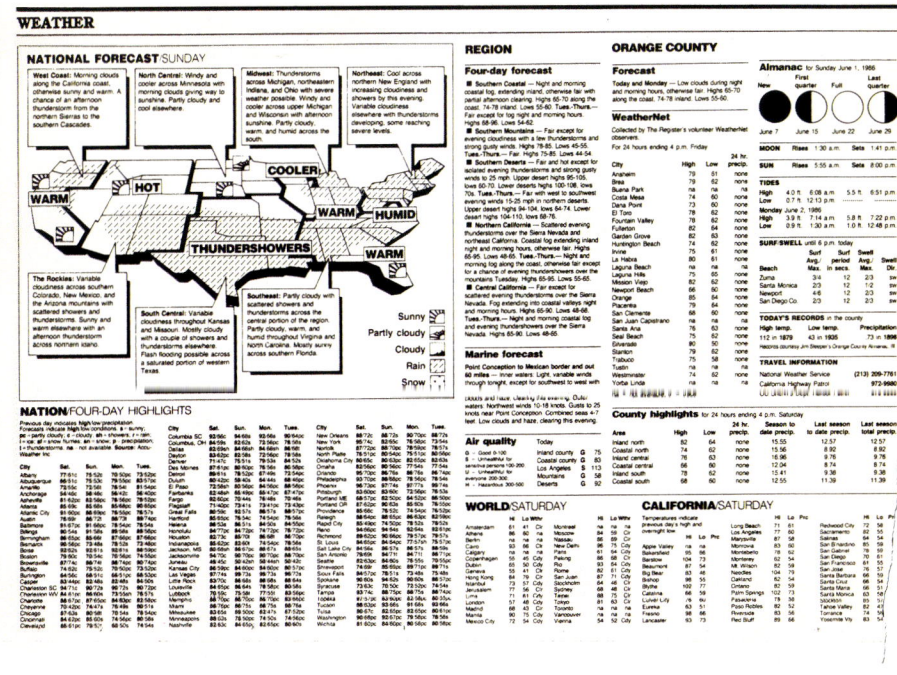

Award of Excellence
THE ORANGE COUNTY REGISTER
Santa Ana, California
Nanette Bisher

Award of Excellence
THE GLOBE AND MAIL
Toronto, Ontario,
Canada
Jim Ireland, Anna Janes

a T-shirt or an empty tin can. And in the marketplace, women squatted before mounds of sweet potatoes and a half-cooked pig carcass, oblivious to helicopters hovering nearby with pipes for oil drilling. A man armed with a bow and arrows and adorned with bird-of-paradise feathers watched his near-naked, barefoot friend kick-start a Yamaha motorcycle.

No tourists came to the nearby West Sepik District when I worked here as a malaria control officer 15 years ago. With a team of half a dozen *bois* and 20 or more carriers hauling aluminum patrol boxes strung from poles across their shoulders, we marched through the remote jungles for weeks, spraying houses with DDT, taking blood samples and passing out anti-malaria medicine. Light aircraft were like flying trucks then, hauling our gear, us and once even a sedated but very large bull to remote and often unlicenced missionary airstrips. Unpredictable weather, rugged terrain, lack of navigational aids and makeshift dirt strips make Papua New Guinea one of the world's most dangerous places to fly. There were no accidents in my district that year. Within six months of my departure, however, three pilots with whom I had flown disappeared into the mountains.

When we break back into the glaring midday sun, the blood returns to my whitened knuckles. The muddy Sepik, Papua New Guinea's longest river at 966 kilometres, slithers off into the expanse of dull green jungle as far as we can see. An occasional flash of a tin roof marks a lonely mission or administration station. In a few small clearings, rows of sweet potatoes grow in mounds like miniature graves. It is an empty, lonely land. The cabin temperature slowly rises as we descend over a vast jungle area of oxbows

WASEMI MAN WEARS KINA SHELLS (FAR LEFT); WOMEN CLOAKED IN TREE BARK

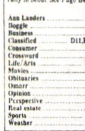

The Toronto Star — SATURDAY MAGAZINE SPECIAL SECTION — Saturday, December 6, 1986

BOOKS
FOR CHRISTMAS

My love for miracles of the imagination

Canada's best-known author, Morley Callaghan, full of years and honors, tells us what books and reading have meant to him in his 83 years.

ONE night back in the '50s when television was making its first impact, my friend Ralph Allen, at that time editor of Maclean's, said to me: "We'd better all start learning to handle pictures and images. People now on there'll be less and less reading of stories or anything else. In fact, we should be worrying about whether reading is on the way out."

I simply couldn't believe this. We argued. I wasn't quite sure why I was so utterly positive I was right, and I remember that on the way home I tried to figure it out, and now I think I did.

See My Love M25

THE TORONTO STAR — BOOKS FOR CHRISTMAS — SATURDAY, DECEMBER 6, 1986 M5

How the past gave our city its future

By Donald Jones

HO HO HO

Historic Toronto

SCIENCE

Hocus-pocus, making it so easy

By Jack Miller

SCIENCE books don't have to sound like text books, although most of them tend to. Here are three of the current crop that show promise, if you're Christmas shopping for a reader.

SCIENCE

COMPUTERS

Bytes of data in layman's language

By George Brett

PERSONAL computers — the tools/toys of the Information Age that have taken over desktops in offices, schools and homes — were supposed to reduce the amount of paper in our lives. Instead, they have created a whole new sub-industry within publishing as computer experts with a flair for layman's language compete to explain to us how our hardware (the computer) and software (the programs on diskette that make the hardware go) work.

Award of Excellence
THE JAPAN TIMES
Tokyo, Japan
Sara Giovanitti

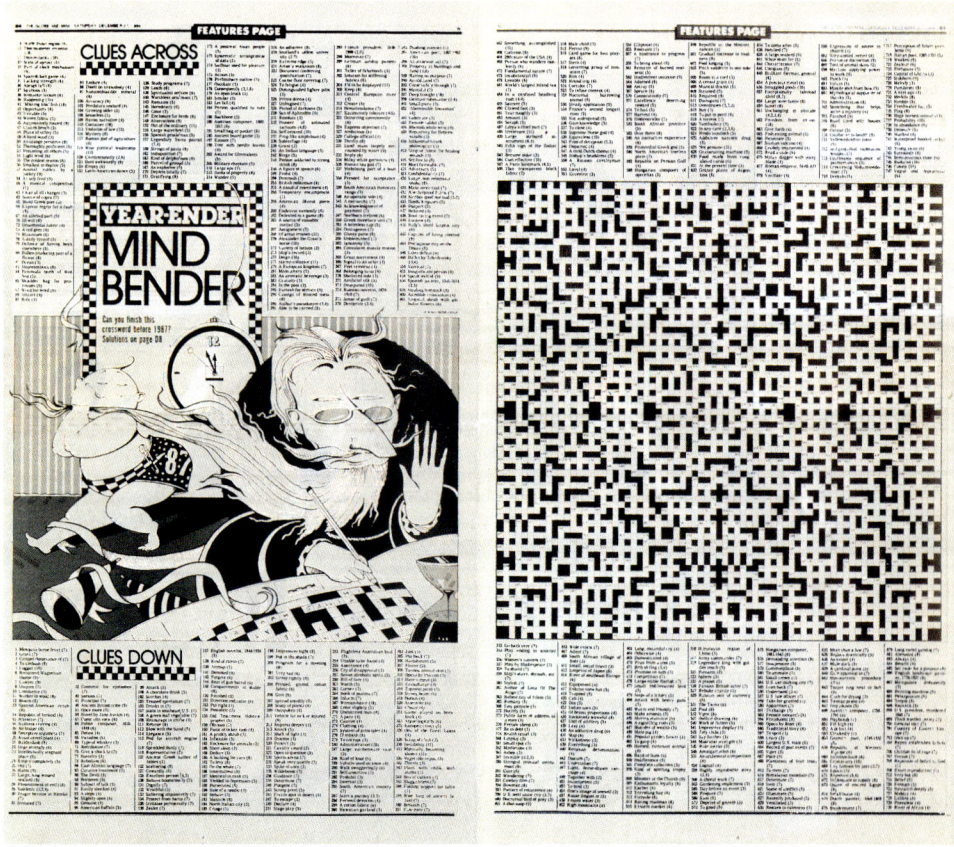

Award of Excellence
THE GLOBE AND MAIL
Toronto, Ontario,
Canada
Eric Nelson,
Deborah Whithey-Culp